D0214386

Film Firsts

THE 25 MOVIES THAT CREATED CONTEMPORARY AMERICAN CINEMA

Ethan Alter

 PRAEGER

AN IMPRINT OF ABC-CLIO, LLC
Santa Barbara, California • Denver, Colorado • Oxford, England

Copyright 2014 by Ethan Alter

All rights reserved. No part of this publication may be reproduced, stored in a retrieval system, or transmitted, in any form or by any means, electronic, mechanical, photocopying, recording, or otherwise, except for the inclusion of brief quotations in a review, without prior permission in writing from the publisher.

Library of Congress Cataloging-in-Publication Data

Alter, Ethan.
  Film firsts : the 25 movies that created contemporary American cinema / Ethan Alter.
     pages cm
  Includes bibliographical references and index.
  ISBN 978–1–4408–0187–7 (hardcopy : alk. paper) — ISBN 978–1–4408–0188–4 (ebook)
  1. Motion pictures—United States. I. Title.
PN1993.5.U6A852   2014
791.430973—dc23   2013034102

ISBN: 978–1–4408–0187–7
EISBN: 978–1–4408–0188–4

18 17 16 15 14   1 2 3 4 5

This book is also available on the World Wide Web as an eBook.
Visit www.abc-clio.com for details.

Praeger
An Imprint of ABC-CLIO, LLC

ABC-CLIO, LLC
130 Cremona Drive, P.O. Box 1911
Santa Barbara, California 93116-1911

This book is printed on acid-free paper ∞

Manufactured in the United States of America

For Jessica, Dylan, and Aeryn—always the firsts in my life.

Contents

Introduction

If one were to point to a single film as representing the dividing line between the classic and contemporary period of American film history, Steven Spielberg's *Jaws* would frequently—and correctly—be cited as the obvious choice. Released in the summer of 1975 to great acclaim and even greater box-office grosses, *Jaws* became an omnipresent blockbuster that provided an industry that had largely been adrift since the collapse of the Hollywood studio system in the 1950s and the various financial and cultural upheavals of the 1960s and early 1970s a template to follow going forward.

Certainly, the mainstream movie landscape that exists today—one dominated by high-concept, thrill-seeking Hollywood entertainments—is made in the image of *Jaws*. But Spielberg's film also encapsulates other changes that have defined the past three decades of film history, from ever-evolving methods of distribution (both theatrically and beyond) to new approaches to movie marketing to the evolution of special-effects technology. Furthermore, the creative risks that the director took with the material—and the resulting challenges he butted up against—were akin, in some ways, to an independent film production . . . although Spielberg had access to more money and resources than the directors who developed that nascent industry in the 1980s before it too became a big business in the following decade.

The release of the first contemporary blockbuster marked the beginning of a wave of other significant firsts that would shape the modern American film industry into the form in which it exists today and what it could resemble tomorrow. *Film Firsts* singles out 25 such features (and their respective firsts) made between 1975 and 2011 that played an important part in shaping the present and potential tomorrow of American cinema. Just as we owe the existence of the modern summer blockbuster to 1975's *Jaws,* the proliferation of computer-generated imagery in contemporary films is the result of 1982's *Tron*, the first movie to make extensive use of CGI, and independent cinema emerged as a commercially viable alternative to studio fare thanks to 1994's *Pulp Fiction,* the first independent film to gross $100 million at the box office.

In some cases, the cited films are significant for what they *did not* bring about—the critical and commercial failure of the first mainstream NC-17 release, 1994's *Showgirls,* for instance, further marginalized that controversial rating; while the unprecedented success of 2000's Chinese-produced martial-arts film *Crouching Tiger, Hidden Dragon*—the first foreign-language film to reach the $100 million mark in America—has not changed the overall marketplace for foreign-made features in this country. And then there are those more recent films that have achieved firsts where the impact has yet to be fully felt; was Kathryn Bigelow's historic 2010 victory as the first female director to receive the Academy Award for Best Director a fluke or has that particular glass ceiling been permanently shattered? And will the first YouTube-branded feature documentary, 2011's *Life in a Day*, prove a one-time experiment or the launching pad for a new film genre: the global video collage? Regardless of the eventual outcome, these specific films can still claim to have achieved a significant first.

Each of the movies profiled in *Film Firsts* will be explored in two sections; *The Film*, which provides background information and a general critical evaluation of the film in question; and *The First*, which addresses the specific first the film is responsible for. (A pair of appendices—or *Film First Files*—per chapter will elaborate on certain aspects of the film and/or the first.) Taken together, these 25 films effectively outline the arc of contemporary American movie history. And as the industry once more stands on the precipice of great change, they provide an understanding of how American cinema has reached this point as well as what the future might hold.

Timeline: 20 Classic Film Firsts

The following pre-contemporary Hollywood films and the respective first each achieved function as a movie-centric historical timeline, illustrating the artistic and industry innovations that served as building blocks for the contemporary era—1975 and beyond—that the rest of the book will explore.

The Birth of a Nation (1915)

The Film: The groundbreaking artistry of D. W. Griffith's Confederate's eye-view Civil War epic can't distract from its ugly racial politics.

The First: In addition to originating a number of cinematic storytelling techniques that are still employed today, *The Birth of a Nation*'s unprecedented commercial success made it Hollywood's first blockbuster.

The Kid (1921)

The Film: Charlie Chaplin's first feature-length film retained the comic buffoonery of his popular shorts, but married it to an emotionally resonant storyline.

The First: As one of the first movie stars to write, direct, and star in his own feature film, Chaplin maintained the kind of creative control over his work and screen image that A-list screen actors continue to aspire to today.

Nanook of the North (1922)

The Film: At a time when most films were manufacturing reality on sound-stages and sets, Robert Flaherty took his camera out into the world to show moviegoers how another culture—in this case, the Inuks of the Arctic—lived.

The First: A pioneering mix of travelogue and documentary, *Nanook of the North* is a touchstone of nonfiction cinema ... even though there are elements of the film that could be considered fiction.

Wings (1927)

The Film: A sweeping love story set against the backdrop of World War I, *Wings* stands as a textbook example of a mainstream silent-era silver screen spectacle.

The First: *Wings* became the first film to win an Academy Award for Best Picture, paving the way for a now-familiar time of the year known as Oscar season.

The Jazz Singer (1927)

The Film: From a narrative standpoint, much of *The Jazz Singer* is a ridiculously melodramatic affair. But something special happens when Al Jolson opens his mouth to sing.

The First: After previous attempts at integrating sound into motion pictures fell flat, the success of *The Jazz Singer* soon made all American movies talk... and occasionally sing.

King Kong (1933)

The Film: Though the stop-motion effects are somewhat dated, *King Kong*'s spirit of adventure endures across the decades.

The First: The lasting achievement of this early creature feature was turning a walking special effect into a three-dimensional character audiences cared about.

The World Moves On (1934)

The Film: A lavish period epic that's generally considered so dramatically bland, even its director, John Ford, didn't care for it.

The First: The wild pre-Code days in Hollywood officially ended when *The World Moves On* became the first film to receive the stamp of approval from a stern new Production Code, which would shape the content of studio productions for decades to come.

Becky Sharp (1935)

The Film: Thackeray's oft-adapted novel *Vanity Fair* gets another retelling in big, beautiful color.

The First: Black and white seemed to pale in comparison to the industry-changing three-strip Technicolor process introduced with *Becky Sharp*.

Snow White and the Seven Dwarfs (1937)

The Film: Walt Disney's passion project remains one of his studio's simplest, most elemental big-screen fairy tales.

The First: Hollywood's first family-friendly animated feature created an entire industry . . . and one enduring animation empire.

Stagecoach (1939)

The Film: John Ford's classic western is a swift, action-packed ride through dangerous territory.

The First: As the first film where John Wayne got to play "John Wayne," *Stagecoach* created an iconic screen presence modern action heroes still measure themselves against.

Citizen Kane (1941)

The Film: *Citizen Kane*'s much-deserved status as one of the greatest films of all time has also made it a target for the dreaded "overrated" label.

The First: Wunderkind filmmaker Orson Welles's directorial debut has become a touchstone of the auteur theory, which argues for the primacy of the director in cinema.

The Robe (1953)

The Film: A big-budget biblical epic where the spectacle often swallows up the drama.

The First: The first film to be shot in CinemaScope, *The Robe* was one example of the myriad ways Hollywood's major film studios sought to combat the upstart medium of television.

East of Eden (1955)

The Film: Elia Kazan's adaptation of the John Steinbeck novel pulsates with raw, rich emotion.

The First: James Dean's first leading role challenged conventions of screen acting and served as a touchstone for every rebellious teenager drama made since.

It Conquered the World (1956)

The Film: Roger Corman's low-budget alien invasion picture offers provocative social commentary amidst the B-movie mayhem.

The First: Corman's first film for the rechristened American International Pictures set him firmly on the path to becoming "King of the Bs" and a mentor for an entire generation of Movie Brats.

Primary (1960)

The Film: Using new camera technology, director Robert Drew got up close and personal with elite members of the country's political class during the pivotal 1960 presidential primary.

The First: One of the earliest examples of Direct Cinema, *Primary* redefined the look, feel, and subject matter of documentary films.

Lilies of the Field (1963)

The Film: Made in the midst of the civil rights era, *Lilies of the Field* treats the subject of race with kid gloves.

The First: When Sidney Poitier became the first black actor to win an Oscar for a leading role, it showcased how far minority performers had come and how far they still had to go.

Bonnie and Clyde (1967)

The Film: Warren Beatty and Faye Dunaway live fast and die young and look real good doing it.

The First: No longer hindered by the dying Production Code, the movie's unprecedented levels of violence and suggestive content made it clear that a post-Code Hollywood would be a wild place.

Night of the Living Dead (1968)

The Film: Zombies may move faster today, but few zombie *movies* are as perfectly paced and genuinely frightening as George A. Romero's debut feature.

The First: *Night of the Living Dead* gave American cinema one of its most enduring boogeymen, and its commercial success represented a major breakthrough for no-budget independently-made horror films.

Easy Rider (1969)

The Film: Frequently remembered as a shrine to hippie culture, Dennis Hopper's cross-country road movie is actually an incendiary critique of that lifestyle.

The First: The box office success of *Easy Rider* highlighted a generational rift in Hollywood that pitted the town's previous masters against an emerging new class.

The Godfather, Part II (1974)

The Film: The parallel narratives running through Francis Ford Coppola's follow-up to his landmark Mafia masterpiece elevate a gangster picture into a father/son drama for the ages.

The First: The first sequel to win a Best Picture Oscar, *The Godfather Part II* was an early symptom of the franchise fever that would later infect the modern movie era.

Chapter 1

Jaws (1975)

The Film: In the face of great odds, an act of artistic hubris that even its director now considers foolhardy became a modern cinematic classic.

Even with all that advance preparation that precedes the making of a major motion picture, sometimes a great film is the result of a series of happy accidents. At least, that's what Steven Spielberg discovered during the course of shooting his movie version of Peter Benchley's blockbuster beach read, *Jaws*,[1] the tale of a great white shark bedeviling a small New England resort town and the three very different men who task themselves with hunting the monster down. Of course, the series of accidents that befell the production didn't seem all that "happy" at the time. The list of things that went wrong during the making of *Jaws* would be extensive enough to fill its own book— and, in fact, it did; *The Jaws Log*, written by the film's screenwriter, Carl Gottlieb, chronicled the numerous challenges the cast and crew confronted on a daily basis and became a best seller in its own right, as well as a source of inspiration for up-and-coming filmmakers. (Bryan Singer and Eli Roth are just two of the post-*Jaws* generation of directors who have gone on record describing *The Jaws Log* as a favorite filmmaking book.)[2]

The fickleness of the ocean tides, inclement weather, and, above all, a non-functioning mechanical shark were the chief culprits for turning what was intended to be a 55-day shoot into a *159*-day shoot that started in the summer of 1974 and finally wrapped in the early fall, long after the beach season had ended.[3] And the rub of it was that Spielberg had nobody to blame for the fiasco that *Jaws* (or, as the crew dubbed it, *Flaws*)[4] very nearly became but himself, as it was his idea to shoot the movie on open water, rather than in the more controlled confines of a water tank on a studio lot.

He had arrived at that fateful decision almost immediately upon accepting the assignment to adapt the book into a movie, a job he had lobbied producers Richard Zanuck and Daryl Brown (who also produced Spielberg's first theatrical feature, 1974's *The Sugarland Express)* for after consuming Benchley's shark tale in a single weekend.[5]

In the moment, none of the logistical concerns that accompanied filming a movie at sea crossed his mind. And, even if they had, it's unlikely that he would have changed course anyway. (The older, wiser Spielberg has expressed different sentiments about his younger self, saying, "Because I was younger, I was more courageous...or I was more stupid. I'm not sure which.")[6] A 27-year-old member of the Movie Brat generation that included rebellious upstart directors like Francis Ford Coppola, Martin Scorsese, and Brian De Palma, Spielberg consciously wanted to challenge the natural order of things within the realm of studio filmmaking. He didn't intend for *Jaws* to have the artifice of classic Hollywood—this was going to be gritty and real[7] ... albeit very much in a commercial way. (Amongst his contemporaries, Spielberg was generally regarded as one of the most box-office minded, to the point where he supposedly petitioned Zanuck to scrap the downbeat ending of *Sugarland* in favor of a happier finale. He didn't win that fight.)[8]

After considering several potential East Coast beachfront locations, Spielberg eventually settled on Martha's Vineyard, Massachusetts, largely because the crew could venture as far as 12 miles away from the island— allowing them to photograph in all directions without the possibility of the cameras spotting land—and still find a sandy floor from which they could set up the equipment and operate the movie's temperamental star: a large mechanical shark.[9] In fact, they came to the Vineyard armed with four different models of the titular great white, a simple fin for ordinary swim-bys, two swimming sharks—one that swam right to left, while the other went left to right—and, finally, the full creature, which had been christened "the great white turd" for reasons that would soon become obvious.[10] The filmmakers' original intention had been to put this feat of special effects engineering on display as often as possible during the course of the movie, starting with the now-famous opening scene where the beast devours a hapless skinny-dipper.[11] But the "great white turd" lived up to its nickname when it was first placed in the water ... and almost immediately malfunctioned and continued to do so on a daily basis for almost the entire duration of the shoot. Suddenly, Spielberg found himself confronted with the very real possibility of having to make a giant shark movie without a giant shark.

At first, the young director did what anyone in his position might do: stall for time. As the crew toiled away on the shark, he turned his attention towards his human stars, which included Roy Scheider as NYPD cop turned small-town sheriff Martin Brody, Robert Shaw as veteran seaman Quint (a role Spielberg had originally earmarked for Lee Marvin), and Richard Dreyfuss as nerdy oceanographer Matt Hooper. With the script still in a state of

YBP Library Services

2074

ALTER, ETHAN.

FILM FIRSTS: THE 25 MOVIES THAT CREATED
CONTEMPORARY AMERICAN CINEMA.
                              Cloth   271 P.
SANTA BARBARA: PRAEGER, 2014

EXAMINES 25 POST-1975 AMERICAN FILMS FOR THEIR
GROUNDBREAKING ASPECTS & INFLUENCE.
LCCN 2013034102
  ISBN 1440801878   **Library PO#** AP-BOOKS

                                    List   48.00   USD
   395 NATIONAL UNIVERSITY LIBRAR   **Disc**   .0%
  App. Date   4/30/14   HUMANITIES 8214-11   **Net**   48.00   USD

SUBJ: MOTION PICTURES--U.S.

CLASS PN1993.5   DEWEY# 791.430973   LEVEL GEN-AC

YBP Library Services

ALTER, ETHAN.

FILM FIRSTS: THE 25 MOVIES THAT CREATED
CONTEMPORARY AMERICAN CINEMA.
                              Cloth   271 P.
SANTA BARBARA: PRAEGER, 2014

EXAMINES 25 POST-1975 AMERICAN FILMS FOR THEIR
GROUNDBREAKING ASPECTS & INFLUENCE.
 LCCN 2013034102
  ISBN 1440801878   **Library PO#** AP-BOOKS

                                    List   48.00   USD
   395 NATIONAL UNIVERSITY LIBRAR   **Disc**   .0%
  App. Date   4/30/14   HUMANITIES 8214-11   **Net**   48.00   USD

SUBJ: MOTION PICTURES--U.S.

CLASS PN1993.5   DEWEY# 791.430973   LEVEL GEN-AC

flux, Spielberg and his actors invented much of their material; the scenes between Brody and his family in particular were created out of an extensive amount of improvisation. Indeed, one of the movie's best scenes (not to mention a classic Spielbergian-brand domestic moment), in which Brody's youngest son pantomimes his father, sprang entirely from Scheider's head in between takes.[12] (The actor also ad-libbed the movie's single most famous line of dialogue: "We're gonna need a bigger boat.")[13]

Once it became clear that the mechanical shark would not be a reliable leading man, Spielberg shifted gears; instead of showing the shark off early and often, he treated it as an object of menacing mystery for the first half of the movie, finally giving the audience their first good glimpse of it roughly an hour in. (Another version of this oft-told story suggests that the decision to hide the creature was made during postproduction by the film's editor, Verna Fields, rather than being initiated by Spielberg.)[14] Although this was a stylistic choice made more out of necessity than artistry, Spielberg himself credits it as being the primary reason that *Jaws* remains such an enjoyable and visceral moviegoing experience. Cue up that opening sequence again, in which the viewer watches the swimmer happily treading water. Then, an instant later, she's dragged around like a rag doll before being pulled into the cold, dark deep. It's a moment that's all the more terrifying because neither she nor the audience knows what's doing this to her; our minds are left to fill in what our eyes can't see, which conjures up all sorts of primal terrors that are more frightening than the image of a mechanical shark could ever be. After the success of *Jaws*, Spielberg would deliberately play the "hide the monster" gambit in other movies, most notably the first *Jurassic Park*, where the film's biggest monster—a T-Rex—is introduced in stages: first the bellowing roar, then the giant foot, and finally the entire beast.

Jaws is often considered the movie where Steven Spielberg officially became Steven Spielberg, both aesthetically and in terms of box-office success. And it's true that the movie carries many of the hallmarks the director has become celebrated for over the years, including an emphasis on family dynamics, fluid action sequences, and a rousing finale constructed to leave audiences cheering . . . even if it doesn't necessarily make a lot of sense. In the case of *Jaws*, the satisfyingly illogical ending finds Brody blowing the shark to kingdom come by putting a bullet through the oxygen canister that's lodged in its mouth. Benchley—who had penned a different ending in the book—complained to Spielberg that this resolution would be patently absurd, but changed his tune when he saw how audiences leapt to their feet after the shark was blown to smithereens.[15] (The creature's fate, by the way, is more than a little reminiscent of the Death Star explosion that closes out the original *Star Wars*—which arrived in theaters two summers later— right down to Brody having to score a direct hit at the exact right angle in order to blow his target up. Perhaps Spielberg's buddy George Lucas made a mental note of how that finale wowed the crowd.)

At the same time, *Jaws* possesses some striking differences from Spielberg's later films; it's very clearly the work of a young director still experimenting with various styles and influences—something he had time to do given the extensive delays brought about by the nonfunctioning shark. The landbound first half, for example, feels indebted to Robert Altman in the way it allows for overlapping conversations in the scenes between Brody and the townspeople, a style that Altman pioneered in his 1970 hit *M*A*S*H*. Meanwhile, the rhythms of the seafaring second half are more languid than the relentless thrill rides Spielberg would go on to make starting with 1981's *Raiders of the Lost Ark*. (Indeed, that film is arguably the more prototypical Spielberg blockbuster than *Jaws*.) One can't help but wonder if Spielberg would have made a more concerted effort to pick up the pace had the "great white turd" floated. That he was able to turn a series of potentially movie-killing accidents to his advantage speaks to his resourcefulness as a filmmaker even at that young age. The *Jaws* that has been thrilling moviegoers for almost 40 years may not be the exact film he set out to make, but here's the funny part: it's better.

The First: With its massive, TV-based ad campaign, ultra-wide theatrical release, and merchandising bonanza, *Jaws* set the template for the way modern-day summer blockbusters are made and marketed.

When *Jaws* swam into 409 theaters[16]—one of the highest opening weekend screen counts ever for a major studio production—on June 20, 1975, it represented a profound shift in theatrical distribution strategy, one that the industry had been building to for some time. During the heyday of the studio system, studio-backed "quality" pictures—that is, those with established stars and bigger budgets, as opposed to genre-oriented, cheaply made B movies—tended to follow a platform-release pattern, opening slowly around the country instead of hitting screens in every city on the same day, as they do today. (Some films were given a wider release, but that was rarely a vote of confidence in the finished product; rather, it was a way to make as much money as possible as quickly as possible off of a disaster.)[17] Studio publicity departments also primarily depended on print-based ad campaigns to market their wares; even after television emerged as a viable means of hawking films, the medium was used sporadically, if at all. It took a series of B-movie producers and independent distributors to demonstrate the value of a distribution plan built around a heavy blanket of TV advertising, coupled with the wider release of the film itself.

Hollywood proved particularly attentive to the case of *Billy Jack*, the 1971 vigilante movie directed by and starring Tom Laughlin. Produced independently, *Billy Jack* was acquired by Warner Bros. and given the standard

platform-release/print-marketing treatment, which netted the movie a medio-
cre $4 million gross. Furious, Laughlin successfully sued Warner Bros. for
mishandling the film and won the right to rerelease *Billy Jack* on his terms.
He opted to employ the "four-wall" strategy for the movie's return to theaters, where a film's distributors rented a screen directly from a theater owner
for a week or more and footed the marketing bill in exchange for collecting
the entire gross. This approach allowed Laughlin to book his film into as
many theaters as he could afford; he then funneled the bulk of his advertising
dollars into television spots that ran in heavy rotation and attempted to
appeal to every potential demographic. All told, Laughlin spent $2.5 million
on TV commercials, an almost unheard of figure at the time. But his gambit
worked: the second run of *Billy Jack* earned $75 million, a sum that Warner
Bros. and the other major studios couldn't ignore.[18]

Coinciding with Hollywood's reappraisal of its traditional distribution
and marketing methods was the dawn of the contemporary blockbuster
age, as represented by two films in particular, 1972's *The Godfather* and
1973's *The Exorcist*. Both films were derived from hugely successful books
that lent them instant brand awareness in the mind of the moviegoing public.
In a portent of things to come, both were also high-class genre pictures—a
gangster film and a horror movie—that would likely have been given the B-
movie treatment not even a decade earlier. On the lookout for the next
mass-market literary phenomenon, Universal Pictures–affiliated producers
Richard Zanuck and David Brown scooped up the film rights to Peter Benchley's *Jaws* before the novel was even published, a smart purchase as it turned
out as the book became an instant best seller as soon as it went on sale in
February 1974. Not wanting to lose any of that momentum, they hurried
the movie version into production,[19] which would become another factor in
the problems surrounding the mechanical shark as the effects team never
had the time to perfect the design of the creature.[20]

Although Universal originally contemplated releasing *Jaws* during the holiday moviegoing season,[21] the extensive production delays scuttled that idea,
and a summer 1975 berth was plotted instead. This wound up working in the
movie's favor as the book sold millions of more copies during that time, stok-
ing the general public's anticipation. If Universal was still dubious about the
film's commercial prospects, a series of test screenings held in the spring of
1975 erased any doubts. The reaction from preview audiences was uniformly
stellar, which convinced the studio to pursue a wide release policy, though
not *too* wide. Universal's head of distribution initially booked the movie
into 600 theaters, but dropped the total count to a still sizeable 409 on the
orders of the studio head, Lew Wasserman, who wanted to ensure the movie's longevity beyond its maiden weekend by limiting supply to increase
demand.[22]

Along with the large screen count, Universal employed two other measures
to goose *Jaws*'s already monstrous commercial prospects. First, they went

all-in on television advertising, spending $700,000 on teasers that aired during prime-time network programming.[23] Additionally, they expanded their marketing arm into the realm of merchandising, slapping the *Jaws* name on such tie-ins as beachwear[24] and less obvious items like lunchboxes and a 500-piece jigsaw puzzle illustrating a scene from the film.[25] All told, Universal's marketing budget for *Jaws* totaled $2.5 million and helped transform the movie into a full-blown cultural event—something the average person couldn't afford to miss.[26]

And very few people did. During the movie's record-setting opening weekend, lines of *Jaws*-saturated moviegoers snaked around all 409 locations where the movie was showing, snapping up tickets for sold-out show after sold-out show. When Monday rolled around, *Jaws* had $7 million in the bank,[27] a number that continued to swell as the summer rolled on. And by the time the beach blankets were put back in the closet and warm weather was a distant memory, the movie's gross stood at a towering $129 million[28]—the first movie in Hollywood history to break the $100 million barrier. When *Star Wars* followed the *Jaws* template to even greater success two summers later (in fact, George Lucas's movie did Spielberg's one better in that it *created* a brand name instead of capitalizing on an existing hit), Hollywood's approach to the making and marketing of big-budget studio fare was permanently altered. Although the limited roll-out pattern continues to be employed for some releases—specifically prestige pictures and independently produced and distributed fare—the majority of mainstream features are released following the same recipe of large screen counts, hefty marketing budgets that focus heavily on television (and now the Internet as well), and, whenever possible, merchandising tie-ins. *Jaws* may have dominated theaters for only a single summer, but its impact is still felt whenever Hollywood flips its calendar to June.

FILM FIRST FILE #1: FIVE TROUBLED PRODUCTIONS THAT BECAME GREAT MOVIES

Battered by technical problems and the complexities of shooting on open water, *Jaws* was a famously difficult shoot that nevertheless resulted in a classic movie. Here are five post-*Jaws* productions that overcame great troubles to enjoy happy endings.

Apocalypse Now (Francis Ford Coppola, 1979)

Production Problems: Where can you start with what was arguably the most disastrous film shoot of all time? To begin with, a typhoon decimated the Philippines-based sets two months into filming. Additionally, the movie's leading man, Martin Sheen (who replaced original star Harvey Keitel a few days into the shoot), suffered a heart attack and was unable to work for over a month. And then there were all manner of budgetary overruns, additional delays, and disagreements with the actors. Through it all, the script lacked an ending, with Coppola inventing one at the 11th hour. (For a comprehensive look at the movie's turbulent production, watch the superb documentary *Hearts of Darkness*, directed by Fax Bahr, George Hickenlooper, and Eleanor Coppola.[29]

Why It's Still Great: Put simply, there's no war movie quite like *Apocalypse Now*. Despite whatever was happening off-screen, scene-for-scene the film is a technical marvel boasting virtuoso direction from Coppola.

Fitzcarraldo (Werner Herzog, 1982)

Production Problems: Just as Coppola squared off against Mother Nature during the production of *Apocalypse Now*, so too were Herzog's ambitions challenged by the natural world while making *Fitzcarraldo*. The film chronicles the exploits of a rubber magnate (played by the director's regular collaborator and frequent off-screen sparring partner Klaus Kinski) who hires an army of locals to haul a 320-ton steamer *over* a mountain to … well, to get to the other side where his preferred river awaits. In the interests of authenticity, Herzog really did have his crew haul a 320-ton steamer *over* a mountain, a challenge that proved almost insurmountable. (Like *Apocalypse Now*, *Fitzcarraldo* inspired a making-of documentary—Les Blank's *Burden of Dreams*—that depicts just how close the movie came to falling apart.)[30]

Why It's Still Great: While his crew may not have been pleased with Herzog's commitment to realism, the Herculean effort it took to make the film helps the audience understand the mixture of ambition and madness that drives the title character.

Tootsie (Sydney Pollack, 1982)

Production Problems: The problems for this gender-bending comedy about a struggling male actor (Dustin Hoffman) who scores a breakout role on a soap opera after disguising himself as a woman started with the script. In that, it took Hoffman—the movie's star and one of its driving creative forces—many drafts and collaborators (including Murray Schisgal, Larry Gelbert, Elaine May, and Pollack himself) until he found a script that he felt comfortable shooting. Hoffman was equally invested in creating a believable female persona, a trial-and-error process that lasted almost two months. (As Hoffman told *The New York Times*, he had it written into his contract that he would only star in the movie if his screen test as a woman was entirely convincing.)[31] Disagreements between Hoffman and Pollack over the film's story and comic tone continued during production, which resulted in a longer, costlier shoot.

Why It's Still Great: Hoffman has delivered some terrific performances during the course of his career, but he's never vanished into a role as completely as he does in *Tootsie*. His absolute commitment to the part is what makes the film so endlessly topical . . . and so hilarious.

Titanic (James Cameron, 1997)

Production Problems: A decade before he helmed this period epic about the doomed ocean liner, Cameron had a notoriously difficult experience making his deep-sea-diving-themed sci-fi movie *The Abyss*. Not only did he willingly return to the sea with *Titanic*, he set an even higher bar for himself, planning a full-scale re-creation of the ship's sinking that would require weeks and weeks of shooting in challenging conditions. Illness and injuries were rampant, and the situation wasn't helped by the director's famous temper, which he sometimes directed against the cast and crew.[32] (One angry employee went as far as to sneak PCP into a serving of lobster chowder, hospitalizing a number of crew members.)[33] The logistical challenges wound up driving up the movie's budget and delaying its release, leading many to suspect that *Titanic* would prove to be Cameron's Waterloo.

Why It's Still Great: Instead of Cameron's greatest defeat, *Titanic* wound up becoming, perhaps, his greatest triumph . . . certainly in terms of its commercial and awards success. Once you make it through the goopy (if still enjoyable) first half, the sinking of the *Titanic* is expertly rendered and the film's conclusion packs an emotional wallop.

Eyes Wide Shut (Stanley Kubrick, 1999)

Production Problems: Always an exacting filmmaker, Kubrick was particularly demanding during the making of what would become his final film. Originally going before cameras in the fall of 1996, *Eyes Wide Shut* finally completed filming in June 1998—a full 15 months later. (Making it, according to the *Guinness Book of World Records*, the longest constant movie shoot in history, lasting some 400 days.)[34] The delays stemmed primarily from the director's perfectionist tendencies, as he demanded countless takes and reshoots and intricate re-creations of New York locations on London soundstages. The length of the shoot required the recasting of two key roles and took its toll on the crew.

Why It's Still Great:　　Although arguably Kubrick's most divisive movie, *Eyes Wide Shut* may also be his most personal film, a dreamlike but moving mediation on love and marriage made with laser-like precision.

FILM FIRST FILE #2: STEVEN SPIELBERG'S $100 MILLION CLUB

Jaws became the first movie in history to cross the $100 million line at the domestic box office, a target that all subsequent aspiring blockbusters were expected to reach. Steven Spielberg himself would surpass that magic number repeatedly throughout the course of his directorial career. Here are the 15 (and counting) members of Spielberg's personal $100 million club, listed by order of total gross (excluding re-releases).[35]

1. *E.T.: The Extra-Terrestrial* (1982): $359.1 million
2. *Jurassic Park* (1993): $357 million
3. *Indiana Jones and the Kingdom of the Crystal Skull* (2008): $317.1 million
4. *Jaws* (1975): $260 million
5. *War of the Worlds* (2005): $234.2 million
6. *The Lost World: Jurassic Park* (1997): $229 million
7. *Saving Private Ryan* (1998): $216.5 million
8. *Raiders of the Lost Ark* (1981): $212.2 million
9. *Indiana Jones and the Last Crusade* (1989): $197.1 million
10. *Lincoln* (2012): $182.2 million
11. *Indiana Jones and the Temple of Doom* (1984): $179.8 million
12. *Catch Me if You Can* (2002): $164.6 million
13. *Minority Report* (2002): $132 million
14. *Hook* (1991): $119.6 million
15. *Close Encounters of the Third Kind* (1977): $116.3 million

And just for completeness's sake, here are the 12 that fell short[36]:

1. *Schindler's List* (1993): $96 million
2. *The Color Purple* (1985): $94.1 million
3. *War Horse* (2011): $79.8 million
4. *A.I.: Artificial Intelligence* (2001): $78.6 million
5. *The Terminal* (2004): $77.8 million
6. *The Adventures of Tintin* (2011): $77.5 million
7. *Munich* (2005): $47.4 million
8. *Amistad* (1997): $44.2 million

9. *Always* (1989): $43.8 million
10. *1941* (1979): $31.7 million
11. *Empire of the Sun* (1987): $22.2 million
12. *The Sugarland Express* (1974): $7.5 million

Chapter 2

Star Wars (1977)

The Film: For a film that has had such an enormous cultural impact, *Star Wars* seems surprisingly small compared to the present-day spectacles it inspired.

If only everyone's initial exposure to *Star Wars*[1] could mirror the way thousands of moviegoers experienced it during the film's first showing on opening day, May 25, 1977. At that point, George Lucas's industry-transforming space opera was just another movie, albeit one that had some viewers—particularly those of the geek persuasion—excited enough to line up hours ahead of time to be the first ones into the theater. Following those initial screenings and over the course of the subsequent holiday weekend, *Star Wars* left mere moviedom behind for pop-culture godhood. And that's the baggage that audiences have had to approach the film with ever since. Parents introduce it to their children like a sacred rite of passage, while older first-time viewers sit down to watch it having already absorbed many of its most famous moments, lines, and images through decades of spoofs, imitators and simple repetition. The mere act of watching *Star Wars* has come to take on the status of a significant life achievement, something that earns a spot on one of those "1000 Things to Do before You Die" bucket lists. And for the truly devoted, it's a gateway to an entire universe that has grown to encompass TV shows, books, graphic novels, video games, music, toys, clothes and pretty much every other form of media and/or merchandise available.

That a movie that today looks so diminutive when placed alongside blockbusters like *Transformers* has inspired a galaxy that's so expansive is one of the great surprises when one revisits *Star Wars* today. Even the subsequent films in the series, to say nothing of the ancillary material, have a larger scope, with storylines, characters, and settings spilling out of the edges of the frame. But the first movie—now officially titled *Star Wars: Episode IV—A New Hope*—is relatively lean and taut. Lucas's original script was famously unwieldy, bogged down by laborious mythology and mystical mumbo jumbo. It took him several years and numerous revisions to streamline the narrative, sorting out what worked from what didn't and soliciting advice from his numerous filmmaker friends, among them Francis Ford Coppola and Willard Huyck.[2] Once Lucas found a studio willing to fund the movie—20th Century Fox—additional changes were made during preproduction as well as throughout the notoriously difficult shoot and in the editing room. (Lucas's then-wife, Marcia, who was working in the industry as an editor, is said to have played an important role in the latter stage, reediting the climactic X-Wing attack on the Death Star into the rousing set piece it is today.)[3] Although Lucas would later have the creative and financial freedom necessary to try things on the set, on the first *Star Wars* there was little margin for error considering that failure could mean the premature end of his career.

Whatever problems bedeviled Lucas offscreen, they don't register in the finished product, at least not in a way that overtly ruins the spell that the movie casts from the moment that iconic John Williams fanfare kicks in and the famous text crawl fills the screen, followed by the appearance of two ships trading laser fire as they soar through space. Even with huge advances made in special-effects technology in the decades since 1977, the first five minutes of *Star Wars* are utterly transporting in a way few contemporary F/X-heavy blockbusters are. That's aided immensely by Lucas's decision to begin the movie *in media res*, an approach that's employed with less and less frequency these days, as studios seem to think that modern audiences won't be able to acclimate to a given high-concept scenario unless it's served up with a whopping spoonful of momentum-crushing exposition. That would be one of the chief arguments against showing a *Star Wars* newbie the prequel trilogy ahead of the ostensible fourth chapter in the series; chronologically that may be the correct order, but it robs the first *Star Wars* (in production order) of one of its chief attributes—the sense that you're discovering a larger universe through the experiences of the movie's main hero and the audience's surrogate, Luke Skywalker. (The sizable quality gulf between the prequels and the original movie would be another reason.)

Much has been written about the way Lucas grafted the typical "hero's journey" narrative as outlined by Joseph Campbell (something that the writer/director himself has freely admitted)[4] onto his outer space extravaganza, and, if anything, the enormous commercial success of *Star Wars* just reinforces the power that kind of mythmaking has when it's done well. Luke is by no means the most interesting character in the movie (indeed, as played by the painfully earnest Mark Hamill, he's kind of a drag), but his blankness is what makes it possible for viewers to project themselves onto him and experience the grand adventure he embarks on firsthand. Although it's more fun to playact as Han Solo, Chewbacca, or even C-3PO—characters with more sharply etched personalities—after the movie, while watching it, Luke functions as the viewer's eyes and ears.

More than Luke and his hero's journey, perhaps the real secret to *Star Wars'* enduring appeal is the fact that it gave the world one of the all-time-great bad guys: Darth Vader. (The character currently ranks as #3 on the American Film Institute's list of the 50 greatest movie villains, behind only Hannibal Lecter and Norman Bates.)[5] From his first entrance, sweeping aboard the Rebel ship in search of Princess Leia, Vader's appearance is so striking, his voice (provided after the fact by James Earl Jones, rather than the actor who was actually in the suit, David Prowse) so memorable, he's both chilling and instantly compelling. Going forward, Darth Vader would become the franchise's central character, with the prequel trilogy essentially transforming the entire six-part *Star Wars* saga into the tale of his corruption and eventual redemption. In this first movie, though, his job is first and foremost to be the physical incarnation of the Empire's might, and, after a few minutes spent in his imposing presence, it's hard to imagine how Luke and his scrappy band of Rebel allies could ever hope to defeat him.

Vader's increased prominence in the sequels and prequels is just one of the ways that Lucas attempts to deepen the emotional and mythological resonance of the series as a whole after the first film. Viewed in the context of the entire franchise, *A New Hope* stands out as the most lighthearted and straightforward of the bunch, a simple adventure yarn pitting the forces of good against the forces of evil complete with a beautiful princess to find and rescue in the midst of the battle. On the other hand, that simplicity, coupled with the screenplay's undeniable dramatic clunkiness, does make one wonder how a movie this modest—save for its special effects, which were groundbreaking at the time and mostly hold up today—could have had such a far-reaching impact on the entire filmmaking industry. When that kind of historical weight is applied to *Star Wars*, it's no wonder that some viewers might come away wondering what all the fuss is about.

And that's really why the experience enjoyed by those first audiences in 1977 is so enviable. Every subsequent generation that has been introduced to *Star Wars* often goes into it all too aware of its importance, either to a specific person in their life or to pop culture at large. Beyond that, the fictional universe that Lucas created (and which is now in the hands of the Walt Disney Company) has expanded so greatly that this particular movie is just one small part of it rather than its defining creative force. Indeed, there are almost certainly individuals out there today for whom the animated *Clone Wars* TV series or *The Force Unleashed* video game is more representative of *Star Wars* than . . . *Star Wars*. Unapologetically earnest and packed with retro charm, *Star Wars* hasn't changed over the years, but the world around it—both on- and offscreen—definitely has.

The First: *Star Wars* launched the modern age of blockbuster filmmaking and all that that entails, from the primacy of the trilogy to the art of merchandising.

If *Jaws* launched the contemporary blockbuster era, *Star Wars* transported it to a new heights. Audiences and the industry at large have been living in the film's shadow for so long, it can be difficult to appreciate just how completely Lucas's space opera, a film that its own studio had next to no confidence in, changed Hollywood's approach to making movies, or at least, making a specific kind of movie. Almost all of the factors that a modern studio weighs before awarding a green light to a big-budget, spectacle-driven production—among them sequel potential, merchandising opportunities, and home entertainment value—can be directly traced back to how 20th Century Fox and in particular George Lucas got the most bang for their buck out of *Star Wars*. And the money was always what impressed the studios the most. Although Lucas and his crew made a number of lasting creative contributions to filmmaking, particularly in the realm of special effects, *Star Wars'* legacy is more commonly defined by its commercial rather than artistic achievements. That's not to suggest there isn't any artistry to it, but the movie's brand of swashbuckling heroics had been seen before, including in the films that had directly inspired Lucas, from Akira Kurosawa's *The Hidden Fortress* to old *Flash Gordon* serials. What hadn't been seen before was a movie that could parlay itself into a full-fledged brand name. To Hollywood's eyes, *Star Wars* wasn't just a piece of summer entertainment, it was a new business model.

Lucas himself deserves the lion's share of the credit for seeing what *Star Wars* could become. To the studio executives at Fox, it was a troubled production (tensions between Lucas and his crew grew so bad that he swore off directing for decades, finally being tempted back behind the camera again for *The Phantom Menace*) that had resulted in an almost certain box-office bomb. On the upside, it wasn't a hugely expensive production—between $10 and $11 million, which in contemporary dollars comes in at around $40 million,[6] an absurdly low number for a contemporary blockbuster—and the studio only paid Lucas a combined $100,000 to write and direct the picture.[7] In exchange for accepting a lower salary, Lucas received a share of the first film's profits, the rights to make any potential sequels himself (while giving Fox first refusal on distribution), as well as the rights to any and all merchandise related to the movie.[8] Beyond the fact that Fox executives had little confidence in *Star Wars* to begin with, at the time neither sequels nor merchandise ranked as the topmost concerns for most studios. The movies themselves were the products they had to sell, not toys, video games or story possibilities for a sequel to a movie that hadn't even opened yet.

Lucas, on the other hand, did have a big-picture view, particularly in regard to where the series could go after the first movie. Certainly, the copious amount of material he threw out of the early drafts of *Star Wars* en route to the script that went before the cameras could have fueled a number of follow-ups. And then there was the curious case of the *Star Wars* "sequel" novel *Splinter of the Mind's Eye*, written by Alan Dean Foster, who also penned the novelization of the first movie.[9] As *Star Wars* was being released, Lucas tasked the author with writing another installment in "The Further Adventures of Luke Skywalker." Legend has it that Lucas's plan for *Splinter* was for it to potentially function as fodder for a sequel, one that could be produced for far less money than its predecessor, should it become even a modest hit. By the time the book finally arrived in stores in March 1978, *Star Wars* was, of course, a mammoth success, and Lucas felt far more secure in the franchise's future.[10] (Although no longer in official *Star Wars* continuity, *Splinter of the Mind's Eye* is still in print and makes for a fun "What If ..." read.) That same year, he told *Time* magazine that he envisioned as many as 12 *Star Wars* movies, which would continue to chronicle the Jedi-in-training's adventures.[11]

Sequels weren't a new invention in Hollywood, of course, but rarely before had an entire saga been planned out in such a grand fashion. In the past, when a movie performed above and beyond expectations, the studio made another one that sometimes related back to the previous movie and other times not. The various Universal creature features from the '30s and '40s are good examples of the former, with Frankenstein, Dracula and the Wolf Man appearing in multiple films that often (though not always) tangentially acknowledged what had come before; on the opposite end of the spectrum was the *Road To ...* series where stars Bob Hope and Bing Crosby played different characters on every globe-trotting adventure. Even the storied James Bond franchise didn't go out of its way to establish a consistent continuity between installments, at least until the current Daniel Craig incarnation.

Direct sequels had started to become more common in the '70s, as films like *The Godfather Part II* and *French Connection II* showed how lucrative it could be to tack another chapter onto a hit movie, but Lucas eventually upped the ante by invoking the trilogy concept. While in the midst of production on the first *Star Wars* sequel, *The Empire Strikes Back*, in 1980, Lucas described plans to make three separate trilogies for a total of nine films—down three movies from his first estimate. After completing *Return of the Jedi*, of course, that number fell again to just a single trilogy of three films as a *Star Wars*–weary Lucas moved on to other pursuits, until circling back to the prequel trilogy a decade later. Regardless of how many trilogies Lucas did or didn't make, the notion of a three-film arc became a central tenet of franchise filmmaking going forward, one that has resulted in such lucrative series as *Back to the Future*, *The Matrix*, and Christopher Nolan's Batman films. These days, it's rare for a studio to begin production on an action-heavy blockbuster *without* thinking at least two films ahead.

The other lesson the studios have been careful to learn from *Star Wars* is to keep a tighter grip on the merchandising rights of their various properties. At the time Lucas made the first movie, virtually all of the major studios, Fox included, lacked a merchandising arm and saw little value in creating one. That allowed Lucas's lawyer, Tom Pollock, to negotiate a deal with Fox that awarded the director 60 percent of *Star Wars* merchandising, with the rights reverting to him in full within two years.[12] The studio didn't have to wait long to realize its mistake. Almost as soon as the movie premiered, moviegoers were ready and willing to snap up anything with a *Star Wars* logo on it. Toys were in particularly high demand; in fact, the toy company Kenner, which had won the licensing rights to create *Star Wars* action figures, was so unprepared for the deluge of orders that they were facing a holiday season with next to no product to offer *Star Wars*–crazed consumers. Their solution was to offer an "Early Bird Certificate Package," a cardboard picture of 12 key *Star Wars* characters whose action figures you would be able to purchase a few months hence, along with a certificate that would allow you to receive four of the figures early.[13]

In the decades since the first film's release, *Star Wars'* galaxy of merchandise has grown to include albums, video games, clothes, costumes, collectibles, and all manner of knickknacks. And, prior to Disney's acquisition of the franchise, all that money went directly back to George Lucas, not Fox. In 2007, Forbes estimated that the *Star Wars* toys alone have sold over $9 billion since 1977, over a third of the franchise's $22 billion total gross.[14] With that kind of profit potential, it's no wonder that so many contemporary blockbusters arrive in theaters complete with fashion accessories, fast-food tie-ins, and more toys than you could ever hope to find space for in your rumpus room. And it goes without saying that no filmmaker since Lucas has been able to strike a deal with a studio that awards them full rights to all these products, although Jack Nicholson famously convinced Warner Bros. to award him royalties from merchandising as part of his *Batman* contract—a lucrative decision, considering that 1989 film banked an estimated $750 million in merchandise sales.[15]

While the advent of the *Star Wars* business model has benefitted Hollywood tremendously in terms of profits, there's no question that it's taken a creative toll on the industry. In the process of trying to craft the next big blockbuster, it's all too easy for both executives and filmmakers to allow their attention to drift away from the content of the movie to its saleable qualities. That's how moviegoers wind up having to choose between forgettable event pictures like *Van Helsing* or *Battleship*, where the movie itself feels like just one more element in a larger marketing plan. Even though they may make for convenient scapegoats, Lucas and *Star Wars* aren't directly at fault for those failures of imagination. It's worth remembering first and foremost that *Star Wars* grew into the empire that it is today because it inspired so much passion and love on behalf of viewers. Without that connection between the storyteller and the audience, the majority of Lucas's savvy business decisions would have come to naught. Despite the quantity of goods sold, the quality of that first *Star Wars* is what hooked viewers at the time of its release and keeps them coming back to that far, far away galaxy decades later.

FILM FIRST FILE #1: FIVE GREAT POST-*STAR WARS* MOVIE TRILOGIES

Like the original *Star Wars* series, the following trilogies prove that great sagas come in threes.

The Lord of the Rings (Peter Jackson, 2001–2003)

Peter Jackson's attempt to bring J. R. R. Tolkien's beloved fantasy series to the screen was a gamble that perhaps shouldn't have worked, but wound up succeeding beyond anyone's wildest imagination. Through spectacular locations, production design, and performances, the movies don't simply recreate Middle Earth—they bring it to life.

The Matrix (Andy and Lana Wachowski, 1999–2003)

What begins as a traditional sci-fi superhero story morphs over the course of three films into a treatise on the relationship between man and machine, as well as the limits of faith in who (or what) you believe to be a higher power. Oh yeah … and the action sequences are pretty spectacular, too.

Paradise Lost (Joe Berlinger and Bruce Sinofsky, 1996–2011)

Thanks in part to the efforts of documentary filmmakers Berlinger and Sinofsky, the case of the so-called West Memphis Three remained a national story for the years that the men were incarcerated, and the release of each new film brought additional attention and support to their cause. The third and final installment concluded with the happiest of endings: their freedom.

The Pusher Trilogy (Nicolas Winding Refn, 1996–2005)

A sprawling crime story set in Copenhagen, each *Pusher* film focuses on a different lead character, but the cumulative impact is a portrait of an (under) world where individuals are pushed to extreme measures to maintain their dominance. It's the laws of the jungle applied to an urban landscape.

The Vengeance Trilogy (Park Chan-wook, 2002–2005)

Chan-wook's trio of bloody revenge pictures—connected by theme rather than storylines—kick-started a worldwide interest in South Korean cinema and kept the local fake blood industry gainfully employed.

FILM FIRST FILE #2: THE MOST MERCHANDISABLE MOVIE FRANCHISES

Star Wars ushered in the modern era of movie merchandising, where studio blockbusters are expected to spawn toys, video games, and even clothing lines that have the potential to earn more money than the film itself. In fact, *Star Wars* merchandise is estimated to account for more than half of the franchise's lifetime gross of $22 billion—with the tie-in goods regularly raking in about $1 billion every year. Here are some other franchises that have proven themselves to be as valuable outside of the multiplex as they are in.

Toy Story

The film series that transformed Pixar from a small computer graphics company and maker of short films into an animation powerhouse has spawned a line of ancillary products that have printed money for the studio ever since the release of the first film in 1995. *Toy Story 3* (2010) alone raked in $2.8 billion in sales of licensed merchandise the year it was released.[16]

Spider-Man

Spider-Man has been one of the most popular superheroes around since he first swung into comic books back in 1962. But the web-head's big-screen franchise, which began in 2002—Spidey's 40th anniversary—increased his popularity, merchandise-wise. For example, even before 2007's *Spider-Man 3* arrived in theaters, sales for toys connected to the film reached $70 million.[17]

Harry Potter

Besides almost single-handedly saving the publishing industry, J. K. Rowling's seven novels about the titular boy wizard spawned a $21 billion cash machine consisting of a lucrative film franchise, a theme park, video games and a $1 billion dollar-a-year product line made up of, among other things, clothes, candy, and magical accessories like wands.[18]

Cars

Although neither *Cars* nor its sequel *Cars 2* are Pixar's highest-grossing movies, the merchandise generated by the franchise has approached the magic $10 billion figure. In fact, one of the main reasons the studio proceeded with a second movie in the first place was to add new products into that lucrative line ... hence the introduction of other anthropomorphic vehicles like planes and boats into a world previously only populated by cars.[19]

Chapter 3

Superman: The Movie (1978)

The Film: Thanks to a verisimilitude-minded director, what began
as a comic book cash grab became a more grounded portrait
of a high-flying hero.

In the wake of *Jaws* and *Star Wars*, Hollywood studios were in the throes
of blockbuster fever by the late '70s, forever on the hunt for the next heavyweight production that could marry the effects-laden, merchandise-friendly
spectacle of George Lucas's space adventure with the built-in name value
and proven mass appeal of Steven Spielberg's based-on-a-bestseller shark
tale. Amidst this feeding frenzy, any producer holding the screen rights to a
piece of material that met these specific requirements could stand to profit
enormously. Ilya Salkind was one such producer fortunate enough in the
right place at the right time with the right . . . well, *rights*. The scion of a family whose history in the movie business dated back to the days of silent pictures, Salkind joined the trade in the late '60s, working alongside his father,
Alexander. In 1974—a year before *Jaws* hit theaters and shattered box-
office records—he made a bold and fortuitous choice that would further
improve the fortunes of the already successful Salkind clan. In search of an
attention-grabbing purchase, he convinced his father and their producing
partner Pierre Spengler to write a not-inconsiderable check to acquire the
big-screen rights to one of the twentieth century's most iconic heroes: the
superpowered stranger from another world known as Superman.[1]

Given the pop culture stature Superman, a.k.a. the Man of Steel, a.k.a. the
Last Son of Krypton had enjoyed in the four decades since gracing the
June 1938 cover of *Action Comics #1*, it may seem surprising that the rights
to his cinematic adventures would be available for purchase. And it's worth

noting that Superman's publisher, DC Comics, required the Salkinds to leap through a number of hoops in order to secure the license, most notably including an "Integrity of Character" clause in the contract designed to ensure that the producers wouldn't destroy the legacy of the publisher's flagship hero.[2] Had the Salkinds waited a year or two more beyond 1974, it's possible that they would have gone home empty handed, beaten to the punch by another producer or even Warner Bros., which was owned DC's parent company, Warner Communications, and may have realized that they had their own potential *Jaws*-sized blockbuster in-house. Besides good timing, what worked in Ilya Salkind's favor was the checkered, largely unimpressive history of translating comic books into other mediums. Although there had been a handful of success stories in the past, most notably the live-action *Adventures of Superman* TV series from the 1950s and the camped-up *Batman* series (which begat a 1966 feature film that's essentially an extralong episode) from the '60s, these productions—much like comic books themselves—were generally regarded as juvenile. Kids might show up to see colorfully clad heroes perform feats of strength, but good luck attracting those adults who were queuing up in droves to see *The Godfather* and *The Exorcist*.

Still, Salkind wasn't dissuaded from his conviction that there was big money to be earned from a Superman feature, and the post-*Jaws* marketplace confirmed that he had made a smart investment. Showmen by nature, he and his producing partners sought to attach high profile, big-name talent to their superhero movie, lending it an aura of artistic legitimacy that the comic book itself perhaps lacked. For the title role, for example, they wooed movie stars like Paul Newman and Robert Redford[3] and offered the directing chair to such proven hitmakers as William Friedkin and Peter Yates. Although none of those choices panned out, they did successfully enlist *Godfather* author Mario Puzo to pen the first draft of the movie's screenplay, a hiring that they trumpeted in the press.[4] That coup was followed by the announcement that none other than Marlon Brando—the Godfather himself—would be playing Superman's father, Jor-El, a glorified cameo role for which he was paid the exorbitant sum of $3.7 million.[5] Brando's hiring proved crucial in two other respects as well; first, it convinced Gene Hackman to jump aboard as Superman's nemesis Lex Luthor, and secondly, it freed the production from having to find a major star to fill the hero's boots and tights, which is how a littleknown actor named Christopher Reeve came to occupy the role that defined the rest of his career.[6]

Despite the aura of respectability that Puzo, Brando, and Hackman brought to the movie, the version of *Superman* that was taking shape was still distinctly kids' stuff. The phone book–sized script that Puzo delivered—it numbered some 500 pages in length, more than enough to support the two movies that the Salkinds intended to produce, which would be shot simultaneously—before departing the project was rewritten by another team of screenwriters who filled it with campy humor, including a scene where Superman randomly flew by actor Telly Savalas, leading him to utter his catchphrase from the hit series *Kojak*, "Who loves ya baby."[7] It was an aesthetic more in line with the old *Batman* series, but the Salkinds seemed less concerned with the movie's tone than with simply getting the production off the ground and into theaters. Their "full speed ahead" approach was typified by the way they eventually secured a director for the project after their initial choice, Guy Hamilton, was forced to drop out. On a Sunday, Alexander Salkind called up Richard Donner, who had just enjoyed a big hit with the horror film *The Omen*, and offered him $1 million to make *Superman* fly.[8] There was no time for pleasantries or a discussion of what his approach to the material might be—they just needed someone on set who was capable of calling "Action."

The Salkinds' almost random hiring of Donner wound up being the wisest decision they made as he came aboard the movie with a creative vision that extended beyond the bottom line and the box office. Born eight years before Superman's first comic book appearance, the director felt a strong connection to the character and wanted to see him handled respectfully on-screen. As a result, he was immediately dismayed to crack open the script to see that camp pervaded every page. Rather than drop out, that discovery convinced him that he *had* to make these two movies, if only to protect the reputation of a twentieth-century American icon. (As he put it in one interview, "I felt this stupid necessity to keep Superman clean.")[9] In the first of many battles with his new employers, he fought for massive script changes that would be overseen by Tom Mankiewicz, screenwriter of several James Bond films and son of Hollywood legend Joseph L. Mankiewicz. Together, they threw out much of the broad comedy (though not all of it; certainly, Lex Luthor's henchman Otis—played by Ned Beatty—is written and performed as an over-the-top buffoon kept around purely for comic relief) in favor of a one-word approach that Donner disseminated to every level of the production: verisimilitude.[10] This version of Superman would be down-to-earth and realistic ... as realistic as the story of a superpowered alien who combats evil and romances attractive female journalists could be, that is.

Donner's determination to achieve verisimilitude in all areas of the film was most keenly felt in the long, trial-and-error-filled process of believably making Reeve-as-Superman take flight. As far as the director was concerned, it was the one element of the film he had to get absolutely right; if Superman couldn't fly, neither would the movie. All kinds of experiments were attempted and abandoned before they finally hit upon a series of methods that worked. The most innovative of these was a process by which the actor was positioned in front of a blue screen and "flew" in place, while being filmed by cameras with a pair of interlocking zoom lenses designed to create the illusion of motion.[11] Due to the superheroic efforts of Donner and his effects team, at the time of *Superman: The Movie*'s[12] release, its now-famous tagline "You will believe a man can fly" really could be considered a promise and not just a marketing tease.

That's less true today, as modern audiences accustomed to digital effects are more easily able to spot the limitations of the analog tools available at the time. But even if the combination of blue screen and interlocking zoom lenses fails to convince when watching the movie today, the joy and exhilaration on Reeve's face, not to mention the smoothness and grace with which he moves—this, despite the sheer discomfort of the harnesses he was required to wear[13]—still feels authentic. Indeed, Reeve's performance is *Superman*'s finest special effect, particularly in the way he effortlessly moves back and forth between his dual identities as dorky Clark Kent and stalwart Superman. In that respect, the movie's finest scene may be one of its quietest: a simple shot of Reeve as he works up the courage to reveal his true self to the object of his affection, Lois Lane. For a brief, fleeting moment, the viewer can glimpse both his identities inhabiting the same body.

In broad strokes at least, *Superman* benefitted almost everyone involved. The Salkinds got the box-office hit they were after, while Donner was able to rescue the character from a camped-up fate. But the trials and tribulations of making the movie had left the director and his producers barely on speaking terms; emboldened by the first film's enormous success and the fact that so much of the second movie was already in the can, the Salkinds dismissed Donner and hired British director Richard Lester to oversee the completion of *Superman II*.[14] This was an especially cruel blow because the second film was shaping up to be (and, in fact, became) a more limber and purely entertaining feature, simply due to the fact that the biggest storytelling hurdle—recounting the character's origin, which Donner devotes almost a full hour to in the first *Superman*—was out of the way.

While it's understandable that Donner wanted to give Superman's backstory the respect and dramatic weight he felt it deserved, the movie's plodding first half regularly verges on being too self-consciously mythic. (Though they're expressly not written that way, the scenes on Krypton almost play as camp, what with the sight of Brando dressed up in a glowing white suit, disinterestedly intoning lines like, "His dense molecular structure will make him strong.") Donner seems far more engaged and at ease during the middle section of the film, when Superman is suited up and patrolling Metropolis, while taking the occasional time out for an interview/date with Lois. It's here that the director's guiding philosophy of verisimilitude proves most successful, as he and Reeve locate the humanity in a hero who might otherwise soar above the kinds of concerns and challenges that would make him a relatable and compelling character. What Donner understands—and what's ultimately key to the movie's success—is that before viewers can believe this Superman can fly, they first have to believe in him as a man.

The First: By proving that there could be such a thing as
a serious superhero film, *Superman: The Movie* established
the template employed by almost every comic book movie
made since.

As someone who had grown up with the comic book version of Superman,
Richard Donner had an abiding respect for the character that burnished his
desire to see him treated seriously on-screen. Similarly, an entire generation
of filmmakers who came of age watching *Superman: The Movie* absorbed
Donner's verisimilitude-first approach and would eventually apply it to their
own superhero spectacles. In fact, the prevailing tone and spirit of the current
comic book movie boom can be traced directly back to *Superman*, with
directors like Bryan Singer openly acknowledging their affection for Donner's film. (It's no accident that when Singer got the chance to helm his own
Superman picture, 2006's *Superman Returns*, he delivered a movie that functions as a continuation of *Superman* and *Superman II*.)[15] Before *Superman*,
few creative types in Hollywood took superheroes seriously, and that showed
in the cheaply made movie serials and campy TV shows that represented the
earliest live-action translations of comic books. These days, however, characters like Superman, Batman, and Spider-Man are approached with an attitude that's closer to reverence.

Granted, that shift in attitude took some time to occur, as the success of
Donner's *Superman* didn't set off a stampede of competing superhero epics.
Apart from three *Superman* sequels (which progressively moved in a more
comic vein after Donner's departure), as well as a Salkind-produced spin-
off, *Supergirl*, and a smattering of low-budget offerings like *Swamp Thing*
and *Red Sonja*, the early and mid-'80s were largely devoid of big-screen
comic book fare. Television remained a somewhat different story, however,
as both of the big publishers, DC and Marvel, had been licensing their characters out for live-action and animated series as well as stand-alone telefilms
even before *Superman: The Movie* hit theaters. Of these small-screen efforts—
which included live-action versions of Wonder Woman, Spider-Man, and
Captain America—the only one that approached its hero with the same level
of seriousness that Donner brought to *Superman* was *The Incredible Hulk*,
based on Marvel's resident Jekyll and Hyde–like beast. The show, which
ran for five seasons from 1978 to 1982 and starred Bill Bixby as scientist
David Banner and bodybuilder Lou Ferrigno as his green-skinned, super-
strong inner monster, may have its campy elements when viewed today, but
there's an underlying feeling of despair and rage that comes through both
in the storytelling and Bixby's performance that distinguished it from its
comic book influenced brethren at the time. Even Reeve's Superman, as sober
as he was in certain moments, was never as tragic or dangerous a figure as
Bixby's Banner.

Eleven years after *Superman*, comic book cinema at last achieved full-scale
liftoff in the wake of Tim Burton's 1989 blockbuster *Batman*—a movie that

had been in the making since 1979, when aspiring producer and supreme comic book fan Michael Uslan took a page from the Salkinds and put together the cash to purchase the film rights to DC's other signature hero.[16] Where the Salkinds had managed to rush *Superman* into production three years after acquiring the rights by sheer force of will (not to mention throwing large wads of money around), it took 10 years and multiple screenplay drafts (one of which was penned by *Superman* savior Tom Mankiewicz)[17] for a *Batman* movie to become a reality. When the film finally was completed, it resembled Donner's *Superman* in the way it took the character seriously, depicting the Dark Knight as ... well, the Dark Knight—an afterhours vigilante who went about his one-man war on crime with a grave sense of purpose. Burton avoided lightening the tone of the character or his universe, running as far away as possible from anything that might be construed as "camp." Stylistically, however, his film does represent a striking departure from Donner's verisimilitude-driven vision. Where *Superman* is meant to take place in the real world (a feeling enhanced by the extensive location shooting in New York, Alberta, and New Mexico), *Batman* unfolds in a highly stylized, highly Gothic version of an American city dreamed up by Burton and production designer Anton Furst. No doubt due to the fact that he was trained as an artist and animator, Burton brings a strong graphic sensibility to *Batman*, with more varied compositions and striking images than are on display in *Superman*. It was the first comic book movie with shots that actually resembled comic book panels.

The comics-derived films that immediately followed *Batman*—which ranged from *The Crow* to *Spawn* to *Blade*—generally sought to replicate that film's formal boldness and darker depiction of its hero. Verisimilitude took a backseat to high style, a trend that blew up in the genre's face when Joel Schumacher took over the Bat-franchise from Burton and put his own distinct visual stamp on the series, a stamp that, unfortunately, happened to resemble a gaudier, tackier version of the '60s TV show. The box-office belly flop of 1997's Schumacher-directed *Batman & Robin* (along with such other high-profile failures as *Judge Dredd* and *Mystery Men*) temporarily cured the studios of their superhero fever. It took Donner disciple Bryan Singer to launch the second wave of comic book super-productions three years later in 2000 by going back to the reality-based model represented by *Superman* for his movie version of Marvel's *X-Men* comic book series. Singer ensured that *X-Men* would possess a level of realism that superhero adaptations had moved away from, playing up real-world parallels to weighty issues like intolerance and puberty and even ditching the colorful costumes that the mutant crimefighters wore on the page for black leather ensembles, a choice that was controversial among fanboys.[18] Not that it stopped them from seeing the movie, of course; *X-Men* eventually powered its way to a $150 million gross, and suddenly, comic books were fair game again.

Like Singer, most of the filmmakers who are part of the post–*X-Men* era of comic book movies were impressionable kids and young adults when *Superman* initially swooped into theaters, so it shouldn't be a surprise that Donner's film remains a touchstone for their own work. Sam Raimi's *Spider-Man*, for example, hewed closely to *Superman*'s structure, devoting the first half entirely to a serious and dramatic telling of the web slinger's origin story before pitting him against the designated villain. (In a reversal from Donner's movie, though, the origin story is actually the strongest part of the film.) Meanwhile, *Iron Man* director Jon Favreau followed in Donner's footsteps by taking a chance on an unconventional casting choice for the title character and, with Robert Downey Jr., wound up with arguably the most successful combination of actor and hero since Reeve donned the Man of Steel's duds.

And then there's Christopher Nolan's rebooted Batman trilogy, in which he jettisoned the stylization of the Burton and Schumacher movies and instead imported Donner's verisimilitude-above-all mantra from Metropolis to Gotham City.[19] Indeed, Nolan's second installment, *The Dark Knight*, strives for an aura of gritty realism that renders it less of a superhero adventure and more of a crime drama that just happens to be about a guy in a costume. (Nolan has cited Michael Mann's *Heat* as a key influence on that film.[20]) DC's attempts to continue the *Superman* franchise—Singer's *Superman Returns* and Zack Snyder's *Man of Steel*—also derive some of their inspiration from their 1978 predecessor, more so in the case of *Returns* than *Steel*, although the latter does feature some noticeable callbacks to Donner's movie, particularly in the Krypton-set prologue. Put in perspective, the film's influence and longevity are entirely appropriate. Just as Superman's 1938 comic book debut revolutionized that industry, almost exactly 40 years later *Superman: The Movie* would do the same for comic book cinema.

FILM FIRST FILE #1: BATTLE OF THE BOX-OFFICE SUPERHEROES

Marvel and DC Comics' stable of superheroes have become Hollywood's biggest superstars, but which single hero reigns supreme atop the domestic box-office charts? Here are the biggest comic-book-based live-action superhero franchises—films of two or more—made since 1978's *Superman*. One note: this list covers solo heroes only, not teams, which means no Avengers, Fantastic Four, or X-Men.[21]

Batman (DC)

Batman (1989): $251.1 million
Batman Returns (1992): $162.8 million
Batman Forever (1995): $184 million

Batman & Robin (1997): $107.3 million
Batman Begins (2005): $206.8 million
The Dark Knight (2008): $534.8 million
The Dark Knight Rises (2012): $448. 1 million
Total: $1.89 billion

Spider-Man (Marvel)

Spider-Man (2002): $403.7 million
Spider-Man 2 (2004): $373.5 million
Spider-Man 3 (2007): $336.5 million
The Amazing Spider-Man (2012): $262 million
Total: $1.37 billion

Iron Man (Marvel)

Iron Man (2008): $318.4 million
Iron Man 2 (2010): $312.4 million
Iron Man 3 (2013): $409 million
Total: $1.03 billion

Superman (DC)

Superman The Movie (1978): $134.2 million
Superman II (1981): $108.1 million
Superman III (1983): $59.9 million
Superman IV: The Quest for Peace (1987): $15.6 million
Superman Returns (2006): $200 million
Man of Steel (2013): $291 million
Total: $808.8 million

Thor (Marvel)

Thor (2011): $181 million
Thor: The Dark World (2013): $202.8*
*****Total: $383.8**
Spider-Man 3 (2007): $336.5 million
*As of January 2, 2014

The Incredible Hulk (Marvel)

Hulk (2003): $132.1 million
The Incredible Hulk (2008): $134.8 million
Total: $266.9 million

Blade (Marvel)

Blade (1998): $70 million
Blade II (2002): $82.3 million
Blade: Trinity (2004): $52.4 million
Total: $204.7 million

The Punisher (Marvel)

The Punisher (2004): $33.8 million
Punisher: War Zone (2008): $8 million
Total: $41.8 million

FILM FIRST FILE #2: FIVE GREAT SUPERHERO-FREE COMIC BOOK MOVIES

Although the majority of the comic book-derived features released since Richard Donner's *Superman* have revolved around superpowered (or just really well-armed) heroes squaring off against colorful, if dastardly villains, there is a subset of the genre that has nothing to do with the capes-and-tights crowd. The following five titles illustrate the wide range of live-action comic book movies ... and comic books in general.

American Splendor (Shari Springer Berman and Robert Pulcini, 2003)

Adapted From: Harvey Pekar's illustrated autobiography of the same name, which was published off and on between 1976 and 2008.

Instead of Superheroes, It's About: The experiences, hopes, dreams, and fears of a Cleveland-based author, critic, and professional raconteur named ... Harvey Pekar. The film version stars a perfectly cast Paul Giamatti as Harvey (although the real Pekar appears in the movie as well) and dramatizes the so ordinary it's extraordinary life story the author chronicled on the page for three decades.

Ghost World (Terry Zwigoff, 2001)

Adapted From: A limited-run series by cult artist Daniel Clowes, originally released over a four-year period between 1993 and 1997 and published as a stand-alone graphic novel in 1997.

Instead of Superheroes, It's About: Two oddball teenage girls (played on-screen by Thora Birch and Scarlett Johansson) whose friendship is largely based upon ridiculing the people and places that make up their impersonal, profoundly shallow hometown. The cynicism and barely restrained fury that marks much of Zwigoff's work finds its strongest outlet in Clowes's slender, sadness-tinged tale.

A History of Violence (David Cronenberg, 2005)

Adapted From: A 1997 graphic crime novel penned by John Wagner and illustrated by Vince Locke.

Instead of Superheroes, It's About: A former trigger-happy criminal (Viggo Mortensen) who gave up the gangster life for a quieter existence as the proprietor of a small-town diner and happily married family man. But his past inevitably catches up with him and forces him to once again adopt the identity he had shed. Although it shares the same basic premise as the comic, Cronenberg's film makes several significant changes to the story and tone, becoming more of a dark comedy than a gritty crime yarn. These alterations have made it one of the director's more divisive films and also a vast improvement on the more generic source material.

Josie and the Pussycats (Henry Elfont and Deborah Kaplan, 2001)

Adapted From: The long-running *Archie* spin-off that originally ran from 1963 to 1982 and has been revived in various other incarnations since.

Instead of Superheroes, It's About: A four-member all-girl rock band that gets up to all sorts of hijinks in between concerts. Produced at the height of the late '90s/early '00s teen pop craze, the film version is a spirited satire of manufactured boy bands like the Backstreet Boys and such bubblegum divas as Britney Spears. Unfortunately, the fans of those artists apparently didn't want to see them spoofed, as the film failed to do much business. A decade on, however, it's a note-perfect encapsulation of that heady time, right down to the Carson Daly cameo.

Scott Pilgrim vs. the World (Edgar Wright, 2010)

Adapted From: Bryan Lee O'Malley's six-volume indie comic sensation, published between 2004 and 2010.

Instead of Superheroes, It's About: A twentysomething Canadian rocker and dreamer (portrayed by Michael Cera on-screen) who is already a legend in his own mind despite not having accomplished much of anything. But the real star of the comics—and the film—is the deft way O'Malley and Wright, in their respective mediums, weave a sophisticated tapestry of pop culture references and anything-goes storytelling.

Chapter 4

Star Trek: The Motion Picture (1979)

The Film: The crew of the starship *Enterprise* embarks on a cinematic adventure filled with grand effects and an even grander scope. Too bad about the lack of any grand drama.

In the decades since its initial theatrical release in 1979, *Star Trek: The Motion Picture*[1] has acquired the alternate title of *Star Trek: The Motionless Picture*. That's a none-too-subtle jab at the film's numerous inadequacies, chief among them the lack of propulsive narrative driving this lavishly produced outer space adventure that returned William Shatner's Captain James T. Kirk, Leonard Nimoy's half-human half-Vulcan science officer Spock, and DeForest Kelley's Dr. Leonard McCoy to the bridge of the *Enterprise* a decade after the original television series was canceled following three low-rated seasons that aired between 1966 to 1969. Despite costing its studio, Paramount, almost three times as much as 20th Century Fox's *Star Wars*—the movie that had paved the way for *Star Trek*'s return as a big-screen property—the first *Star Trek* film has less than half of the thrills of George Lucas's brainchild.

Given all the smirks and snide remarks that have been directed at *The Motion Picture* over the years, it's tempting to rise to its defense, insisting that it's been massively underrated in the *Trek* canon. But no, it really is that dry and motionless, a movie whose grand ambitions have clearly been compromised by a difficult production process marked by creative compromises, extensive delays, and behind-the-scenes disagreements. It's telling that the lasting achievement of *The Motion Picture* is that it proved financially successful enough to encourage the studio to make a second film, 1982's *The Wrath of Khan*. That installment course-corrected the mistakes of its predecessor and firmly established *Star Trek* as a viable film franchise.

Star Trek's journey from television screens to movie theaters began in 1975, when Paramount first approached series creator Gene Roddenberry about penning a script for a potential movie. But Roddenberry's initial effort, entitled *The God Thing*, wasn't well received at Paramount,[2] an early sign that cracking this project wouldn't be easy. Roddenberry's at times contentious relationship with his collaborators—particularly producer Harold Livingston, who is credited as the sole screenwriter for what would become *The Motion Picture* (although the script actually has several authors, including Alan Dean Foster, who wrote the original story treatment)[3]—continued throughout the making of the movie. This appeared to be a case where all the parties involved agreed that the film required a bold vision; it's just that none of them was able to completely agree on what that vision should be.

On the original series, Roddenberry's voice was always the one that rang through loud and clear. *Star Trek* was his creation, and as TV is generally a more writer-friendly medium, he was able to maintain greater control over what appeared on the screen. Movies don't always work in a similar fashion, with screenwriters often being required to put the director and the studio's vision ahead of their own. In transferring his creation from one medium to another, Roddenberry went from being the driving creative force behind *Star Trek* to being part of a team that included Paramount, Livingston, and the movie's eventual director, Robert Wise, the veteran studio craftsman whose credits included *West Side Story*, *The Haunting*, and *The Day the Earth Stood Still*. (Funnily enough, Wise was the fourth name listed on an internal studio memo that suggested potential directors for *The Motion Picture*; also on the list were such filmmakers as George Lucas, Steven Spielberg. and, at the head of the pack, Francis Ford Coppola.)[4] Certain cast members, specifically Shatner and Nimoy—who didn't want to revisit his signature character, Spock, and had to be cajoled into participating in the feature—were also quick to share their story suggestions.

Despite the competing chorus of voices behind the scenes, Roddenberry's influence is still present in *The Motion Picture*, specifically in regard to the larger themes the film attempts to tackle. But the movie also possesses a look and feel that represents a striking departure from his vision for TV series. Gone are the bright, colorful uniforms; the rugged spirit of adventure (Roddenberry often described his original conception for *Star Trek* as "*Wagon Train* to the stars,"[5] a reference to a '50s television western that followed pioneers traversing the American frontier); and the earnest mix of thoughtfulness and good humor that made the show so memorable to the small but devoted fan base who tuned in week after week. Taking its cue from the muted outfits all Starfleet personnel are now apparently required to wear, *The Motion Picture* is a more somber and restrained trip through the cosmos. Part of that stems from the story's premise; instead of venturing into deep space on a mission of exploration, the *Enterprise* is tasked with confronting a mysterious force of great destructive power. It's because of the unprecedented nature of this threat that Kirk, who has been trapped at a desk job since his initial five-year tour of duty ended, is able to reclaim control of his former ship and pilots it into an encounter with a remnant from Earth's distant past, the NASA-launched satellite *Voyager 6*, which has evolved into a sentient machine in the centuries since it left the planet. The being, now known as V'ger, has at last returned to meets its creators in an effort to further understand the nature of existence, blowing to smithereens anything that blocks the path toward its self-enlightenment.

Although the philosophical questions raised by this storyline are authentically *Star Trek*, the film doesn't dramatize them successfully, certainly not the same way the series did in its finest hours. In fact, for much of the film's running time, there's very little in the way of drama at all. Large sections of *The Motion Picture* are given over to the crew staring out through the viewscreen on the *Enterprise*'s bridge, reacting to all the majestic space phenomena they pass on their way to rendezvous with V'ger. Considering how little is happening on the ship, it's no surprise they'd rather spend most of their time gazing out the window. Out of the large cast, only two individuals—Kirk and Spock, naturally—have discernible character arcs. A stranger aboard a newly retrofitted *Enterprise* with a new, younger captain whose job he's taken, Kirk has to come to terms with the fact that time moves on and he can't simply pick up where he left off as if nothing has changed. Meanwhile, Spock is still struggling to divest himself of his emotions and follow the Vulcan path of pure logic; through a one-on-one encounter with V'ger, he comes to understand and embrace his own unique position as a man who is literally of two worlds.

These narrative threads are too flatly written and performed to generate much interest, though. The stiff acting is surprising considering how charismatic the cast was on the original series, charismatic enough that Paramount made a point of reuniting them for the movie instead of recasting their roles or starting over with new characters. Then again, the budgetary limitations of the show demanded a more intimate, character-driven kind of sci-fi storytelling that gave the actors dramatic material to play. Here, the sheer scale of the production dwarfs the characters and the men and women playing them; even Shatner gets lost amidst the sound and light show happening outside the *Enterprise*. (*Star Trek* fans would have to wait for *The Wrath of Khan* to really see the actor unleash the full range of his Shatner-tude.) Another reason the film may seem light on story is that a number of dialogue-driven scenes had to be scaled back or eliminated altogether to make room for the labor-intensive special-effects sequences, which were being dropped into the movie at the last possible minute as the filmmakers rushed to meet the studio-mandated December release date. As Wise himself has said, it was the first movie he had ever directed that didn't have a sneak preview simply because it wasn't ready in time; the first time he saw a finished print of his movie was at its premiere at the Smithsonian's National Air & Space Museum in Washington, D.C.[6]

Even if the F/X-heavy scenes wound up hurting the movie overall, they are, both then and now, the most impressive element of *The Motion Picture*. They also happen to be the material that boasts the clearest authorial voice, one belonging not to Roddenberry but to F/X pioneer Douglas Trumbull, who first gained notice for his groundbreaking work on Stanley Kubrick's *2001: A Space Odyssey*. (He's responsible for one of that movie's most famous sequences, David Bowman's hallucinogenic trip through the Star Gate.) When the original effects house Paramount hired to handle the big set pieces proved to be not up to the task, Trumbull was brought in and applied his distinctive techniques (including multiplane exposures of airbrushed artwork)[7] to the design and execution of the V'ger scenes. Trumbull's touch is so apparent, one almost expects to see the *Enterprise* go cruising past *2001*'s Star Child. These sequences fill the big screen of a movie house in a way the rest of the film fails to do and are also, no doubt, one of the reasons *The Motion Picture* performed as well as it did at the box office, grossing $82 million (roughly $250 million in today's dollars) during its run—a number that indicated the movie found an audience beyond the show's Trekkie fanbase. Whatever its flaws, *Star Trek* as a franchise owes its continued existence to *The Motion Picture*, as its success paved the way for additional movies and, eventually, more *Trek* TV series as well.

The First: After more than a decade in dry dock, *Star Trek* boldly ventured into movie theaters, becoming the first TV franchise to cross the final frontier that separated the small screen from the big screen.

The dawn of the TV age is generally regarded as a crisis point for the film industry and it's true that in the wake of television's ascent in the late '40s and early '50s, the major studios worked hard to devise ways to entice viewers away from their sets and back into theaters. New technologies like CinemaScope and such gimmicks as 3D were introduced to remind audiences that movies could offer a viewing experience far more immersive and spectacular than those small black-and-white images that flickered in their living rooms at home. Behind-the-scenes, however, the heads of the studios recognized the financial promise of the new medium and weren't about to allow a potentially lucrative revenue stream to pass them by. Major players like 20th Century Fox and Warner Bros. built TV production arms that made shows for the various networks, while Paramount tried to go one better, establishing the Paramount Television Network in 1949 (they also had a substantial interest in the DuMont Television Network, which launched in 1946) only to run afoul of the FCC and shut it down several years later.[8] The studio's next foray into TV occurred after it was purchased in 1966 by the Gulf + Western Corporation, which would also purchase Desilu—the television production company founded by *I Love Lucy* stars Lucille Ball and Desi

Arnaz—the following year. *Star Trek*, which premiered on NBC in September 1966, was a Desilu series, and the sale of the company put it under the control of Paramount.⁹

Almost from the day it premiered, *Star Trek* seemed destined for cancellation, but despite meager ratings, NBC stuck with it for three seasons, due in large part to an impassioned (and, at the time, unprecedented) letter-writing campaign by the show's fans geared toward keeping it on the air.¹⁰ Eventually the numbers took their toll and the show departed the airwaves in 1969 after 79 hour-long adventures. Paramount Television took those episodes and quickly sold them into syndication (in fact, old episodes of *Star Trek* started airing only months after the series had been canceled), where the show wound up flourishing. Around the same time, networks and television producers began to look past a show's overall ratings number in favor of a breakdown of its audience demographics. When viewed this way, *Star Trek* was a significant success story, with its repeats attracting an exceptionally desirable demographic of young people.¹¹ Paramount knew they had a lucrative property on their hands—the only question was how to exploit it.

The studio's first attempt at bringing back *Star Trek* was an animated series produced in conjunction with Filmation (the same animation house behind such Saturday morning nostalgia pieces as *The Archie Show* and *Fat Albert and the Cosby Kids*) which lasted 22 episodes from 1973 to 1974. Around the same time, they began discussing the idea of taking the series to the big screen and hired Roddenberry to write the first pass at a script in 1975.¹² The idea of reviving a dormant TV series as a film was new territory for a studio; the closest equivalent would have been 1966's *Batman*, an adaptation of the then-popular TV show, but that series was still producing first-run episodes when the movie version was released in theaters. As the film version *Star Trek* languished in development, Paramount grew serious about launching another TV network with a new *Star Trek* series serving as their flagship program. Suddenly, all work on the feature ceased, and Roddenberry's energies were directed toward launching what came to be called *Star Trek: Phase II*, an all-new series that would reunite the original crew of the *Enterprise*, sans Leonard Nimoy, who declined to return. Sets were built, screen tests were shot and scripts were commissioned, including the Alan Dean Foster short story "In Thy Image," which everyone agreed would make a great pilot for the revived *Trek*.¹³

Then in November 1977, only weeks before the premiere episode was due to start filming, Paramount abruptly changed its mind one more time and pulled the plug on *Phase II*, announcing instead that *Star Trek* would be back as a major motion picture. Two factors drove this decision—first, the studio's decision to abandon plans for a TV network, and secondly, the release of a little movie called *Star Wars*. In the wake of that film's incredible success, the hunt was on for another science-fiction blockbuster, and Paramount happened to have a candidate already in their portfolio, one whose title even echoed *Star Wars*, even though it had preceded George Lucas's movie by a decade. After that announcement, things finally began to move quickly; Robert Wise was hired as director in March 1978, and filming began in August. With the original cast already in place for *Phase II*, Paramount ported them over to the film version and even managed to lure back a reluctant Nimoy. Keeping the original crew intact guaranteed that the hardcore *Star Trek* fans would turn up on opening day and, with any luck, spectacle-hungry nonfans would tag along as well.

When *The Motion Picture* finally opened following its tumultuous production, the reviews were not especially kind. But the film's subsequent box-office success was a signal to Hollywood that a mass audience would turn out to see a feature film that had been derived from a TV series, even if it was a series they might not have seen in its original run. This knowledge allowed the studios to take a closer look at their television production arms in search of defunct shows that could potentially find another life in theaters. Beyond giving them a movie that would come with built-in name recognition as well as an established fan base, studios already held the movie rights to these properties through their TV divisions. In the years after *Star Trek: The Motion Picture*, Paramount would go on to launch two other film franchises based on shows produced by Paramount Television—*The Naked Gun* series (adapted from the short-lives spoof *Police Squad!*) and *The Brady Bunch* movies (derived from the '70s family comedy)—while 20th Century Fox made two movies based on the popular Fox television series *The X-Files*, and Universal Studios brought the Universal Television series *Miami Vice* to the big screen as well. And that's not counting the numerous other TV-derived features made by studios that didn't produce the original series, such as *Serenity*, *I Spy*, and *McHale's Navy*. In this post–*Star Trek* world, cancellation doesn't have to mean the end of a television show—just a warm-up for a major motion picture.

FILM FIRST FILE #1: FIVE FILMS THAT BEGAT SUCCESSFUL TV SHOWS

Star Trek: The Motion Picture was the first time a TV series moved to the big screen, a leap that has since been replicated by such diverse titles as *The Fugitive*, *The X-Files*, and even *The Beverly Hillbillies*. But there have also been plenty of productions that have gone in the opposite direction, with major motion pictures giving way to ongoing television shows. In fact, this tradition predates the first *Star Trek* feature; films like *The Odd Couple*, *M*A*S*H*, and *Planet of the Apes* are just some of the ones that inspired TV shows that aired well before *The Motion Picture* started shooting. Here are five post–*Star Trek: The Motion Picture* movies that spawned successful TV series.

Buffy the Vampire Slayer

Movie Version: Released July 1992 by 20th Century Fox
TV Version: Aired 1997–2001 on The WB; 2001–2003 on UPN
Joss Whedon's self-aware send-up of conventional horror movie tropes (specifically, the blonde cheerleader-type who is always instant monster bait) didn't click with moviegoers, largely because of problematic execution— director Fran Rubel Kuzui wasn't the best person to bring the script to life. When the series began five years after the film's release, Whedon was in firm creative control from the get-go and, over the course of its seven-season run, expanded on the initial premise in daring and provocative ways, producing a show that has some of the most passionate fans around, even a decade after it aired its final episode.

Friday Night Lights

Movie Version: Released October 2004 by Universal Pictures
TV Version: Aired 2006–2011 on NBC
Peter Berg's big-screen version of the hugely influential nonfiction sports book by journalist (and his cousin) Buzz Bissinger is a gripping account of the social and economic role that high school football plays in small-town Texas. The subsequent TV show, which Berg was also heavily involved in, proved to be an even more evocative portrait of a community where football is king, populated by characters viewers grew to love . . . and in some cases love to hate.

La Femme Nikita

Movie Version: Released domestically April 1991 by the Samuel Goldwyn Company
TV Version: Aired 1997–2001 on USA; a second series, *Nikita*, aired 2010–2013 on The CW
Luc Besson's French action thriller has such an irresistible hook—a former criminal is recruited into a top-secret organization and trained as an assassin— it's no surprise that it's resulted in two TV shows. The first was a Canadian production that ran for five seasons and got a good deal of mileage out of Nikita's conflicted feelings about her new profession and her employers. The second delves further into various conspiracies and double-crosses that make up the modern spy game. Neither are as thrilling as Besson's movie, but their knotty narratives can be fun to unravel.

Parenthood

Movie Version: Released August 1989 by Universal Pictures
TV Version: Aired 1990–1991 on NBC; a second series aired 2010– present on NBC

Ron Howard tried twice to turn his successful 1989 comedy about the nonstop stream of hilarity and heartache that raising kids entails. The first attempt died off after only 12 episodes, but the second version lingered around longer, never becoming a ratings monster but recognized by critics and audiences alike as quality television.

Stargate

Movie Version: Released October 1994 by MGM
TV Version: Aired 1997–2002 on Showtime; 2002–2007 on SciFi Channel
Roland Emmerich's 1994 sci-fi blockbuster about an interstellar portal that opened the universe to mankind seemed intended to launch a *Star Wars–* (or *Star Trek–*) like feature film franchise, but made a much better fit for television instead. Three years after the film hit theaters, the TV sequel *Stargate SG-1* premiered on the small screen and ran for 10 seasons on two different networks and in syndication. It also spawned two spin-off series and a fan community that came to rival Trekkies.

FILM FIRST FILE #2: IS TELEVISION BETTER THAN CINEMA?

Throughout the first decades of its history, television existed in the shadow of feature films; although it often reached a wider audience, as an artistic medium it was rarely awarded the same kind of stature. Starting in the late '80s and early '90s, that impression radically changed. Today, television is not only regarded as being the artistic equal of cinema; some believe it has surpassed it. Here are a few of the common points that are raised when someone strives to make the case that TV is better than the movies.

Characters Are Given More Time to Develop

Example: *Breaking Bad* (AMC, 2008–2013)
Feature films can only immerse you in the lives of their characters for a limited amount of time. A successful television series, on the other hand, invites you to observe them for anywhere from 10 to 22 hours a year over multiple years. This allows for the kind of in-depth character development that films can sometimes only hint at. Over the course of *Breaking Bad*'s five-season run, for example, viewers watched a seemingly ordinary high school chemistry teacher transform into a drug kingpin, and every step of this metamorphosis was chronicled in compelling detail.

Television Can Take a Novelistic Approach to Storytelling

Example: *The Wire* (HBO, 2002–2008)

Prior to transitioning into television, *The Wire* creator David Simon was a journalist and author, and he approached his groundbreaking HBO series as if he were writing a book, allowing storylines to spill over between episodes, introducing seemingly minor elements early on that would later have major ramifications, and lavishing attention on the smallest detail. Drawing on his own experiences as a Baltimore crime-beat reporter, Simon crafted a series that's widely regarded as one of the medium's all-time great achievements and one that plays even better when consumed in one sitting rather than weekly installments ... just like a great novel.

Television Writers Can Construct a Complex, Elaborate Mythology

Example: *The X-Files* (FOX, 1993–2002)

Long-form storytelling can be especially beneficial in science-fiction and fantasy shows, where the writers have the time to make their alternate, often more fantastical reality feel authentic and build in mysteries and puzzles that keep viewers engaged. Of course, sometimes the mythology grows so complex that no one can make head or tails of it, including the creators (a problem that plagued the paranormal procedural *The X-Files* in its final years, as well as such descendants as *Lost*), but early on at least getting to know the world is part of the fun.

Television Is Just Funnier

Example: *NewsRadio* (NBC, 1995–1999)

Are there still great movie comedies made every year? Sure. But the majority of the finest, funniest, and most consistently inventive comedies around are on the small screen. NBC's mid-'90s workplace sitcom set in a New York radio station was just one example of a TV series that was frequently more hilarious than most of the comedies churned out by a Hollywood studio during that same era. Television also happens to be where the majority of the comic superstars in front of and behind the camera spring from, going all the way back to the days of Woody Allen and Mel Brooks and still today in the era of Will Ferrell and Steve Carell.

Chapter 5

Tron (1982)

The Film: A traditional adventure story rendered for the digital age, *Tron* celebrates the then-burgeoning video-game industry and provides the medium with a road map for its future.

By the time *Tron*[1] arrived in theaters during the summer of 1982, coin-operated video games were celebrating the first decade of their existence. It was in 1971 that the precursors to the contemporary arcade consoles—*Galaxy Game* and *Computer Space*—arrived on the scene,[2] but the real game changer came the following year, when the fledgling Atari company installed a machine bearing the name *Pong* in the Silicon Valley watering hole Andy Capp's Tavern.[3] A simple game of electronic tennis accompanied by a soundtrack of digitized bleeps and blorps, *Pong* became a pop culture phenomenon, and soon an entire industry sprang up to service the increased demand for similar coin-eating distractions. Games as varied and addictive as *Asteroids*, *Donkey Kong*, and, especially, *Pac-Man* followed in *Pong*'s wake, continually expanding the young medium's potential and keeping it from joining the ranks of passing fads. As 1982 rolled around, the arcade era of gaming was arguably at its zenith, which naturally meant that the film industry was interested in finding a way to make some money off the whole thing.

In the midst of the video-game revolution, a young filmmaker named Steven Lisberger began experimenting with a process known as backlit animation—where light is shown through animated mattes, giving them a distinctive, vaguely electronic glow. Struck by the visual similarities between backlit animation and video games, Lisberger used the process to create the character of Tron—deriving his name from the very word "elec*tron*ic."[4] Tron made his first appearance in a short but eye-grabbing piece of animation that depicted him smashing two discs together above his head.

The positive reaction that clip generated told Lisberger that his creation had the potential to be the right hero at the right time . . . even though Tron didn't have an actual story line or even a personality yet.

After making the rounds at various studios and production companies, Lisberger found a willing investor in Walt Disney Company, which in the early '80s was in the midst of a creative lull that had left it with the status of being a second-rate place to work. Beyond the opportunity to tap into the lucrative video-game market, the studio was drawn to *Tron* because it hearkened back to its founder's own history of artistic and technological innovation in service of storytelling.[5] Just as Walt Disney's first feature-length production, *Snow White and the Seven Dwarfs*, broke new ground in traditional hand-drawn animation, the studio saw the potential to once again be innovators by funding Lisberger's grand experiment. For a company that has been known for exerting a great deal of creative control over its films, Disney seemed willing to give *Tron* a wider berth, providing Lisberger and his production team with all the necessary resources, and then mostly leaving them alone to make the movie as they saw fit.

That sense of creative freedom is strongly felt in the finished product, which may borrow story elements from other sources (most glaringly, *Star Wars*), but sets them down in a world the majority of moviegoers at that time had never seen or even imagined before—one that exists inside a computer. The gist of the plot involves roguish software designer/expert hacker Flynn (played by Jeff Bridges, doing a spirited impression of Harrison Ford's Han Solo) being zapped into an electronic mainframe maintained by the corporation where he used to work. Once inside this digital universe, he has to locate the stalwart security program Tron (Bruce Boxleitner) and enlist his help in shutting down the tyrannical Master Control Program in charge of this operating system. Accomplishing this mission requires participating in a series of gladiatorial games (tricked out with newfangled arcade flourishes, like glowing identity discs), plus a perilous journey across a grid patrolled by computer-animated hovering crafts straight out of *Space Invaders*.

Along with video games, personal computers were still novelties in 1982, which gave Lisberger license to be imaginative in his rendering of a computerized world. With the help of noted graphic artists Syd Mead (who designed the movie's memorable light cycles) and Moebius (who created the circuit-laden costumes that Tron and the other programs wear),[6] the first-time director generated an environment that reflects some of the design elements of early arcade games—lots of simple geometric shapes and primary colors—but feels far more expansive than one-screen classics like *Pac-Man* and *Donkey Kong*. Both at the time and still today, *Tron* doesn't look or sound like any other depiction of a digital world; even its eventual sequel *Tron: Legacy* (which was made almost 20 years later, with newcomer Joseph Kosinski taking over from Lisberger) is more conventional in its style than its predecessor, embracing a sleeker, more sterile design. While *Legacy*'s look may appear more "modern," it lacks the personality of Lisberger's vision. Despite being set in a supposedly cold electronic environment, there's a pronounced warmth to *Tron* that exudes both from the movie's bright, colorful imagery (with hand-painted reds and blues popping off the screen) as well as its generally optimistic attitude toward the still-young computer revolution.

The film wears its geek cred proudly, with Lisberger casually dropping technical jargon into the dialogue (one of the characters is named "RAM," for example) and dramatizing the social structure of Tron's world with an eye toward replicating how a computer functions. Much is made of the relationship between digitized "programs" like Tron and flesh-and-blood "users" like Flynn or Tron's human surrogate, Alan; although users have the ability to create programs, left unchecked, their electronic creations can swallow the entire system, as the Master Control Program attempts to do, aided and abetted by a corrupt corporate executive on this side of the computer screen. Made at a time when the fledgling computer industry was still something of a Wild West environment, the overarching plot of *Tron* argues in favor of free and unrestricted access to the digital frontier. And despite the machinations of the MCP, that frontier is quite deliberately presented as an inviting, welcoming place—a horizon "users" should happily explore rather than shrink away from. Indeed, *Tron*'s closing shot—in which the nighttime skyline of Los Angeles morphs into the electronic grid that constitutes Tron's universe—foretells the way that modern society would become inextricably linked to computers ... and suggests that we'll ultimately be better for it.

Although *Tron* anticipates a brave new world, at heart it remains an old-fashioned adventure story. Like the gunslingers in vintage Western novels, Flynn is the loner who wanders into a strange town and has to confront the outlaw running the place before continuing on his way; even if the landscape and his weapons of choice are different, his purpose remains the same. Bridges' lively performance helps make up for the limitations in Lisberger's script, which doesn't possess the same mythic grandeur of Lucas's pulp-inspired *Star Wars*. Dramatically, *Tron* is often stiff and static, as the filmmakers' interests clearly lie in the setting rather than with the characters. Viewers come out of *Star Wars* wanting to *be* one of the characters. With *Tron*, they come away wanting to visit a similar video-game realm, but not necessarily as Flynn or even as Tron.

Despite a strong promotional push by Disney, *Tron* never came close to matching *Star Wars* in the box-office department either, stalling out at $33 million—enough to qualify as a modest success, but not the phenomenon that the studio hoped for. Nevertheless, the movie has left its mark, not just on Hollywood (where its use of computer-generated imagery ushered in a sea change in the realm of special effects) but also within the video-game industry. If you examine how gaming has evolved since 1982, game designers have embraced the open-world approach that Lisberger presented in *Tron*—the idea that an entire universe exists outside of the game arena. One can plot a direct line from *Tron* to video games like the *Grand Theft Auto* or *World of Warcraft* franchises, where players allow their avatars to freely explore a sprawling digital world, while also taking part in missions and side games. Obviously, Lisberger's film isn't solely responsible for this shift—the huge technological leaps in game technology, as well as the advent of more sophisticated home gaming consoles and the evolving demands of the audience, are even more important factors—but the connection is clear. Made to capitalize on the medium's present, *Tron* also points to its future.

The First: As the first major studio feature to make extensive use of computer-generated special effects, *Tron* can be credited (and blamed) with ushering in the era of the CGI blockbuster.

About a month before *Tron*'s release in July 1982, moviegoers got a sneak peek of what the future of blockbusters would look like courtesy of a single scene snuck in toward the end of *Star Trek II: The Wrath of Khan*, in which a piece of far-future technology known as the Genesis Device transforms a dead space rock into an Earth-like environment, filled with life-sustaining oceans and lush forests. To accomplish this effect, the filmmakers enlisted the aid of the Graphics Group, a team of computer animation specialists that existed within the computer division at George Lucas's production company, Lucasfilm. Accepting the challenge, the animators designed and executed a minute-long sequence depicting the birth and rapid evolution of a new planet, a clip that deeply impressed the filmmakers, studio executives, and audiences alike. What made the scene so groundbreaking was the way the animators lent it a sense of motion, programming the camera to fly over the digitally generated environment as it if were soaring through actual space.[7] Today, the effect may look somewhat primitive, but at the time, it hinted at the untapped potential of marrying computer animation with feature filmmaking. (As for the Graphics Group, they would eventually be sold from Lucasfilm to Apple founder Steve Jobs and rechristened as . . . Pixar.)[8]

If *Star Trek II* was the overture to the CGI (known in full as computer-generated imagery) age of blockbuster filmmaking, then *Tron* functions as its first full movement. Where computer animation constitutes only one minute of *Khan*'s nearly two-hour runtime, it accounts for almost 20 minutes of *Tron*, with several major sequences—most notably the light cycle race—being generated entirely by computers. It is worth noting, of course, that the majority of *Tron* was still created with more traditional animation and live-action techniques, as well as the director's backlit animation process. Lisberger shot the bulk of the film on soundstages, where the sets and costumes all shared the same color scheme: black and white. Each individual frame of celluloid was subsequently treated as an animation cel, with animators painting colors onto the outfits and backgrounds in multiple layers, which would eventually be composited to produce one image.[9] It was a painstaking process that required a great deal of time and manpower, but it also produced the unique look that Lisberger had hoped to achieve.

Nevertheless, there remained aspects to *Tron*'s digital world that couldn't be realized via analog animation methods and for those specific elements, Lisberger turned to 3D computer animation, a medium that had its origins in the '40s and '50s but really started to be used in earnest in the '60s and '70s, generally in short cartoons and advertisements. In those cases, computer-generated imagery was employed primarily to make an impression or sell a product rather than fit into an existing narrative. Lisberger, however, wanted sequences that would both demonstrate the capabilities of the technology and also advance his story. It was a fresh approach to computer animation and one that necessitated both the filmmakers and the animators developing a common language.[10] For the filmmakers, the hurdle was understanding exactly what the existing computer technology could accomplish and plotting their story accordingly. The animators, meanwhile, were now required to take into account narrative elements like character point of view, length of time, and action occurring in a defined physical space—all things that often weren't part of the experimental and/or commercial projects that represented the bulk of their output up to that point.

Complicating matters further was the fact that, in the early '80s, there weren't one-stop shops for all your computer imaging needs—the role that giant effects houses like Industrial Light & Magic and Weta Workshop fill today—not to mention little in the way of industry standardization. Instead, the nascent industry consisted of a handful of companies, each of which had proprietary software that specialized in specific areas. Thus, Lisberger was required to employ four separate computer animation houses to realize his singular vision for *Tron*, Digital Effects, Information International Inc. (or Triple I), Math Applications Group Incorporated (or MAGI) and Robert Abel and Associates.[11] Each of these companies was assigned specific sequences based on their skills and software, sequences that included the digitization process that transports Flynn into the computer, the light cycle chase during which Flynn and Tron escape from the games arena and into the rest of the mainframe, as well as the so-called Solar Sailer vehicle that transports the heroes to the Master Control Program's lair. As an example of the way the scenes were divvied up, MAGI's history with simulating light rays within their computers—something they began experimenting with in the '60s for their U.S. government contracts[12]—made them the natural choice to execute the light cycle race. Meanwhile, Robert Abel and Associates designed Flynn's transition from the real world to the digital world drawing on their experience creating abstract animations.[13] Lisberger sketched out each computer-animated sequence down to the minutest detail, creating detailed storyboards that featured multiangle views and specified the camera's location in the shot. Armed with that information, the animators worked to design sequences that felt like organic parts of the movie, rather than product demonstration reels.

It's a testament to the working relationship that the filmmakers and the different animation teams established that all of *Tron*'s CGI-based sequences feel of a piece with each other and the movie as a whole. Watching the film without any knowledge of how it was made, you'd have little reason to suspect that each of those individual scenes was the product of a different company with a different skill set—the overarching aesthetic of the film established by Lisberger retains its primacy throughout. (Funnily enough, the computer-animated sequences prove more visually dynamic than the live-action scenes, as the animators had more freedom to move the camera through the 3D space. The technical demands of shooting on celluloid that would later be painted on and composited like traditional animation cels clearly limited Lisberger's ability to vary his composition and framing. For much of *Tron*, the camera remains still and locked down while filming human actors on physical sets.)[14]

And while some of the design looks clunky today, overall the computer animation in *Tron* appears less dated than other CGI-intensive features, and not just those made in the '80s—even movies that were considered state-of-the-art eye candy five years ago haven't aged all that well. That's primarily because Lisberger wasn't interested in employing the technology to mimic the real world.[15] What he understood even then is that CGI-technology is most effective when it is used to create a distinct on-screen reality instead of attempting to directly recreate the world outside of the movie theater. We're persuaded by (or at least accepting of) the computer animation in *Tron* because it transports us to an environment that's convincingly different from our own. Although it's worth noting that not every blockbuster has to create a world out of whole cloth to make its computer-animated effects transporting. A film like Joss Whedon's *The Avengers*, for example, is set in a recognizable version of present-day Earth that happens to be populated by superpowered heroes and villains, and it's their CGI-enhanced feats of derring-do that make the movie just unreal enough to seem real.

Even if the general public didn't go wild for *Tron* in 1982, numerous creative types within the industry—including a young Disney employee named John Lasseter, who joined Lucasfilm's Graphics Group the following year and became a creative force in the company when it transformed into Pixar, which today, of course, is one of the leading lights in computer animation —came away from the film extremely impressed by the potential of CGI.[16] Two years later, the sci-fi adventure *The Last Starfighter* (the plot of which also hinged on video games) boasted almost 30 minutes' worth of CGI-effects and from that point, there was no looking back. Each passing year brought more advances and refinements in computer technology, more companies specializing in CGI and more expensive studio films in need of effects that could best be accomplished by digital wizards sitting at their keyboards.

In the short term, *Tron* may not have launched a franchise, but it did start a lasting revolution within its industry on par with *Pong*.

FILM FIRST FILE #1: THE 5 BEST MOVIE-CREATED VIDEO GAMES

Tron began its life as a movie, but the game depicted on-screen eventually found its way into actual arcades as well. (Subsequent *Tron*-inspired games have been produced for home consoles like Xbox and PlayStation.) Not all of the following movie-invented video games are playable in real life, but you'll probably come away from the films wishing they were.

Fix-It Felix, Jr.

As Seen In: *Wreck-It Ralph* (Rich Moore, 2012), the Disney cartoon that showed viewers what life was like for their favorite arcade game characters when the players all went home.

Type of Game: A *Donkey Kong*–like platformer in which the player assumes the identity of hammer-wielding handyman hero Fix-It Felix, Jr., who restores the mess created by the game's destructive bad guy, Wreck-It Ralph.

Can You Play It? Disney made a Flash version of *Fix-It Felix* available on its official site and also for download to mobile devices.

Starfighter

As Seen In: *The Last Starfighter* (Nick Castle, 1984), a *Star Wars*-meets-*Tron* sci-fi adventure about an ordinary kid who achieves a high score and is promptly rocketed to a distant galaxy to play the game in real life.

Type of Game: A futuristic flight simulator with a hefty dose of action, as players must battle an alien armada from behind the cockpit of a weapons-laden starcraft.

Can You Play It? Not easily. After scuttling plans to release a *Last Starfighter* game in 1984 on the heels of the movie's release, Atari put it on the market in 1986 under a different name due to licensing issues.[17] And while Nintendo did make a *Last Starfighter* game in 1990, it turned out to be a modified version of an earlier game, *Uridium*, originally produced in 1985 for the Commodore 64.[18] It's currently out of print.

Beat-Beat Revelation

As Seen In: *The FP* (Brandon Trost and Jason Trost, 2011), a low-budget cult comedy set in a near future where gangs of young thugs do their fighting in arcades rather than on the streets.

Type of Game: A music game that bears more than a passing resemblance to *Dance Dance Revolution* and requires players compete head-to-head to see who is best at keeping a beat and putting their feet on the right lit-up squares.

Can You Play It? *Beat-Beat Revelation* is sadly unavailable, but *Dance Dance Revolution* is the exact same game and can be readily purchased in advance of your next party/gang war.

Cloak & Dagger

As Seen In: *Cloak & Dagger* (Richard Franklin, 1984), in which Henry Thomas plays a video-game-obsessed kid whose favorite digital hero, Jack Flack, comes to life in the form of Dabney Coleman, just in time to help the boy get to the bottom of a murder case that involves the FBI and killer spies.

Type of Game: An adventure/puzzle game where you assume the identity of Flack and retrieve items and solve cases while avoiding bad-guy bullets.

Can You Play It? In an early example of synergy between the film and video-game industries, the filmmakers and Atari agreed to turn a preexisting game entitled *Agent X* into the *Cloak & Dagger* game seen in the movie. The arcade version of *Agent X* was similarly re-titled to fit the film. Subsequently, a home console version was developed, but never released.[19]

eXistenZ

As Seen In: *eXistenZ* (David Cronenberg, 1999), a horror-tinged tale about a developer of virtual video games that you plug directly into your body for a gaming experience that's even more realistic than reality.

Type of Game: Pure virtual reality, to the point where you're not entirely sure whether you're in the game or the "real world."

Can You Play It? No, and that's probably a good thing considering what it does to the characters' minds.

FILM FIRST FILE #2: 1982, THE SUMMER THAT CHANGED HOLLYWOOD

Tron opened in July 1982, in the thick of that year's extraordinary summer movie season. At the time, few probably could have foreseen how influential many of the titles released during the four-month window from May to August would become over the years. Here are some other notable alumni from the summer Class of '82, as well as the specific influences they had on Hollywood going forward.

Conan the Barbarian (May 14):

Arnold Schwarzenegger was already a celebrity thanks to his bodybuilding career, but it was his role as the muscle-bound pulp hero in John Milius's bloody fantasy adventure that set him on the path to becoming one of the era-defining action stars of the '80s and '90s.

Rocky III (May 28):

Some have described the third entry in the heavyweight *Rocky* franchise as the first movie to use MTV-like editing techniques in its musical montages, marrying rousing pop music to a fast-paced stream of images.

Poltergeist (June 4):

Simply put, you wouldn't have *Paranormal Activity* without *Poltergeist*, which makes an ordinary suburban home seem as terrifying as a Gothic castle after an evil spirit moves in.

E.T.: The Extra-Terrestrial (June 11):

By surpassing *Star Wars* to become the highest-grossing film of all time at that point, *E.T.* intensified the interest in the box-office horse race that now dominates the industry as well as entertainment journalism. That the movie also scored an Oscar nomination for Best Picture became a sign that "kids' movies" could be taken seriously by adults.

Blade Runner (June 25):

It's hard to think of a contemporary sci-fi film set in a dystopian future that hasn't in part been influenced by Ridley Scott's richly detailed vision of twenty-first-century Los Angeles. The film's impact is obvious on everything from *The Matrix* to the television remake of *Battlestar Galactica*.

The Secret of NIMH (July 2):

After decades as the only major animation studio in town, Disney's supremacy was challenged by upstart Don Bluth, who founded his own company to make this cult favorite. Although the film was only a modest success, his example gave other studios and animators the courage to compete with the Mouse House so that, today, Disney no longer has a monopoly on the animated-feature business.

Chapter 6

Parting Glances (1986)

The Film: Bill Sherwood's slice-of-life drama is less remarkable for what it's about than who it's about.

The opening sequence of *Parting Glances*[1] presents a scene of almost banal domesticity. In it, two young lovers are enjoying a lazy day in Central Park before heading back to their Upper West Side abode. Once through the door, they head straight for the bedroom, doffing various articles of clothing along the way. Sometime later, we hear the shower running, and the curtain is pulled back to reveal the lovebirds contentedly clasped in each other's arms, the very picture of happiness. What makes this seemingly innocuous scene so surprising, though—at least to audiences in 1986 when the film was released—is that couple we're observing isn't a guy and a girl, but a guy and a guy. It's a measure of just how far public acceptance of homosexuality has come that most contemporary moviegoers wouldn't bat an eye at the film's prelude. At the time, however, watching a gay couple do something so ordinary was, in a very real sense, extraordinary.

It's not that audiences in 1986 were unfamiliar with the concept of committed gay relationships. The Stonewall riots that roiled New York in the summer of 1969 had forced an end to the era when homosexuality was something the public at large pretended didn't exist, requiring gay men and women to hide their true selves from the world lest they face ostracizing at best and violent abuse at worst. Galvanized by Stonewall, the '70s saw the emergence of a new activist phase of the gay rights movement, which in turn gave individuals the courage to open up about their own sexuality. Pop culture played a role in reflecting the changing social paradigm as well. The film industry—somewhat grudgingly, it must be said—tackled the issue of homosexuality in movies like 1970's *The Boys in the Band* (based on the play by

Matt Crowley, which opened Off Broadway the year before Stonewall) and 1982's *Personal Best* and *Making Love*, the latter of which was the first studio-backed mainstream film to dramatize the experience of coming out of the closet. While none of these titles proved big commercial hits, they were by and large positively received by the gay community if only by virtue of the fact that they offered up representations of homosexual characters that weren't overtly malicious or hateful.

But aspiring feature filmmaker Bill Sherwood, for one, wasn't particularly impressed with the few gay-centric films being made within the industry. And he had a point; invariably, most of those movies made *too* much of the characters' sexuality, treating them as objects of curiosity rather than human beings. Sexual orientation became their sole defining feature, instead of just one part of who they were. Sherwood felt he had yet to see a film that captured the pride he felt in being gay so he took it upon himself to make a movie that would.[2] Originally trained as a classical musician, a career path that led him to Juilliard for a time, Sherwood switched tracks to writing and film-making, helming several shorts while a student at Hunter College. In 1983, he was working as a secretary at New York's CBS affiliate[3] when he put pen to paper to write the screenplay for what would become *Parting Glances*. Well aware that no studio would be interested in his script, Sherwood decided to raise the money independently, a task that took some six months. Production finally commenced in September 1984 for a seven-week shoot, followed by an additional week of photography in March 1985 (a delay that was due both to logistical issues and a temporary lack of funds). The film was shot entirely on location in New York and Sherwood made a point of filling the cast with both gay and straight actors; one-half of the central couple, for example, was a married father of three.[4]

From the beginning, Sherwood's intention with *Parting Glances* was to make a naturalistic love story starring a gay couple, and the opening sequence proved key in establishing that tone. In an interview, the director explained that one of his concerns about the majority of the films that had depicted gay culture up until that point—citing 1985's *Kiss of the Spider Woman* as an example—was the way they spent much of their running time having the characters avoid any outward signs of affection, like hugging or even kissing. Instead, they would delay those moments, so when the two men finally locked lips, the kiss would register more for its shock value than romance. As he explained in an interview, "This is why I had two men kissing right from the start in *Parting Glances*, to get it over with right away and allow us to get on with their interaction with other people and with what's going on in their lives."[5]

And Sherwood certainly wastes little time getting on with his lovers' lives after their midday makeout session. After they towel off, a slightly awkward expository sequence introduces us to who these guys are and why this isn't as ordinary a day for them as it initially appears. Twenty-eight-year-old

Michael (Richard Ganoung) is an editor and aspiring author, while his strapping boyfriend, Robert (John Bolger, the aforementioned married family man), works for an unspecified global aid organization, and this is their last 24 hours together before Robert's employer dispatches him to Africa on a lengthy overseas mission. Prior to his departure, they have a number of going-away functions to attend, including a dinner with Robert's closeted boss, Cecil (Patrick Tull), a farewell party their artist friend Joan (improv comic—and later breakout star of *The Drew Carey Show*—Kathy Kinney) is throwing at her downtown loft and, finally, drinking and dancing at an after-hours NYC nightclub. Michael also wants a reluctant Robert to say goodbye to their friend Nick (Steve Buscemi in one of his earliest feature-film roles), who has been diagnosed with AIDS and thus—given the disease's high fatality rates and the medical community's limited knowledge for how to combat it at the time—likely won't be alive when he returns home from Africa.

Despite the looming specter of Robert's departure, Sherwood keeps the pace of the duo's farewell tour relatively unhurried, not to mention entirely free of melodramatic revelations and surprise twists. *Parting Glances* is almost defiantly low-key, but it's also never dull, and above all, it achieves Sherwood's goal of capturing some of the exceptional ordinariness of gay life in the '80s. Almost two decades removed from Stonewall, Robert and Michael are able to live their lives as openly as any straight couple, and that's significant progress that can't be deterred by obstacles such as AIDS or—in a perhaps too on-the-nose scene involving a mouthy cab driver—the continued presence of homophobia.

Although *Parting Glances* eschews sermonizing and overt political commentary, Sherwood does use the film's structure as an opportunity to explore various aspects of New York's gay and lesbian scene as it existed in the early '80s, with each pit stop the central couple makes highlighting a different facet of the community at large. Robert's boss, Cecil, for example, represents a relic from the pre-Stonewall age; married to a wealthy woman who doesn't suspect (at least, not that she lets on) his true orientation, he plays at being a straight man at home and work and, whenever the pressure gets to be too much, sneaks off on vacations to exotic locales with *very* tight-lipped employees to indulge his proclivities. (His most honest moment in the film comes when he confesses to Robert that he'll miss having him around because, "Now I have no one to talk to at the office.") Unable to comprehend that way of life, Michael finds Cecil's behavior largely repugnant, while his lover is more understanding and even sympathetic to his boss's plight. Joan's party, meanwhile, is both a toast to and a gentle ribbing of the downtown avant-garde art scene where gay and straight couples mingle over canapés and alcohol, exchanging catty comments and pithy observations. (This section of the movie also feels like Sherwood's answer to *The Boys in the Band*, in that it chronicles a party where there are no dramatic histrionics, emotional breakdowns, or mind games played by the mostly gay attendees.)

While Robert and Michael are both likable characters and effective tour guides through this community, by far the film's most resonant personality is Nick, due to both Buscemi's edgy, unsentimental performance and the obvious care that Sherwood has invested in writing that role. It's no accident that he—and not Robert or Michael—gets the last line of the movie, as well as one of its most poignant scenes, a hallucinatory visit from a dead friend clad in a suit of armor who returns from the great beyond to inform him how boring heaven is and to enjoy life for as long as possible. And that's the message of *Parting Glances* in a nutshell: life is filled with endless possibilities for happiness and romance, regardless of sexual orientation. So be who you are and love who you love, freely and without fear, for as long as you can.

The First: With *Parting Glances* Bill Sherwood set out to make the first narrative feature that realistically captured his community and addressed the most serious problem it faced: AIDS.

Among the many ways that the nascent independent film industry impacted the cinematic landscape in the early '80s is that it allowed for filmmakers from different social and ethnic minorities the opportunity to depict their communities on-screen. That wasn't always the case; for example, during the civil rights era, the majority of mainstream films tackling the thorny subject of race relations were helmed by white filmmakers. Even the 1961 film version of *A Raisin in the Sun*, which stars an almost entirely African American cast and was written by a celebrated black author, was brought to the screen by Daniel Petrie, a Canadian-born Caucasian. Likewise, prior to *Parting Glances*, the few high-profile "gay films" that managed to make it to movie theaters—most notably *The Boys in the Band* and *Making Love*—were directed by heterosexuals, William Friedkin and Arthur Hiller, respectively. (Experimental and underground cinema was a different story; Andy Warhol and Kenneth Anger were just two early pioneers in depicting gay culture on-screen, albeit in highly stylized art films that weren't intended for, and almost never reached, a mass audience.)

But the advent of a vibrant—and more importantly, commercially successful—independent cinema, which started to coalesce in the late '70s thanks to surprise hits like John Sayles's 1979 debut *Return of the Secaucus Seven*, granted new opportunities to voices that had previously gone unheard. Around the time that Bill Sherwood began work on *Parting Glances*, Wayne Wang had recently released 1982's *Chan Is Missing*, which took place in San Francisco's Chinatown and featured a large cast of Asian American actors and nonactors. Meanwhile, Gregory Nava's 1983 film *El Norte* depicted

the hardships two Mexican immigrants face both before and after they ille-
gally cross the border into the United States. The positive response that
greeted those movies indicated that there was a hunger—both within their
respective communities and outside them—to see different cultures presented
on-screen by filmmakers with firsthand experience. The timing seemed right
for a positive gay love story from an openly gay filmmaker, and Sherwood
had the right instinct and initiative to fill that void. It should be noted that
he wasn't alone in sensing an opportunity, though; as Sherwood was getting
Parting Glances off the ground in New York, California-based director
Donna Deitch was in the process of making her lesbian-themed drama *Desert
Hearts* in Nevada. In fact, the two movies would go on to compete for the
attention of distributors when they started screening in 1985.[6]

Sherwood had another goal in mind with *Parting Glances* as well, one
born out of his anger and frustration at the lackluster response that the
American medical establishment, not to mention the federal government,
was showing toward the ongoing AIDS crisis.[7] Initially surfacing in the
United States in the mid-'70s, the disease had swept through the gay community by 1983, claiming thousands of lives. The severity of AIDS, coupled with
the sheer lack of knowledge about its origins and transmission, inspired
waves of misinformation and fear, which in turn resulted in gay men often
confronting acts of violence and hostility. Although it was frequently in the
news—where the coverage naturally dwelt on the high casualty rates and
conflicting reports about treatment and prevention—when Sherwood sat
down to write his film in 1983, AIDS had yet to be readily addressed in a dramatic medium, be it film, television, or theater. (The first significant play to
confront the crisis, Larry Kramer's *The Normal Heart*, wouldn't premiere
until the spring of 1985.) Thus, with *Parting Glances*, Sherwood intended
to put a human face on the disease, showing moviegoers what AIDS had cost
his community, but also their resilience in the face of this unprecedented
threat.

As brave as Sherwood was for tackling the subject at a time when no other
film would, it is possible to take *Parting Glances* to task for not depicting the
damage wrought by AIDS as starkly as it might. In fact, the word "AIDS" is
almost never used (it was similarly left out of the press materials),[8] and
there's no reference to the toll it had already taken on New York's gay population. Based purely on what we're shown in *Parting Glances*, you'd never
know that, in 1984, the city's hospitals were still filled with once healthy
men wasting away to nothing, while grassroots activist groups like ACT UP
were protesting in the streets to bring some much-needed attention and
money toward research. (For an eye-opening look at that era, make a point
of seeing David France's Oscar-nominated 2012 documentary, *How to Sur-
vive a Plague*.) Even the movie's AIDS-afflicted character hasn't yet borne
the full brunt of the disease; although Nick and his circle of friends know that

his death is imminent and most likely inescapable, he's still of relatively healthy mind and body during the course of the movie.

While audiences at the time would probably have been able to fill in the blanks, seen from today's perspective, *Parting Glances* appears guilty of trying to have its cake and eat it too. Yes, AIDS is addressed in the film—a first for an American narrative feature—but in a somewhat idealized way that doesn't risk offending or upsetting moviegoers. To see the pain the disease inflicted on its victims and their loved ones presented on-screen, viewers would have to wait until 1989's *Longtime Companion*, which depicts the deaths of several of its gay characters from AIDS. Unlike *Parting Glances*, that drama became a modest theatrical success, grossing almost $5 million, and earned a Best Supporting Actor nomination for Bruce Davison, who has one of the movie's most memorable scenes in which he urges his dying lover to just "let go." Given how Sherwood's film had largely faded from view by 1989, perhaps it's no surprise that *Longtime Companion*'s backers felt emboldened to bill it as the first feature film to deal with AIDS.[9] (Although if we're keeping close score, both *Longtime Companion* and *Parting Glances*—which was first filmed in 1984 and completed in 1985 but not released until 1986—were beaten to the punch by the 1985 TV movie *An Early Frost*, which starred Aiden Quinn as a closeted lawyer diagnosed with the disease.)

Even if Sherwood's treatment of AIDS is lacking in some respects, it's worth noting that his approach is tonally appropriate with the movie he's making. After all, *Parting Glances* isn't intended to be a film specifically about AIDS—it's a film about a contemporary gay couple and the different people in their lives, one of whom happens to have AIDS. As the writer/director told the *Los Angeles Times*, "I intended the film as an homage to New York City, and also to the gay community, which in spite of this (AIDS) crisis we are living through, continues to be such a life force."[10] When viewed through that lens, it's clear that we're meant to focus on Nick's life and not his eventual death. To dwell on the character's illness to the point where it winds up exclusively defining him would be to commit the same sin as the movies Sherwood made *Parting Glances* as a reaction to. One also can't discount the commercial considerations involved; Sherwood intended for the film to be seen by as wide an audience as possible, and at that particular time, in that particular market, it was unlikely that a more serious and somber examination of the impact of AIDS on gay life would have sold many tickets, let alone found a distributor.

As it was, *Parting Glances* traveled a bumpy path to theaters, with many buyers passing on the film out of concern that it would never find an audience outside of the gay community, even with its inclusive tone and upbeat message. And when it was eventually acquired for distribution (by the now-defunct company Cinecom, which also released the Talking Heads concert film *Stop Making Sense* and Merchant Ivory's *A Room with a View*) and opening in theaters during the winter of 1986, it wound up being over-shadowed by two other gay-themed movies released that year, Donna Deitch's aforementioned *Desert Hearts* and the British production *My Beautiful Laundrette*, which became a breakout vehicle for director Stephen Frears and star Daniel Day-Lewis. *Parting Glances* finished its run with a final gross just under $1 million—not a pittance, but also not the crossover hit its makers might have hoped for.[11]

Four years later, in 1990, Sherwood himself would die from AIDS, without having the opportunity to make another film. But his one and only feature would prove to have an impact beyond its initial theatrical release. One can see *Parting Glance*'s influence reflected most directly in a number of the slice-of-life gay romances that have been made since, such as Rose Toche's *Go Fish* from 1994 and Andrew Haigh's *Weekend* from 2011. It also served as a stepping-stone to what was labeled the New Queer Cinema in the early '90s, independent movies by gay directors that dealt with homosexuality, as well as AIDS, in an open, honest—and frequently much blunter and confrontational—fashion. (Examples would include Todd Haynes's *Poison*, Gregg Araki's *The Living End*, and Tom Kalin's *Swoon*.) It's only appropriate that a movie that was made, in part, to celebrate life has gone on to enjoy such a long one.

FILM FIRST FILE #1: THE FIVE MOST MEMORABLE GAY ROMANCES

Parting Glances contains one of the earliest and most authentic depictions of a gay couple seen in a feature film. The following pairs of screen lovers feel like descendants of Michael and Robert in that their romance is entirely believable, even if it doesn't always last.

Ely and Max

From: *Go Fish* (Rose Troche, 1994)
Played by: V. S. Brodie and Guinevere Turner
Their Story: Set up by a mutual friend, the younger Max and the older Ely don't click at first, due to their different temperaments and relationship status (Max is single, Ely is technically not). But when they meet again at a party sometime after their disappointing first date, they've both grown and changed a bit and wind up hitting it off famously. Soon, Ely has broken things off with her girlfriend, and the duo embrace full-fledged coupledom.
Why They Click: The (slight) age divide works in their favor thing; Ely's added years of experience impress Max, while Ely is affected by Max's confidence and strong sense of self.

Ennis and Jack

From: *Brokeback Mountain* (Ang Lee, 2005)
Played by: Heath Ledger and Jake Gyllenhaal
Their Story: Hired to keep watch over a Wyoming farmer's flock of sheep, rugged cowhands Ennis and Jack take an almost instant shine to each other, even though the exceptionally taciturn Ennis tries hard to fight those feelings. By the end of the summer, though, they're enjoying a full-blown love affair that continues even after one of them goes to his grave.
Why They Click: Like the song says, opposites attract; Jack's more outgoing, forceful personality prods the reclusive Ennis out of his shell, releasing all the volcanic emotion he otherwise keeps stored away.

James and Jamie

From: *Shortbus* (John Cameron Mitchell, 2006)
Played by: Paul Dawson and PJ DeBoy
Their Story: An ex-call boy and a one-time child actor, this duo have mostly overcome troubled pasts—although James is still wrestling with some serious issues—to make a loving home for each other. Now, working under the theory of the more equaling the merrier, they've decided to invite a third man to join their union.
Why They Click: They're both invested in each other's happiness and don't seem to possess a jealous bone in their respective bodies, which explains why they're open to the idea of a three-man household.

Jules and Nic

From: *The Kids Are All Right* (Lisa Cholodenko, 2010)
Played by: Julianne Moore and Annette Bening
Their Story: A picture-perfect lesbian couple—married for years with two great kids and a comfortable California lifestyle—Jules and Nic are well settled in their ways. Perhaps too settled . . .
Why They Click: They're like two sides of the same brain; Nic represents the logical, thoughtful portion, while Jules is the imaginative (if often impractical) dreamer.

Glen and Russell

From: *Weekend* (Andrew Haigh, 2011)
Played by: Chris New and Tom Cullen
Their Story: A one-night stand that quickly becomes something more, Glen and Russell spend the weekend before Glen's departure for a two-year trip abroad talking, making love, taking drugs, and talking some more. In

the process, they get to know each other more fully in two days than some couples do in a lifetime.

Why They Click: They're both thoughtful and inquisitive, not to mention sexually compatible.

FILM FIRST FILE #2: A CINEMATIC TOUR OF NEW YORK IN THE '80s

Beyond being a realistic portrait of gay life in '80s New York, *Parting Glances* is also a vivid time capsule of the city's Upper West Side circa 1984. Like the city itself, that neighborhood has been through some significant changes since then, but it remains perfectly preserved in Bill Sherwood's film. If you want to piece together your own tour of what other well-known New York nabes looked like during that era, leave your walking shoes by the door and just watch the following '80s films, all of which were shot on location.

Neighborhood: Alphabet City, Manhattan
Movie: *Alphabet City* (Amos Poe, 1984)

Neighborhood: Battery Park, Manhattan
Movie: *Desperately Seeking Susan* (Susan Seidelman, 1985)

Neighborhood: Bedford-Stuyvesant, Brooklyn
Movie: *Do the Right Thing* (Spike Lee, 1989)

Neighborhood: Brooklyn Heights, Brooklyn
Movie: *Moonstruck* (Norman Jewison, 1987)

Neighborhood: Greenwich Village, Manhattan
Movie: *The Pope of Greenwich Village* (Stuart Rosenberg, 1984)

Neighborhood: Harlem, Manhattan
Movie: *The Brother from Another Planet* (John Sayles, 1984)

Neighborhood: Long Island City, Queens
Movie: *Coming to America* (John Landis, 1988)

Neighborhood: Lower East Side, Manhattan
Movie: *Downtown 81* (Edo Bertoglio, 1981)

Neighborhood: Times Square, Manhattan
Movie: *The King of Comedy* (Martin Scorsese, 1982)

Neighborhood: SoHo, Manhattan
Movie: *After Hours* (Martin Scorsese, 1985)

Neighborhood: South Bronx, The Bronx
Movie: *Wild Style* (Charlie Ahearn, 1983)

Neighborhood: Upper East Side, Manhattan
Movie: *Hannah and Her Sisters* (Woody Allen, 1986)

Chapter 7

She's Gotta Have It (1986)

The Film: Spike Lee's feature film debut pulsates with an energy that reflects its rough-and-tumble production.

She's Gotta Have It[1] is a movie that probably shouldn't exist. Not that it doesn't deserve to; on the contrary, it's an important and influential piece of filmmaking—a fundamental building block of its director Spike Lee's career as well as contemporary black cinema in general. But before, during, and after its ultra-fast shoot in the summer of 1985, Lee had to clear so many hurdles (mostly of the financial variety) that the movie could have collapsed at any point. In fact, that had happened to the then 28-year-old Brooklyn resident and award-winning NYU grad the previous year, when the film that was supposed to have been his feature-length debut—*Messenger*—fell apart due to lack of funds. Still smarting from that failure, Lee threw himself into work on a new screenplay in the fall of 1984, coming up with the eye-catching title almost before he penned a single word of dialogue. "I want it to be different from my other work," Lee wrote in his journal at the time. "First of all the protagonist will be female. . . . It will be told through her eyes. . . . I want a happy ending. Plus, it will be more commercial than the previous films, and it won't be a totally BLACK thing."[2]

Although Lee may have set out intending to write a commercial film, potential investors didn't necessarily see it that way. The writer/director endured rejection after rejection for funding from private investors as well as organizations like the American Film Institute, in many cases due to concerns over the movie's content. And it's true that Lee was deliberately out to push buttons with the film—why else pick the title *She's Gotta Have It*? As the name suggests, sex plays a central role in the story, which revolves around single gal Nola Darling (Tracy Camilla Johns), who is happily involved with three very different men. There's slick egomaniac Greer Childs (John Canada Terrell), hyperactive hustler Mars Blackmon (Lee), and nice, but very possessive guy next door Jamie Overstreet (Tommy Redmon Hicks). Nola flits between each guy, aware of—but completely uninterested in—their desire to be the only man in her life. The movie takes great pains to point out that she's not some heartless tease; rather, she's an empowered, confident woman with a healthy sexual appetite who is up front about her wants and needs. Lee's stated intention with the movie was to explore the double standard he saw between the way men with lots of sexual partners are treated versus women with more than one lover. "[Men] are encouraged to have and enjoy sex, while it's not so for women. If they do what men do they're labeled whore, prostitute, nympho etc."[3]

While Lee made sure to position Nola as the movie's heroine as he wrote the script, he found that the subject matter still made some people— particularly those he hoped would fund the movie—uncomfortable and not just due to its sexual content. From a marketing standpoint, there wasn't an obvious precedent for the kind of movie Lee wanted to make, and, despite the strength of the script and the passion of the filmmaker behind it, the risk of financial failure scared people off. Refusing to abandon (or tone down) the project, though, Lee eventually cobbled together enough money to get the movie on celluloid in a marathon 12-day shoot in his home borough of Brooklyn. Of course, his financial woes didn't stop once the film was in the can ... really, they had only just begun. Postproduction fees, cast and crew salaries, and other costs pushed the total price tag well north of $100,000[4]—a pittance by studio standards, but a huge number for an independent filmmaker depending on the kindness of friends, family, and strangers for cash. Lee would eventually make all that money back, following the sale of the movie to an established distributor (Island Pictures, the film arm of the Island Records label) and an almost $8 million box-office haul. But he didn't know any of that during the two weeks he spent shooting the film or the roughly four-month editing period that followed. All that mattered to him at that point was getting his film made, by any means necessary.

Over the course of his career, Lee's name has, unfairly or not, become synonymous with provocation; movies like *Jungle Fever*, *Malcolm X*, *Bamboozled*, and, of course, *Do the Right Thing* take political and social issues that people are often reluctant to discuss and put them front and center, daring the audience to look away. They are also frequently viewed as extensions of the director's public persona, which remains that of an outspoken, highly opinionated individual who isn't expressly concerned with remaining diplomatic. *She's Gotta Have It*, though, showcases a lighter, more playful side of Lee; compared to the more forceful movies that would follow, this one plays first and foremost as a relatively straightforward relationship comedy, at least in terms of its substance if not necessarily its style.

That's not to say that this film is without its opinions or, for that matter, its provocations. Certainly, *She's Gotta Have It* is highly critical of male vanity, calling attention to the way each of Nola's suitors preen for her, hoping to be singled out as her favorite. At the same time, Lee is careful not to present his heroine as encouraging these kinds of adolescent displays of bravado for her pleasure; if anything, she finds the guys' behavior as ridiculous as the audience is intended to. By far one of the director's most upbeat characters, Nola is comfortable with her sexuality and lifestyle choices even when the people around her are telling her she's wrong. Sometimes the constant criticism does get to her, however; in one scene, we hear from a sex therapist who counseled her through a difficult period, reassuring her that she's not an addict for simply enjoying sex. And toward the end of the film, there's a dream sequence where Nola imagines herself being taunted and then set on fire by three women who accuse her of "corrupting our men." It's interesting to note that this is also one of the few scenes in the movie to directly address the subject of race, a topic that's central to many of Lee's best-known films, particularly *Do the Right Thing*. On the one hand, this may have been a calculated appeal for the film to reach a wider audience. But, considering the era in which the movie was made, Lee also clearly recognized that just making a relationship comedy with an all-black cast was already an act of social commentary; he didn't have to explicitly call attention to the characters' race to make viewers understand what was unique about *She's Gotta Have It* or its heroine.

In his journal, Lee reminds himself that he must "love and respect"[5] Nola, and he holds to that promise in the movie, almost to a fault. As written by Lee and played by Johns, Nola is so confident and self-assured, she can be difficult to relate to; there doesn't seem to be much of an inner life beneath her sunny exterior. We hear about her occasional doubts and uncertainties from other people, but rarely see them reflected in her face or expressed in her own words. Even when she addresses the camera directly—as several characters do, following the documentary aesthetic Lee establishes early on—she remains somewhat remote and unknowable, an ideal rather than a fully rounded human being. (One could make the same case about the various men she bounces between, who represent types—the out-of-his-depth youngster, the player, and the boy next door—rather than distinct individuals.) Other questionable choices on Lee's part include a story thread involving Nola's lesbian friend Opal (Raye Dowell), who is depicted as having a somewhat predatory interest in her pal, as well as a scene in which Jamie forces himself on Nola in a rough sexual encounter that borders very closely on rape. That this sequence ends with the implication that she's enjoying being treated this way makes it all the more unpleasant and out of step with the rest of the movie. (In the years since *She's Gotta Have It*, Lee has cited that scene as his biggest regret, suggesting it "makes light of rape.")[6]

If the film's narrative and characterizations aren't quite as sharp as in some of Lee's later work, *She's Gotta Have It* does showcase many of the formal trademarks that have become part of his house style. Early on, for example, there's an extended montage of guys pitching their best (and worst) pickup lines directly into the camera, a device the director would use to memorable effect (albeit with very different content) in both *Do the Right Thing* and *25th Hour*. Later on, the movie's documentary-style realism is interrupted by a fanciful dance sequence filmed in color; that sudden and unexpected intrusion of fantasy into otherwise grounded, real-world narrative has since become another staple of Lee's work, with similar moments cropping up in *Crooklyn* and *He Got Game*. At the time, though, both of these scenes—as well as other striking elements like the fractured chronology, jazz score (written and performed by the filmmaker's father, Bill Lee), and eye-catching shots (like the introduction of Mars, which features Lee riding directly into the frame atop a bicycle)—were the product of a young filmmaker whose sensibility was shaped by his limited resources, ferocious will, and the sense that he had nothing to lose. *She's Gotta Have It* exists because Lee refused to let it slip away, despite the overwhelming odds facing him. That experience informed how he made not only this movie but the majority of his other films going forward.

The First: As the first post-blaxploitation hit, *She's Gotta Have It* opened the door for a new generation of African American filmmakers to tell different kinds of stories on-screen.

Thirteen years before Spike Lee first wrote the words "She's Gotta Have It" in his journal, another determined African American writer/director poured his blood, sweat, tears, and a healthy chunk of his bank account into making an independent feature that seemed on the verge of collapse throughout its rushed production. Despite the numerous challenges that stood in its way, the film was completed and released in theaters, whereupon it became a sensation, one that reaped impressive profits and launched a wave of movies starring black actors and aimed at black audiences (most of which, admittedly, were made by white directors and producers). The filmmaker was Melvin Van Peebles, and the movie was 1971's *Sweet Sweetback's Baadasssss Song*, the story of a well-endowed sex show performer who is falsely fingered as the culprit in a murder case and proceeds to fight the racist cops and rigged justice system by going on the run, relying only on his fists (and his penis) to escape from difficult situations en route to a freer existence across the Mexican border.

African American audiences at the time weren't showing up in droves for the story or the filmmaking; what galvanized them was simply the image of a black man defying authority instead of acquiescing to it, which had been the status quo for dark-skinned characters in Hollywood for decades. And while studio-backed movies like 1967's *In the Heat of the Night* tried to combat this portrayal from within the system, it took an independent production like *Sweet Sweetback* to really explode it, especially once the majors saw how much money stood to be made from movies where black characters were the (anti)heroes. The commercial success of Van Peebles's film, followed by the similarly large grosses racked up by *Shaft* three months later, begat one of the defining genres of the '70s: blaxploitation. Between 1971 and 1979, blaxploitation pictures with titles like *Superfly*, *Coffy*, and *Blacula* became sizable hits and made movie stars out of performers like Pam Grier, Richard Roundtree, and Fred Williamson. But the genre had run its course by the time the '80s rolled around—the victim of a lack of innovation and, subsequently, declining attendance—and Hollywood went back to mostly ignoring the black moviegoers, outside of the occasional prestige project like 1984's *A Soldier's Story* (starring a young Denzel Washington) or 1985's *The Color Purple* (starring a young Whoopi Goldberg), both of which, again, were directed by white filmmakers.[7] And while those movies were finely crafted, they lacked a certain authenticity. After seeing *The Color Purple*, Lee wrote in his journal: "The movie is weak. . . . WE, I GOTTA MAKE OUR OWN GODDAMN FILMS. FUCK HAVING THESE WHITE BOYS FUCK UP TELLING OUR STORIES. WE GOTTA TELL OUR OWN AS ONLY WE CAN."[8]

Interestingly, although Lee—who was born in 1957—came of age right in the middle of the blaxploitation era, he's often said that he was not a fan of the genre during its heyday, not catching up with defining films like *Shaft* or *Superfly* until years after their release. "I just wasn't interested in those types of movies," he told Nelson George in a 1986 interview, adding, "I was going to see quality films."[9] And, indeed, the form and content of *She's Gotta Have It* owes less to blaxploitation and more to movements like the French New Wave and such directors as Martin Scorsese and even Woody Allen. (In his journal, Lee specifically mentions renting Allen's 1983 black-and-white feature *Zelig* for visual reference.)[10] Perhaps the movie that seems to have had the most direct influence on Lee's debut feature was the 1979 slice-of-life story *Killer of Sheep*, directed by Charles Burnett, who was then part of an Los Angeles-based, African American led film movement known as the L.A. Rebellion. Also filmed in black and white on an ultra-low budget, Burnett's film followed a working-class black family living in the Watts neighborhood of L.A. *Killer of Sheep*'s episodic structure, as well as the way it depicts the everyday lives of black characters without calling overt attention to their race, is certainly reflected in *She's Gotta Have It*. Despite winning accolades on the festival circuit, Burnett's film never received a substantial theatrical release, largely due to licensing issues over the film's soundtrack, which made use of several popular songs. (Those rights were eventually cleared and the film was released in theaters and on DVD in 2007.)[11]

Lee's film might have gone the same route had it not been for the interven-
tion of John Pierson, a fellow NYU alum who started out programming repertory theaters before moving into distribution and producing. Pierson saw
an early cut of *She's Gotta Have It* at a private investors screening at their
alma mater. Although the film was in an exceedingly rough state, lacking
sound effects or music (there were projector issues as well), Pierson immediately saw its potential and invested $10,000,[12] as well as his time and effort
in helping Lee secure high-profile playdates at film festivals, all the while with
an eye toward landing the film an established distributor. *She's Gotta Have It*
had it first public screening at the San Francisco International Film Festival in
March 1986 and even a power outage 20 minutes into the film—which lasted
almost a half hour, during which time Lee took to the stage for an
impromptu Q&A session—didn't dampen the audience's enthusiasm, something the distributors in the crowd took note of.[13]

After a flurry of postfestival meetings with different companies, Pierson
and Lee eventually signed with Island Pictures, the film division of the well-
known record label of the same name. The film opened at New York's
now-defunct Cinema Studio on August 8, 1986, and from its initial showings, the theater was packed and remained so for the entire month. Pierson
recalls ticket buyers regularly being turned away at the door and visits from
such luminaries as Eddie Murphy, who brought 14 people to see the film.[14]
The movie continued to expand around the country over the next few
months, and by the end of its run, it had grossed $7.5 million[15]—an eye-
opening number for an independent film at the time, particularly one that
was viewed as only having niche appeal. It was clear that a market existed
for serious (and seriously funny) movies about contemporary African American life, if enterprising filmmakers both in and outside Hollywood could
figure out how to serve it.

The impact of *She's Gotta Have It* was slowly but surely felt within the
industry. One year later, Robert Townsend wrote and directed *Hollywood
Shuffle*, a satirical send-up of Hollywood's stereotypical treatment of black
actors. Keenen Ivory Wayans's blaxploitation spoof *I'm Gonna Git You
Sucka* followed in 1988, the same year that Lee returned with his sophomore
feature, *School Daze*, a collegiate musical that dealt more directly with racial
issues than *She's Gotta Have It*. But it was in the early '90s that the number
of new movies from black filmmakers started to substantially increase. For
example, 1991 saw the release of *New Jack City* from Mario van Peebles
(son of *Sweet Sweetback*'s director), *Straight out of Brooklyn* from Matty
Rich, *Daughters of the Dust* from Julie Dash (who had been active in the
L.A. Rebellion in the '70s, but hadn't directed a feature in over a decade prior
to *Daughters*), and, most famously, John Singleton's *Boyz n the Hood*, for
which Singleton became the first black filmmaker to receive an Oscar nomination for Best Director. (It took almost 20 years for another black director
to receive the same recognition—Lee Daniels secured a nod in 2010 for his

film *Precious*. To date, Spike Lee has yet to be nominated in the Best Director category.) With the arguable exception of *New Jack City*, these movies were very much removed from what the blaxploitation genre represented, instead telling personal stories about the present-day black experience. Additionally, the success of *Boyz* paved the way for another long-running subgenre, the hood film—movies that dealt with the social problems facing predominantly black urban neighborhoods.

Despite the positive industry changes that *She's Gotta Have It* helped bring about, the opportunities for both established and new black filmmakers continue to wax and wane, especially at the studio level. Even Lee, who now has a long and proven track record directing both big-budget and independent features, frequently finds himself struggling to find funding for his movies, just he did back in the *She's Gotta Have It* days. For example, his 2012 film *Red Hook Summer* was entirely self-financed and self-distributed largely because, as he put it in an interview, "Hollywood is really superhero land now. It's harder to make adult films today without people flying..."[16] (In 2013, Lee made headlines by bypassing Hollywood in favor of the online crowdfunding platform Kickstarter to bankroll a planned feature.) Fortunately, the challenge of getting a movie made still seems to energize the director instead of sapping his drive. When it comes to finding a way to make a movie he's passionate about, Lee's still got it.

FILM FIRST FILE #1: THE LOST SPIKE LEE JOINTS

Spike Lee's determination has rescued a number of films from collapse. But here are five projects even he couldn't see to fruition.

Inside Man 2

What It Was: The sequel to Lee's biggest commercial success, *Inside Man*, a star-powered bank heist thriller starring Denzel Washington, Clive Owen and Jodie Foster.

Why It Collapsed: Although the original earned almost $90 million for Universal Pictures, the studio declined to fund the follow-up due to budget concerns, a decision that Lee is still flummoxed by.[17]

Messenger

What It Was: The film that was supposed to have been Lee's directorial debut was a drama about the life of New York City–based bike messenger.

Why It Collapsed: The Screen Actors Guild declined to approve a waiver that would have allowed Lee to hire nonunion actors; short of funds, the director was forced to shut down the production just before filming started.[18]

Rent

What It Was: The big-screen version of Jonathan Larson's smash hit Broadway musical, in which a crew of young bohemian types rock out while trying to make a living on New York's Lower Side.

Why It Collapsed: Lee (who is namechecked in one of *Rent*'s lyrics) actively pursued the job when the film rights were held by Miramax, but the studio declined to give it a green light.[19] A film version was eventually released in 2005, directed by Chris Columbus.

Untitled Joe Louis Project

What It Was: Lee teamed up with celebrated writer Budd Schulberg, who wrote *On the Waterfront*, to tell the story of boxer Joe Louis's groundbreaking 1936 bout against Max Schmeling.

Why It Collapsed: Sadly, it never even got started as, no studio proved willing to put up the cash despite the dynamic duo of Lee and Schulberg.[20]

Untitled Jackie Robinson Project

What It Was: A biopic about the legendary baseball player who shattered the sport's color barrier.

Why It Collapsed: Lee and frequent collaborator Denzel Washington came close to making the film, but failed to secure the rights from Robinson's widow, and eventually both the director and his star moved on.[21] (In 2013, Warner Bros. released the Robinson biopic *42*, directed by Brian Helgeland.)

FILM FIRST FILE #2: FIVE A-LIST AFRICAN AMERICAN DIRECTORS

Although directing opportunities for black filmmakers remain limited at the studio level, here are five directors who have managed to achieve a certain level of financial and creative success within Hollywood.

Tyler Perry

Arguably the most powerful black filmmaker working today, the playwright turned media mogul owns his own studio in Atlanta, where he writes, directs, produces, and acts in his various movies and TV shows.

Directorial Debut: Tyler Perry's *Madea's Family Reunion* (2006; $63.2 million)

Biggest Hit: Tyler Perry's *Madea Goes to Jail* (2009; $90.5 million)

Tim Story

To date, still the only black director to have helmed a major comic book movie franchise—2005's *Fantastic Four* and its 2007 sequel—Story's other credits include hits like *Barbershop* and *Think Like a Man*.
Directorial Debut: *Barbershop* (2002; $75.7 million)
Biggest Hit: *Fantastic Four* (2005; $154.6 million)

Antoine Fuqua

After getting his start in music videos, Fuqua has gone on to helm such big-budget star vehicles as *King Arthur* and *Shooter*.
Directorial Debut: *The Replacement Killers* (1998; $19.2 million)
Biggest Hit: *Olympus Has Fallen* (2013; $98.9 million)

Allen and Albert Hughes

The Hughes brothers broke through with the inner-city crime tale *Menace II Society*, before moving into the studio system with movies like *From Hell* and *The Book of Eli*.
Directorial Debut: *Menace II Society* (1993; $27.9 million)
Biggest Hit: *The Book of Eli* (2010; $94.8 million)

F. Gary Gray

After getting audiences laughing with the stoner comedy *Friday*, Gray made his mark as an action director, taking on thrillers like *The Negotiator* and *Law Abiding Citizen*.
Directorial Debut: *Friday* (1998; $27.4 million)
Biggest Hit: *The Italian Job* (2003; $106.1 million)

Chapter 8

The Thin Blue Line (1988)

The Film: A real-life legal thriller, *The Thin Blue Line* is a better potboiler than most screenwriters could dream up.

The "wrong man" scenario is a classic narrative device for any piece of fiction set in the legal realm, one that rarely fails to get the audience rooting for the innocent victim being railroaded through an uncaring justice system, as well as the one person—usually a dogged lawyer with more passion than common sense—who goes to Herculean lengths to help them. The more stacked the deck is against the accused protagonist, the better, even if the absurdly heightened circumstances end up rendering the tale a fantasy on the level of a J. R. R. Tolkien knockoff. It's precisely that lack of realism that appeals so strongly to an audience; as almost any adult who has endured an extended stint on jury duty knows, the real-world mundanity of the legal process—where impassioned speeches and last-minute bombshell testimonies are few and far between and cases often drag on for years and years before even seeing the inside of a courtroom—can be deeply frustrating, to the point where a satisfying verdict seems an impossibility. In 45 minutes, two hours, or 500 pages, however, a TV episode/feature film/best-selling airplane read will reward the innocent, punish the guilty, and above all, leave those following along feeling that justice has been done.

Viewed in those terms, Errol Morris's 1988 documentary *The Thin Blue Line*[1] appears to be the very model of a classic legal thriller. Over the course of a tense, wholly involving 108 minutes, Morris—who spent several years working as a New York City-area private detective in the early '80s while his film career was on hold[2]—spins a yarn about a gross miscarriage of justice that was perpetrated against one innocent man, exposing the lies at the center of the prosecution's case and even pulling a semiconfession out of the actual guilty party. It's even paced like a potboiler, with a slow burn opening followed by wild twists and turns as the details of the crime and its aftermath unfold. What makes this particular thriller so unique, however, is the fact that the story Morris is telling happens to be 100 percent true. Not only that, but the "characters" we see and hear on-screen are the actual men and women involved in the case, from the wronged man, to various law enforcement officials, to the probable killer. What Morris achieves with *The Thin Blue Line* was something unique to documentaries at the time: he uses the conventions of narrative filmmaking to build a fine piece of nonfiction police work.

In an interview, Morris once half-jokingly remarked that, "My films never end up where they're supposed to end up."[3] That was certainly the case with *The Thin Blue Line*, which started its life as a public television–funded profile of Dallas-based psychiatrist Dr. James Grigson, who was frequently brought in by the prosecution on death penalty cases to register his professional opinion on whether the accused was capable of killing again. His verdict almost always aligned with the prosecution and sealed the fate of many a Death Row–bound inmate, earning him the nickname Dr. Death, a moniker he seemed to wear almost proudly.[4]

In doing the prep work for his Grigson documentary, Morris was introduced to Randall Dale Adams, a drifter who was tried, convicted and sentenced to death—in part because of Dr. Death's testimony—for the fatal shooting of a police officer one night in 1977. As the director/P.I. spoke with Adams (who strongly maintained his innocence) and dug into the details surrounding the murder, the more he realized that the official version of events didn't add up. And so the Dr. Death film went on the shelf, and the beginnings of what would become *The Thin Blue Line* took shape as Morris spent the next two years doing exhaustive research, interviewing everyone from the original investigating police officers, to the presiding judge, to Adams's defense team to the convicted man himself.

Most importantly, he sat down with David Harris, the 16-year-old who had been in Adams's company in the hours leading up to the murder. As the movie's chronology of events outlines, the two had met earlier in the day when Harris gave Adams a lift—in a car he turned out to have stolen—to a service station after the older man's car ran out of gas. They continued hanging out together late into the evening, grabbing a bite to eat and taking in a movie at the drive-in, before Adams returned to the hotel room he was sharing with this brother. Around midnight, Harris's vehicle was pulled over by officer Robert Wood, primarily because the headlights were out. Wood was shot at point-blank range and the car peeled away, headed back toward Harris's hometown of Vidor, Texas, where he openly bragged to his pals about killing a cop—a boast he promptly backed away from when the Dallas police started to question him. Instead, he put them onto Adams's trail, insisting that his "friend" had been the one driving. And, for their part, the police were more than happy to point the blame at someone other than Harris because, as a minor, he wouldn't face the death penalty. Adams, on the other hand, was 27 and could thus be prosecuted to the full extent of the law for killing one of the Dallas PD's own.[5]

Finding this crucial witness proved to be an adventure in and of itself for Morris; Harris had just been released from a seven-year stint in California's San Quentin prison and was serving out his parole in Vidor, which had long been a major hub of Ku Klux Klan activity. Morris's first meeting—off-camera—with Harris took place in a local bar, and the filmmaker came away from their encounter with the strong sense that his life could very well be in danger.[6] Sometime later, when Morris had finally persuaded the skittish young man to be filmed, Harris missed his call time on the day of the inter-view because he was in the process of murdering another man—a crime that landed him on Death Row.[7] (He was executed in 2004.[8]) Eventually, the director lugged his camera to the prison to get the interview on film, only to have an equipment malfunction halfway through their conversation. Refus-ing to give up, he returned the next day with a microcassette recorder and captured the crucial statements that would give The Thin Blue Line its now-famous ending, where Harris all but confesses on tape to killing the police officer that night in 1977 and allowing Adams to take the fall.[9] The starkness of the film's finale—just a series of tight close-ups of the recorder, with the wheels of the audio tape turning and Harris's disembodied voice emanating from the tiny speaker—is just as powerful, if not more so, as a "You can't handle the truth!"-style courtroom confessional.

That sequence is just one example of the heightened visual style that Morris brought to The Thin Blue Line, which was, in part, conceived as a reaction to the reigning cinéma vérité school of nonfiction features, as repre-sented by films like Frederick Wiseman's High School and the Maysles broth-ers' Salesman. Those documentaries were fly-on-the-wall portraits of real people, places, and events; nothing was staged for the camera, and overt commentary was discouraged in favor of an observational approach. Morris, however, rejected the notion that only the vérité style could be con-sidered the model of documentary truth. As he put it: "There's this false idea that style equals truth. If you adopt a certain style, then out pops truth. It's a stupid idea. Truth isn't guaranteed by style. Truth, to the extent that we can ever grab a hold of it, is the product of a lot of hard work and investiga-tion."[10]

Morris announces his intention to depart from the traditional documen-tary playbook in the opening scenes of The Thin Blue Line. Gone is the hand-held camerawork the defines so many vérité films in favor of a series of carefully composed shots of, among other things, the Dallas skyline, set to an original score penned by noted composer Philip Glass. This represented a distinct change from the nonfiction norm, with the specific combination of music and image lending the film the appearance of a commercial feature.

And Morris's interviews with his various subjects—or, in the parlance of documentary slang, "talking heads"—were also unique, as he conducted them while sitting next to the camera, forcing the interviewees to stare directly into the lens while responding instead of gazing off to the side where the director would typically be sitting in a more standard Q&A arrangement. Morris would later perfect his patented interviewing technique by inventing what his wife dubbed "the Interrotron," a teleprompter-like device that uses a two-way mirror to project a person's face onto a screen that's positioned in front of a camera lens. This way, a person can stare into the camera while still making direct eye contact with the person he or she is speaking with.[11]

Perhaps Morris's most radical departure from the "approved" documentary style was his decision to incorporate reenactments into the film. Although early documentaries from pioneering directors like Robert Flaherty (*Nanook of the North*) and Merian C. Cooper and Ernest B. Schoedsack (*Grass*) made liberal use of re-created and otherwise staged scenes, that practice had fallen out of favor in the *vérité* era. But the power and, ultimately, the persuasiveness of *The Thin Blue Line* hinges on the reenactment of the central crime that Morris repeatedly cuts back to during the course of the film, presenting the same series of events before, during, and after the shooting from multiple points of view. It's a device that has since become a staple of true-crime documentaries, to say nothing of narrative features and TV shows. (One can see the movie's influence in the flashy crime-solving theatrics on CBS's popular *CSI* franchise, for example.) Flourishes like that help *The Thin Blue Line* entertain like a great piece of fiction, but the film ultimately resonates because it tells nothing but the truth.

The First: Through his thorough investigation of the Randall Dale Adams case, Errol Morris crafted a movie that, quite literally, became a lifesaver.

Most filmmakers dream of making a movie that changes someone's life for the better, although the specific circumstances of that change is often nebulous, like inspiring a person to pursue his or her passion or reach for a goal that previously seemed out of reach. When *The Thin Blue Line* arrived in theaters, it had a more direct and immediate impact on one man's life: it paved the way for Randall Dale Adams's eventual release from prison. While Morris himself has taken great pains to say that a movie alone isn't responsible for overturning a conviction,[12] it's also clear that had the director not deviated from his original plan to make a documentary about James "Dr. Death" Grigson, Adams would almost certainly have continued to serve out his life sentence. Specifically, it was the evidence that Morris gathered in the course of making the film—evidence that he then provided to the defense team and that later appeared in court—that helped the wronged man clear his name. These unprecedented actions for a documentary filmmaker meant that Morris was no longer just chronicling the story ... he had become *part* of the story.

Adams hadn't been languishing in prison waiting for a dogged private eye and filmmaker to help rescue him, of course. Since the original trial, he and his defense lawyers had fiercely protested his conviction, as well as the death sentence that the judge had initially handed down, pointing out the gaping holes in the prosecution's case. The appeals and calls for a retrial went nowhere until, three days before Adams was scheduled to die in the electric chair, the U.S. Supreme Court issued a stay of execution that would have paved the way for a new trial. Rather than proceed down that path—which could very well end with Adams winning, considering the unreliable witness testimony that the prosecutors used to convict him in the first place—the district attorney had his sentence commuted from death to life imprisonment. That ruled out the possibility of a retrial, and, as the Texas appeals court had already upheld his original conviction, the case of Randall Dale Adams was for all intents and purposes closed[13] unless new evidence was unearthed that exposed the police and prosecutorial machinations that tilted the case in their direction.

Enter Morris, whose detective instincts were stirred by the inconsistencies in the original police investigation as well as the subsequent trial. Armed with his camera and the help of longtime Adams legal counsel Randy Schaffer, Morris built his own version of a case file, one that was filled with probing on-camera interviews that exposed some of the prejudices, distortions, and outright lies that helped bring about the original guilty verdict in addition to the usual assortment of legal documents, police reports, and independent research. (Also instrumental to his case were those reenactments, which allowed him to visualize the specific sequence of events that the jury had been forced to re-create in their minds based on flawed testimony.) The challenge before him was now twofold: assembling the results of his one-man investigation into a compelling feature film, while still ensuring that the evidence he had collected would benefit Adams as well as himself.

Even once the film was completed following a protracted and difficult editing process, *The Thin Blue Line* didn't secure the convicted man's immediate release. Before that could happen, the independently financed documentary would need to find a distributor. Morris's first stop was the San Francisco Film Festival in March 1988, after which he traveled on to Adams's old stomping ground in Dallas for the U.S.A. Film Festival. In both venues, the film was met with an extremely positive response and the still-young distributor Miramax—run by Harvey and Bob Weinstein—quickly moved in to acquire it, with plans to play up its true crime story hook rather than advertising it as a traditional documentary. At the same time that *Line* was inching closer to a theatrical release, it was also officially made part of Adams's defense by being submitted as evidence for his pending appeal.[14]

Things finally began to gather steam in the latter half of 1988. First, *The Thin Blue Line* opened in theaters in August, and while it didn't set the box office on fire—instead finding its widest audience on home video[15]—it did win critical raves and brought Adams's plight some much-needed media attention. That December, Morris traveled to Dallas for Adams's three-day hearing in front of District Court Judge Larry Baraka, during which Schaffer drew on both the film and the director's additional catalogue of evidence to decimate the prosecution's arguments. In the end, the judge decided in favor of a retrial, a ruling that the state criminal appeals court seconded in March 1989. By the end of the month, Adams had been released from prison, and the new D.A. dropped all charges against him. (As for the all-but-confessed killer, David Harris, he was never put on trial for the police officer's murder, having already by then been placed on Death Row for another killing.)[16] Interestingly, one of Adams's first actions as a free man was to sue Morris for the life rights to his story, allowing him to profit from any books and feature films based on his experiences. The two eventually settled out of court with Schaffer—who had helped Morris throughout the making of the film—this time sitting across the table from him.[17] After cowriting his own account (entitled *Adams v. Texas*) and speaking out in the press about his experience, Adams chose to leave the spotlight and eventually moved to a small town in Ohio. He died in 2010 of a brain tumor.[18]

His directing career buoyed by *The Thin Blue Line*, Morris never had to take a second job as a private investigator again, devoting himself to film-making full time. His subsequent documentaries have covered a wide swath of subjects and include such titles as *Fast, Cheap & Out of Control*, *Mr. Death*, and the Oscar-winning *The Fog of War*. (He's also occasionally returned to the true crime well, most notably with 2010's *Tabloid*, which chronicles an obscure '70s case involving a Mormon missionary and the beauty queen who allegedly kidnapped him.) And, in fact, several of those movies have proven to be artistically superior to *The Thin Blue Line*. Still, the importance of that particular film to his own career and contemporary documentaries in general cannot be overstated. Morris restored a cinematic flair to a form of filmmaking that had, over time, become undervalued for its artistry. (Perhaps *too* cinematic for some; the nominating committee overseeing the Best Documentary Feature Oscar category famously declined to nominate the film for that award and, in fact, didn't even finish watching it.)[19] Furthermore, the film's demonstrated ability to affect change encouraged some of Morris's contemporaries as well as successive generations of documentary filmmakers to be activists as well as artists as they document causes they believe in. *The Thin Blue Line* showed that documentary could have as substantial an impact outside of a movie theater as it could inside it.

FILM FIRST FILE #1: FIVE MUST-SEE "STRANGE BUT TRUE" CRIME DOCUMENTARIES

The Thin Blue Line follows the twists and turns of the Randall Dale Adams case with more panache than a lot of fictional crime dramas. Here are five other documentaries that chronicle crimes too strange to be the stuff of mere fiction.

Brother's Keeper (Joe Berlinger and Bruce Sinofsky, 1992)

The Crime: One morning in 1990, William Ward—one of four undereducated, largely illiterate brothers who lived in isolation on a remote farm in upstate New York—was found dead in his bed, and his sibling Delbert was arrested and charged with second-degree murder.

Why It's Stranger Than Fiction: Convinced that they had their man—especially after he confessed to the murder in front of the police, a confession that he later said was coerced—prosecutors proposed several motives for Delbert's alleged actions, including the notion of him performing a "mercy killing" due to William's illness. These arguments failed to convince a jury, and Delbert was found innocent in court.[20]

Capturing the Friedmans (Andrew Jarecki, 2003)

The Crime: In 1989, a small Long Island community was rocked by a case involving local family man and computer teacher Arnold Friedman and his 18-year-old son Jesse, who were both arrested and pleaded guilty to charges of sexually abusing a number of young boys.

Why It's Stranger Than Fiction: First, the details about the crimes that were allegedly committed remain murky, as the accused, the victims, as well as law enforcement officials offer contradictory accounts of what was going on in the Friedman home. (To this day, Jesse Friedman maintains his innocence.) Secondly, the family appeared in an extensive amount of home movie footage during the course of the trial that offers an unprecedentedly intimate depiction of the toll outside events took on their lives together. And finally, there's the unlikely way the documentary itself came about; Jarecki had initially set out to make a documentary about children's party clowns, and one of his subjects happened to be David Friedman, the now-grown son of Arnold and brother of Jesse and the person who filmed the bulk of the home movie footage. Needless to say, after learning this piece of information, Jarecki changed focus, and the clown movie fell by the wayside.[21]

Roman Polanski: Wanted & Desired (Marina Zenovich, 2008)

The Crime: Easily one of Hollywood's most notorious true crime cases, celebrated director Roman Polanski was arrested in 1977 for sexually assaulting a 13-year-old girl. He faced six charges overall, including rape and child molestation.

Why It's Stranger Than Fiction: In a narrative that could come right out of one of Polanski's thrillers, the director initially pled guilty to one charge and served 42 days of a 90-day psychiatric evaluation sentence. As he faced final sentencing, however, he came to believe that the judge presiding over the case intended to deliver a harsh ruling and fled the country for France. To this day, he has yet to return to the United States either of his own accord or via legal proceedings. (Although the latter came close to happening in 2009, when U.S. authorities requested Polanski's capture while he was in Switzerland and he was placed under house arrest while the two countries discussed extradition. Ultimately, Polanski was released and returned to France.)[22]

Tabloid (Errol Morris, 2010)

The Crime: In 1977, former American beauty queen Joyce McKinney was accused of kidnapping her ex-boyfriend, Mormon missionary Kirk Anderson, from his church in England. She then transported Anderson to a remote cabin in the British countryside, where she allegedly chained him to a bed and raped him.

Why It's Stranger than Fiction: McKinney maintained her innocence throughout the ensuing court case, arguing any sex that occurred was consensual. (She also became a tabloid fixture, a position she did little to discourage.) She wound up flying home to America under a false identity before the trial concluded, but English authorities declined to extradite her when the FBI caught up to her in 1979. Five years later, she would be arrested again for allegedly harassing Anderson at his job at the Salt Lake City airport.[23]

The Imposter (Bart Layton, 2012)

The Crime: In 1994, 13-year-old Nicholas Barclay vanished from his hometown of San Antonio, Texas. Three years later, he was supposedly found in Spain and returned to his family. But the person who came home wasn't Nicholas ...

Why It's Stranger Than Fiction: Instead, it was Frédéric Bourdin, a French con man with a long track record assuming the identities of missing and/or dead children. Bourdin managed to live with Barclay's family for five months—who maintained they never suspected a thing—until the ruse was uncovered and he received a six-year prison sentence. After several more arrests, he eventually married and started a family.[24]

FILM FIRST FILE #2: FIVE DOCUMENTARIES THAT MADE A DIFFERENCE

In addition to being a terrific film, *The Thin Blue Line* played an instrumental role in freeing an innocent man from prison. The following nonfiction features also made a substantial societal impact.

Paradise Lost: The Child Murders at Robin Hood Hills (Joe Berlinger and Bruce Sinofsky, 1996)

In 1994, a trio of Arkansas teenagers—who later became known as the West Memphis Three—were tried and convicted of the brutal murder of three young boys. Even at the time, the prosecution's case was deemed problematic, and this film, as well as its two sequels, steadily chipped away the verdict and inspired others to start a campaign geared toward securing a new trial. In 2011, the state agreed to let the WM3 record Alford pleas—allowing them to plead guilty while still maintaining their innocence—and they were released from prison with time served.[25]

Super Size Me (Morgan Spurlock, 2004)

To showcase the effect of a steady diet of fast food, documentary filmmaker Morgan Spurlock used himself as a guinea pig, eating nothing but McDonald's meals for 30 days. The result wasn't pretty for Spurlock's health *or* for the casual dining titan. *Super Size Me* brought renewed attention to the high caloric levels and large portion size (like McDonald's own "Supersize" option, which offered customers a 7-ounce serving of French Fries and a 42-ounce soft drink) of fast food meals. By the end of 2004, McDonald's had done away with supersizing altogether, although they insisted the decision wasn't due to Spurlock's film.[26]

Dear Zachary: A Letter to a Son About His Father (Kurt Kuenne, 2008)

Kurt Kuenne's highly personal documentary about the death of his best friend, Andrew Bagby, is the stuff of Greek tragedy: in 2001, Bagby was allegedly murdered by his ex-girlfriend Shirley Jane Turner, who then fled to Canada, where she later gave birth to their son, Zachary. Bagby's grieving parents were awarded custody of the child while the pending murder charges kept Turner in prison. However, she eventually persuaded a judge to release her on bail and won back shared custody of Zachary. Then in 2003, she drowned both herself and her son. Seven years after the murder-suicide and two years after the film's release, the Canadian government officially approved a bill—nicknamed "Zachary's Bill"—that would refuse bail to individuals formally charged with serious crimes if doing so protected their children.[27]

The Cove (Louie Psihoyos, 2009)

To prove that Japanese fishermen were hunting dolphins—both to sell to international marine parks, as well as for meat—in a secluded cove nearby the whaling town of Taiji in southeast Japan, director Psihoyos and activist Ric O'Barry secretly planted cameras around the area and filmed the resulting slaughter. Although the film didn't put an end to the annual hunt, it did inspire a new wave of activism both in and outside of Japan aimed at publicizing the killing and discouraging the purchase of dolphins and/or dolphin meat from the Taiji region.

Gasland (Josh Fox, 2010)

After receiving an offer from a natural gas company to lease his land for drilling, Josh Fox took his camera on a cross-country trip about the United States to research the standards and practices of the natural gas industry, uncovering stories about shady business dealings and the potential contamination of drinking water. A highly controversial film that's been both celebrated and severely criticized, *Gasland* (and its sequel, *Gasland II*) has succeeded in turning natural gas drilling—and the country's energy policy in general—into a topic of serious conversation.

Chapter 9

sex, lies, and videotape (1989)

The Film: It may seem relatively tame now, but at the time of its release, Steven Soderbergh's frank look at marital dissatisfaction and sexual dysfunction got audiences hot under the collar.

Steven Soderbergh's debut feature, *sex, lies, and videotape*[1] possesses one of those film titles that doubles as both an evocative name and an accurate description of the movie's content. All three of the titular elements play a crucial role in the film, which the writer/director shot in Baton Rouge, Louisiana, during the late summer of 1988 and premiered at the Sundance Film Festival in Park City, Utah, the following January. The sex (or, in some cases, lack thereof) and lies are provided by the story's central married couple, repressed Ann (Andie MacDowell) and duplicitous John (Peter Gallagher), as well as Ann's self-conscious sister Cynthia (Laura San Giacomo), who is carrying on an affair with John unbeknownst to Ann. Meanwhile, John's old college pal Graham (James Spader) turns up in town with the videotape and accompanying video camera, which he uses to film women talking about their sexual histories for his own pleasure.

Obviously, this is a combustible combination of ingredients, not to mention personalities, and Soderbergh wastes little time setting off the dramatic fireworks, although *sex, lies, and videotape* remains largely free off any outsized melodrama. But don't mistake the film's even-handed temperament for a lack of passion; lust—be it for the physical act of sex or an intimate emotional connection—permeates the film. But Soderbergh largely avoids arousing the audience through traditional sexual imagery, an approach reflected in the way the movie's most erotic moments are those centered around the exchange of words rather than bodily fluids. Indeed, the film only contains three sequences that can be considered conventional sex scenes, none of which feature any nudity. As Soderbergh wryly put it: "I didn't want to risk alienating people in the audience with something like nudity. I'd rather risk it alienating them with ideas."[2]

Two of these scenes also employ a distinct stylistic touch whereby the viewer is invited to watch the lovers on-screen—John and Cynthia, the only characters who we're shown having sex during the course of the film—cavort while listening to Ann discuss her own conflicted feelings about sex first to her psychiatrist and later to Graham. In both cases, her conversations serve as a counterpoint to her husband and sister's coupling. They may be in the process of baring their bodies, but she's baring her soul and thus achieves an honesty with her (non-sexual) partners that Cynthia and John prove unable to find with each other. That's also why, later in the film, when Cynthia breaks off the affair, she points out that she and John have nothing to talk about. And rather than try to argue the point, he agrees, with a resigned smile.

The directness and lack of overt moralizing in Soderbergh's depiction of a troubled marriage and adulterous fling distinguished *sex, lies, and videotape* at the time of its release, but it was probably the videotape element that piqued the audience's interest most. Camcorders had only recently become widely available for personal use, and there was still a fascination with the technology and the ways in which it could be employed in intimate situations. The now-familiar notion of a "sex tape," for example—which, in effect, are the kinds of videos Graham is making even though he doesn't record any actual sex—was still a novelty at that time. (On the DVD commentary track, Soderbergh himself points out that the movie was released only a year after Rob Lowe's infamous video-recorded encounter with two young women at the 1988 Democratic National Convention.)[3] Furthermore, the way in which the women Graham interviews willingly open up their lives for his camera presages the advent of reality show video diaries, as well as the way anyone with a webcam can record their own thoughts and feelings and share them with the world via YouTube and other video-sharing platforms. Rather than coming across as a voyeur, Graham and his camera function as a kind of confidant, and one could make the case that that is how video technology itself has evolved, at least in the realm of personal use. Provided they're aware of its presence, the camera lens promises an intimacy that can make those in front of it want to reveal a private piece of themselves. And it's precisely that kind of intimacy that functions as a turn-on for Graham. For him, the notion of using his camera to film women having sex doesn't carry the slightest hint of arousal. He requires the same genuine human connection that Ann does, although he'd prefer for that connection to be through the TV screen rather than face-to-face.

As his career evolved, Soderbergh would become known and celebrated for the diversity of material he tackled onscreen, as well as his fascination with the mechanics of filmmaking. And when placed alongside such later movies as *Out of Sight, Che,* and even *The Girlfriend Experience, sex, lies, and videotape*'s straightforward simplicity almost makes it seem like the work of a different filmmaker. Soderbergh himself acknowledged that he deliberately sublimated the common urge felt by most first-time filmmakers, which is to throw in as many visual gimmicks as possible to show audiences and, more importantly, potential employers that you know how to do more with the camera than simply turning it on and calling "Action." Instead, he wanted the material and the cast to occupy center stage.[4] One can still spot distinct authorial flourishes around the edges of the frame, though, from the way he allows dialogue from one scene to play over another (a device he credits to Mike Nichols's *The Graduate*[5] and would later employ in such movies as *Out of Sight* and *The Limey*) and shooting in actual locations rather than sets and soundstages, a choice that was primarily motivated by cost in this case, but many of his subsequent, higher-budgeted studio features are distinguished by their extensive use of location shoots.

Even as its commercial success—the movie eventually grossed $25 million on a $1.2 million budget—substantially raised the profile of independent film in America, artistically, *sex, lies, and videotape* cast a smaller shadow over the indie world than you might expect, at least in the short term. Part of that was due to the fact that Soderbergh was consciously not attempting to break new stylistic ground, instead working within the key of the films that influenced him, specifically the relationship dramas of the '70s. The movies that would go on to shape the next decade of indie cinema—films like *Reservoir Dogs*, *Clerks*, and *El Mariachi*, all of which also graduated from Sundance to mainstream success—had a style or, at the very least, subject matter that spoke to young audiences and filmmakers in a way that Soderbergh's chronicle of the sexual dissatisfaction of a thirtysomething married couple perhaps didn't. Many of the directors that made the trip to Park City in the '90s wanted to be the next Tarantino, not necessarily the next Soderbergh. On the other hand, more recent indie fare like Lynn Shelton's *Humpday* and Andrew Haigh's *Weekend*—both of which hinge on the characters sorting out their complicated feelings about sex and its importance or lack thereof to their relationships—seem to carry at least the partial influence of *sex, lies, and videotape*. In that respect, the lasting contribution of Soderbergh's stylistically low-key debut was making audiences and filmmakers alike comfortable with the notion that sex is a subject worthy of thoughtful conversation, not mere titillation.

The First: The success of *sex, lies, and videotape* put the Sundance Film Festival on the industry and cultural map and became a motivating factor in getting studios to take a serious look at the commercial prospects of independent cinema.

For a generation of filmmakers and film lovers, Sundance is more than just an annual movie festival: it's a full-fledged brand with name recognition that translates far beyond the boundaries of its home base in Park City, Utah.

In addition, the eponymous festival and Institute—which offers filmmaking labs, workshops, and fellowships for aspiring writers and directors—the Sundance franchise has grown to encompass a national cable channel that screens indie movies and original series, as well as a one-night-only version of the festival that sends select movies to various cities around the United States and abroad for special Sundance-branded screenings. The value for an up-and-coming director of having his or her film associated with an independent film-devoted festival (as opposed to festivals like Toronto or Cannes, which program a mix of studio and indie fare) that has that kind of global reach can't be overstated. It can mean a shot at appearing at other major festivals, a path to awards attention and, most importantly, a distribution deal. And even if the movie winds up attracting little commercial attention, the Sundance name at least gives it a higher profile out of the gate. Admission means that one also gets to experience being in Park City itself while the festival is in full swing. For a little over a week, the town is teeming with agents, producers, distributors publicists, journalists, and fellow filmmakers, making it a bustling marketplace for anyone that's shopping around a completed movie or even just a simple pitch.

That wasn't the environment that Steven Soderbergh encountered when he took *sex, lies, and videotape* to Park City in the winter of 1989, though. In his journal, which was published in book form after the movie became a hit, the then-26-year-old filmmaker described a low-key welcome at a minor regional festival where volunteers seemed to outnumber industry professionals and audiences. (In fact, Soderbergh decided to join the volunteer corps almost on a whim during his stint in Park City, ferrying other guests such as Jodie Foster around while hiding the fact that he had a movie that was screening at the festival.)[6] His impressions of Sundance as something of a small-time operation weren't entirely off base. At that point in time, the festival had little industry or media cachet. The celebrity enjoyed by the Sundance Institute's founder Robert Redford, coupled with the festival's dedication to low-budget, sober-minded adult dramas lent the event an aura of respectability, but not much in the way of excitement.[7] As Peter Biskind damningly wrote of Sundance's early years in his book *Down and Dirty Pictures*: "No agents showed up, few publicists, and fewer press. There was no reason to; the films, with few exceptions, were eminently forgettable."[8] The few movies that did find distribution mostly sank without a trace after leaving Park City. In fact, some specialty distributors specifically kept their movies away from Sundance, feeling that its appearance there would immediately result in box-office death.[9] But the prejudice could cut both ways, with Sundance being equally cautious about the films it admitted. Indeed, *sex, lies, and videotape* almost didn't make it into the '89 lineup; then–festival director Tony Safford was unimpressed by the movie and only gave it the okay after pressure from a persistent member of the selection committee, Marjorie Skouras.[10]

It's worth noting as well that Sundance didn't really become "Sundance" until 1985. Prior to that, it was known as the Utah/US Film Festival (later just the U.S. Film Festival), which was founded in 1978 in large part as a way to persuade more filmmakers to shoot their movies in Utah. A local resident and real estate developer himself, Redford served as the chairman of the festival's inaugural edition and later went on to found the Sundance Institute, providing a place for filmmakers to come to make the kinds of movies that might play at the Utah/US Film Festival. When financial woes threatened to kill off the event, Redford was persuaded to bring it under his institute's umbrella, and the 1985 edition was the first to carry the name Sundance.[11] Four years later, the festival was still struggling to turn around the perception of it being a place where audiences yawned through and politely clapped after a series of bland, if well-meaning movies. According to Soderbergh's journal, the first Sundance screening of *sex, lies, and videotape* on January 22, 1989, didn't exactly upend the festival's sedate aura. Instead, the director describes a somewhat muted premiere, where the film was met with some "good laughs ... and applause at the end."[12]

It wasn't until the day after that screening that Soderbergh received an inkling that something bigger was happening; compliments filtered back to him from both people associated with the festival and random attendees on the street. Then the next screening sold out, and the screening after that, and more positive reviews and requests for interviews and meetings filtered back to the director. By the time of the film's fourth and final screening on January 28, the buzz was so strong people were rumored to be scalping tickets. That same night, *sex, lies, and videotape* won the Dramatic Competition Audience Award, which countered Soderbergh's original suspicions about how genuinely audiences seemed to enjoy the film.[13] As he wrote: "Festival audiences ... or rather, *this* festival audience is very sympathetic. I've seen films that weren't going down too well where the audience was really trying to hang in there. So I don't know how much is the film and how much is the audience being kind."[14]

Despite the movie's popularity, Sundance still had yet to become the place where million-dollar distribution deals were made overnight and Soderbergh returned to Los Angeles after Park City without a guaranteed theatrical release in hand. Part of the issue was that the movie's $1.2 million budget had originally been financed by RCA/Columbia Pictures Home Video, which meant that the video rights—a prize asset for any distributor—were already spoken for.[15] But the Sundance buzz did win Soderbergh meetings with a number of interested distribution companies, as well as major producers like Sydney Pollack.[16] A little over a month after playing Park City, the movie found a home with Miramax, owned by brothers Bob and Harvey Weinstein, who saw *sex, lies, and videotape* as the breakout mainstream commercial hit they had been looking for.[17] The film's profile was further elevated after it played the Cannes Film Festival in May 1989 and beat out Spike Lee's *Do the Right Thing* for the prestigious Palme d'Or. Getting onstage to accept his award, Soderbergh famously said, "Well, I guess it's all downhill from here."[18]

Of course, that prediction didn't prove true for the director or his film. After Cannes, Miramax set their eyes on an early August release date opposite the Yahoo Serious comedy *Young Einstein* and the Sylvester Stallone vehicle *Lock Up*. The next step was to create the right marketing campaign that would expand the movie's audience beyond the art house crowd. But the process of sculpting that campaign resulted in strained relations between the Weinsteins and Soderbergh, who wasn't comfortable with the tenor of some of their ideas.[19] Tensions came to a head over the film's trailer; the director had cut his own version that excluded any footage from the movie itself in favor or a concept piece where lines of dialogue from the film played out over shots of a video camera. Unimpressed, the Weinsteins commissioned their own version, which played up the film's racy subject matter and was scored to an overexposed pop song. "Miramax hated my trailer, and I hated theirs," Soderbergh wrote, summing up the impasse.[20] Eventually, a compromise cut was agreed upon that revealed the movie's provocative edge without overselling it. Despite Soderbergh's trepidations, the campaign made an impact; opening in limited release on August 4, *sex, lies and videotape* performed beyond anyone's expectations and eventually graduated from a handful of theaters to a wider release, reaching cities most indie films never reached. The film's final $25 million gross was almost unheard of at the time for an independent film and made both Miramax and Sundance—where the movie's improbable journey had begun and which Soderbergh happily talked up—names to watch within the industry.[21]

Sundance's star continued to rise in the early '90s, as directors like Quentin Tarantino and Robert Rodriguez entered Park City relative unknowns and emerged riding major waves of buzz. The turning point arrived in 1994, as Kevin Smith's *Clerks*, Steve James's *Hoop Dreams*, and, especially, Tarantino's *Pulp Fiction* all premiered at Sundance and went on to great acclaim and commercial success. With that, the festival's reputation as America's premiere launching pad for indie films was firmly established. Meanwhile, Soderbergh—after a rough patch in the mid-'90s—would land his first big studio gig with 1998's *Out of Sight* and has worked steadily both in and outside of the Hollywood system ever since. He's also made the occasional trip back to Sundance, most memorably in 2009 when he showed up to screen an early cut of his latest feature, *The Girlfriend Experience*, and participate in a twentieth-anniversary panel for *sex, lies, and videotape*. And on that visit, he didn't even have to volunteer to serve as a driver.

FILM FIRST FILE #1: THE SUNDANCE CLASS OF '89

Steven Soderbergh is the most famous filmmaker to emerge from the Sundance Film Festival's 1989 edition, but several other films attracted positive buzz that year as well. Here are some of Soderbergh's fellow Class of '89 alumni and where they are now.

Martin Donovan

1989 Sundance Entry: *Apartment Zero*, a Buenos Aires–set thriller starring a then-little known Colin Firth as a recluse who suspects his new roommate might be a serial killer.

Post-Sundance Credits: *Mad at the Moon* (1992); *Somebody Is Waiting* (1996)

Where He Is Now: The Argentinean-born filmmaker most recent writing/directing credit is 2008's *The Bandit K*.

Michael Hoffman

1989 Sundance Entry: *Some Girls*, in which a college student (Patrick Dempsey) visits his girlfriend's family for Christmas, and strange events ensue.

Post-Sundance Credits: *Soapdish* (1991); *A Midsummer Night's Dream* (1999); *The Last Station* (2009)

Where He Is Now: In 2012, Hoffman directed a contemporary remake of 1966's *Gambit* starring Cameron Diaz and Colin Firth.

Michael Lehmann

1989 Sundance Entry: *Heathers*, the cult black comedy starring Winona Ryder as a wannabe mean girl and Christian Slater as the rebel who helped her understand the price of popularity.

Post-Sundance Credits: *Hudson Hawk* (1991); *The Truth About Cats & Dogs* (1996); *40 Days and 40 Nights* (2002)

Where He Is Now: Lehmann primarily directs episodic television on such series as *True Blood*, *Californication*, and *Bored to Death*, but helms the odd studio picture now and then, among them the 2007 comedy *Because I Said So*.

Nancy Savoca

1989 Sundance Entry: *True Love*, a romantic comedy about a recently engaged couple whose relationship is tested by the arduous process of planning the wedding. The film won the dramatic Grand Jury Prize at Sundance that year.

Post-Sundance Credits: *Dogfight* (1991); *The 24 Hour Woman* (1999); *Dirt* (2003)

Where She Is Now: The New York–based Savoca released her sixth theatrical feature, *Union Square*, in 2012.

Jonathan Wacks

1989 Sundance Entry: *Powwow Highway*, the winner of that year's Filmmaker Trophy Dramatic award and a film exploring the difficult circumstances confronting a group of modern-day Native Americans living on a troubled Montana reservation.

Post-Sundance Credits: *Mystery Date* (1991); *Ed and His Dead Mother* (1993)

Where He Is Now: Mostly retired from filmmaking, Wacks entered academia and currently serves as the director of Brooklyn College's Barry R. Feirstein Graduate School of Cinema.

FILM FIRST FILE #2: THE SONS OF SUNDANCE

It's an age-old story: a scrappy young film festival with a proudly independent spirit launches a couple of significant titles, and it soon ages into the role of established institution. Meanwhile, a number of new festivals arrive on the scene looking to become the next hip, cool indie cinematic happening. These are some of the festivals that have sprung up in the wake of Sundance and are steadily gaining mainstream attention.

Fantastic Fest

Founded In: 2005
When: September
Where: Austin, Texas
What: As the name suggests, this festival devotes itself to science fiction, horror, outlandish action movies, and other fantastical genre entertainments. Although many of the movies are low-budget cult fare, the festival has screened some high-profile titles, among them Mel Gibson's *Apocalypto* and Paul Thomas Anderson's *There Will Be Blood*.

Slamdance

Founded In: 1995
When: January
Where: Park City, Utah
What: After their movies received rejection notices from Sundance, a group of filmmakers decided to host their own festival in the same city and at the same time. Two decades later, it's almost as much of an institution as its Park City counterpart. Unlike Sundance though, Slamdance is organized and programmed entirely by filmmakers who are particularly looking to feature work by first-time directors.

South by Southwest

Founded In: 1994
When: March
Where: Austin, Texas

What: Originally an offshoot of the South by Southwest Music Conference and Festival (which dates back to 1987), the film portion of the event has become a major attraction itself. The 2005 edition served as the launching pad for the mumblecore movement, premiering such films as *The Puffy Chair*, *Mutual Appreciation*, and *Kissing on the Mouth*.

Tribeca Film Festival

Founded In: 2002
When: April
Where: New York, New York
What: Launched in part to bring businesses back to Manhattan's downtown area after the events of September 11, 2001, Tribeca casts a wide net in its programming and has a strong international focus as well. In 2009, the festival hired Geoff Gilmore, previously Sundance's festival director, to be the Chief Creative Officer of its parent company, Tribeca Enterprises.

True/False Film Fest

Founded In: 2003
When: February/March
Where: Columbia, Missouri
What: A documentary-centric festival, True/False offers a place where nonfiction fans and filmmakers can congregate to view movies covering all manner of real-world issues. In the past, the festival has screened such acclaimed documentaries as *Murderball*, *Touching the Void*, and *Man on Wire*.

Chapter 10

Blade Runner: The Director's Cut (1992)

The Film: While the director's cut of Ridley Scott's seminal science fiction drama hits many of the same notes as the original theatrical version, it plays a very different tune.

Having final cut on a film—which essentially amounts to deciding which version of a movie goes out into the world without any interference—is a contractual privilege enjoyed by a relatively small and select group of filmmakers, particularly those working at the studio level where executives generally get the last word on their investments. So when a director who initially lacks final-cut privileges is later granted the opportunity to unveil his or her desired version of a movie months or years after its theatrical release, the expectation typically is that this new "director's cut" will differ substantially from its previous incarnation. What's most surprising, then, about the producer-approved cut of *Blade Runner* that moviegoers saw in theaters in 1982 versus *Blade Runner: The Director's Cut,*[1] which the film's maker, Ridley Scott (who did not have final-cut privilege on the theatrical version), gave his blessing to in 1992 prior to its theatrical rerelease is how few substantive changes there appear to be on the surface.

After all, both versions of Scott's futuristic film *noir* about a grizzled ex-cop (Harrison Ford) tasked with pursuing a pack of illegal "replicants" (the movie's jargon for androids) through the mean streets of Los Angeles circa 2019 tell the same story, have a majority of the same scenes and even share the same running time (give or take a few seconds). And where other director's cuts can boast a significant amount of notable additions and/or deletions, the '92 version adds only one new sequence—a brief vision of a unicorn that runs through the mind of Ford's replicant hunter (a.k.a. "blade runner:"), Rick Deckard—and eliminates another, an upbeat ending that depicts Deckard escaping into the wilderness with the movie's femme fatale, Rachael (Sean Young), herself a replicant. Hands down, the biggest change between the two cuts is something that's heard—or to be more accurate, *not* heard—rather than seen: the elimination of Deckard's pulpy voice-over narration that accompanies the theatrical version.

Compared to the extensive revisions seen in alternate director-overseen cuts like Francis Ford Coppola's *Apocalypse Now Redux* or Peter Jackson's extended versions of his *Lord of the Rings* trilogy, these alterations seem fairly minor. At the same time, though, their impact is, in many ways, more pronounced. Where the longer cuts of *Apocalypse Now* and *The Lord of the Rings* don't fundamentally alter much about those movies beyond their runtime, *Blade Runner: The Director's Cut* proves a strikingly different viewing experience from *Blade Runner*. With those small but potent tweaks, Scott fundamentally alters both the tone of the film and its driving thematic concerns. If the theatrical cut is somewhat akin to a detective yarn laced with sci-fi trimmings, the director's cut is a full-throated piece of speculative fiction strongly rooted in issues of identity and memory. It's the version that ultimately feels more in line with the work of Philip K. Dick—the celebrated sci-fi author who wrote the novel upon which the movie is loosely based, 1968's *Do Androids Dream of Electric Sheep?*—than a crime writer like Dashiell Hammett.

The evolutionary leap that *Blade Runner* made between these two cuts is only appropriate since, from its earliest inception, the film was always something of a work in progress, one that the director kept tinkering with trying to find the right combination of elements that would best meet his artistic goals while still keeping the audience engaged. Scott himself wasn't the originator of the project, which started as the brainchild of Hampton Fancher, a struggling actor-turned-screenwriter who was in need of extra cash and felt there was money to be made in the science-fiction realm. Turned on to Dick's work, he got in touch with the author himself and wound up securing the rights to translate *Do Androids Dream of Electric Sheep?* from the page to the screen.[2] But dramatizing the dense, difficult novel proved a challenge, and Fancher went through multiple drafts trying to crack it, altering a number of story points and adding the *noir* flavor, with the character of Deckard deliberately taking on some of the same voice and mannerisms of one of the genre's best-known stars, Robert Mitchum. Even the title went through multiple changes, acquiring and shedding such names as *Android* and *Dangerous Days* before finally settling on *Blade Runner*—a phrase coined by author William Burroughs for a book that had nothing to do with the eventual movie.[3]

Even as he struggled to settle on the right title, Fancher's script made the rounds amongst various directors, including Scott, who had just completed the 1979 blockbuster *Alien*, a gripping sci-fi/horror hybrid that proved there was more to the genre than the light space opera of *Star Wars*. Initially, the director was reluctant to commit to another dark futuristic piece, instead dallying with the grander mix of spectacle and adventure offered by the movie version of Frank Herbert's *Dune* that Italian producer Dino de Laurentiis was trying to get off the ground. (That film was eventually made with David Lynch at the helm in 1984.) But he ultimately departed that project for several reasons, one of which was the untimely death of his elder brother, Frank. He committed to the movie that would be *Blade Runner* not long after and worked closely with Fancher—as well as Fancher's eventual replacement, David Peoples—to refine and hone the script.[4]

Given the personal backstory that preceded Scott's direct involvement in *Blade Runner*, his specific influence on the film's narrative seems most deeply felt in the replicants' motivations for coming to Los Angeles in the first place. Advanced models designed and built by the L.A.-based Tyrell Corporation for use on off-world colonies, these cybernetic organisms have been programmed to self-terminate after four years, a way to avoid them developing messy human emotions. But one particularly thoughtful replicant, Roy Batty (Rutger Hauer), is unwilling to accept his fate and, along with a small group of like-minded androids, escapes a life of space servitude to make the pilgrimage to their corporate "father's" pyramid-shaped house with the unlikely-to-succeed scheme of requesting a longer life span. One can only assume that Scott felt a strong connection to the idea of a dying man bargaining with his creator for more time on this Earth, and, indeed, the film itself seems far more taken with Batty than with its ostensible hero, Deckard. (Batty's role feels even more prominent in the director's cut—despite not having any additional screen time—due to the elimination of Deckard's voice-over, which shifts the movie away from a first-person point of view.) A large part of that is due to Hauer's charismatic performance, but it's also a deliberate decision on the director's part to emphasize the tragedy of the character's plight, even as Batty engages in assault, murder, and all the other attributes typically associated with your average cinematic heavy. By the end of the film, it's made clear that those actions are the replicant's way of raging against the dying of the light, an end that will claim not only his artificial life, but also all memory of the very real things he's witnessed. It's only in his final moments that Batty comes to a kind of acceptance of his fate, delivering a haunting monologue that serves as his own eulogy.

As involved as he must have been in shaping the film's story, it was in the visual design of *Blade Runner*'s dystopian future that Scott brought the full weight of his influence to bear. It's not an exaggeration to say that *Blade Runner*'s striking, lived-in vision of twenty-first-century Los Angeles—a hellscape where flying cars soar between fire-belching smokestacks and towering skyscrapers, while on the streets below, waves of people shuffle through overcrowded streets marked by signs of urban blight—has profoundly impacted the way American filmmakers have depicted the world of tomorrow on-screen ever since. A director who has frequently remarked on the pleasure he takes in creating detailed worlds in his movies,[5] Scott's inspiration for *Blade Runner*'s universe was a fusion of the "city on overload"[6] feel of early '80s New York City with the "future medieval"[7] skyline of Hong Kong, filtered through the boldly graphic art and design work glimpsed in *Heavy Metal* magazine.[8] Certainly, the pronounced Asian influence on the movie's futuristic production design was something new at the time it was made and reflected, in part, the changing face of the real Los Angeles. The 2019 glimpsed in *Blade Runner* isn't "realistic" per se, but it is all-enveloping and, thanks to a deft mixture of tabletop models and set-dressed locations, possesses a tactile quality that many of the digitally generated futurescapes that followed haven't always shared. Dick himself was deeply impressed by Scott's visual interpretation of his book; after attending a private screening of footage from the film, he remarked that the images on-screen capture precisely what was in his mind when he wrote the book.[9] (The author died in March 1982, four months before the movie's theatrical release.)

A stern taskmaster on set, Scott was thrilled to see that his exacting demands on the crew had paid off. As early screenings of a work print (a rough cut of a feature assembled by the editor that frequently lacks completed sound and visual effects and music) indicated, though, his careful attention to the movie's visuals arguably came at the expense of the characters and the story. Trying to clarify the narrative for confused test audiences, Scott decided that narration might be the best way to fill in any gaps. From the beginning, however, that approach seemed doomed to fail, as both the director and his star were unimpressed with the voice-over dialogue that had been submitted by the writers—in one recording session, Ford can be heard muttering "Goddamn, this is bizarre"[10] after intoning one particularly pulpy bit of prose—and for the final taping, Ford was required to read his lines without Scott present,[11] which might account for his flat, affectless monotone that's heard in the completed theatrical cut. Rather than supplement the movie's plot and Deckard's personality, the narration actually distracts from both, due to Ford's poor delivery and the dialogue's penchant for stating the obvious instead of providing fresh insights. At the producers' behest, Scott was also required to scrap his original downbeat ending in favor of a "happily ever after" finale, with Deckard running off into the wilderness with Rachael, a trip spliced together out of leftover second-unit footage from Stanley Kubrick's *The Shining*.[12] Again, whatever intrigue there is to Deckard's character is largely undone by this unnecessary addition, which resolves his complicated situation in the most simplistic way possible.

Eliminating the voice-over and the happy ending alone are enough to make the director's cut of *Blade Runner* a substantially different (and significantly better) movie. Deckard still remains something of an aloof, detached protagonist—Ford had a famously difficult time making the film, and that's felt in his stiff performance—but that attitude complements the revised thrust of his character arc, namely the growing realization that he himself is likely a replicant. The theatrical cut dances around that particular plot thread, but the director's cut makes it more explicit with the inclusion of Deckard's unicorn fantasy that Scott had shot but been blocked from using.[13] (The sequence is intended to echo a moment toward the end of the film, where one of Deckard's fellow cops leaves an origami figure of a unicorn at his doorstep, a hint that the vision has been implanted in the blade runner's artificial mind.) The character's journey toward self-awareness was the story that Scott and his screenwriters had intended for him all along but were unable to effectively realize in the theatrical cut, due to disagreements with the producers, Scott's lack of final-cut privilege and their own uncertainty over how the film would be received.

Even after the release of the director's cut righted those wrongs, *Blade Runner* continued to be refined and changed. Fifteen years later, in 2007, Scott assembled a version that was billed as "The Final Cut" and featured spruced-up visual effects, as well as alternate lines of dialogue, sound effects, and shots (including one that was specifically reshot with a stunt double), along with other assorted nips and tucks. In contrast to the jump the film took between the theatrical cut and the director's cut, though, the "Final Cut" feels less like a reinvention than a refinement of the material. Still, it's satisfying that, three decades after its initial release, *Blade Runner* at last exists in the form that Scott always intended. Until he feels the urge to improve it again.

The First: The positive response to *Blade Runner: The Director's Cut* helped Hollywood see the artistic and commercial incentive in releasing alternate versions of films—even those that were once considered failures.

Browse through any DVD section either online or at a brick-and-mortar store and you'll be greeted with an avalanche of choices, frequently for the same film. Phrases like "Director's Cut" or "Extended Edition" or "Unrated Version" adorn the box art for both new and older titles, promising that even if you've seen the movie before, you haven't seen it like *this*. And sometimes, these alternate cuts make good on that promise, incorporating new material or restructuring existing scenes in ways that enhance your knowledge of and appreciation for the film. More often than not, however, they turn out to be *exactly* the same movie you've already seen, just with a few extra swear words and maybe a bonus bit of nudity. The tease worked, though; you paid to see the movie again and thus contributed more money to its bottom line. And that's really what the film's backers are hoping for; a superior version of the movie—as in the case of *Blade Runner: The Director's Cut*—is just a bonus.

It's largely because of DVDs—and laserdiscs and VHS tapes before them—that a healthy market for director's cuts and other such alternate versions exists in the first place.[14] Prior to the advent of the home entertainment revolution, moviegoers typically only had one cut of a movie to choose from, the one that was playing in theaters. And while longer versions—including those that the directors themselves approved—occasionally played at repertory houses, in international markets, or on television (for example, the L.A.-based television station Z Channel aired Michael Cimino's original full-length cut of *Heaven's Gate* that was pulled from theaters in favor of a reedited shorter version[15]), they weren't often available in wide circulation.

That began to change in the mid-'80s once viewers were able to literally bring films home with them on video, and the studios came to recognize that releasing an alternate cut might generate commercial interest.[16] One of the most high-profile of these rereleases was a 1989 restored version of David Lean's 1962 Oscar-winning epic *Lawrence of Arabia* supervised by the director himself and boasting improved sound and image quality along with several never-before-seen sequences.[17] This new cut of *Lawrence* was released in theaters prior to turning up on home video, which only made it seem like more of an event.

The deluxe treatment that was awarded to *Lawrence of Arabia* was something Scott hoped to replicate with *Blade Runner* when Warner Bros.—which had distributed the film in 1982 and watched it do a fast fade at the box office—contemplated taking the movie back into theaters in the early '90s as its anniversary approached. Not the '82 cut, but rather a rare 70mm print that the studio's Director of Film Preservation and Asset Management, Michael Arick, had unearthed in a screening room's archive in 1989. At first, Arick was unaware that this version wasn't the theatrical cut; it was only after he loaned the print to the Los Angeles-based Fairfax Theater for a classic films series that he—along with a dedicated audience of fans that turned up for an early Sunday morning screening—discovered it lacked both the narration and the upbeat ending that had been tacked on to the cut viewers originally saw in theaters. After viewing the print in 1990, Scott identified it as an early cut (though not his official director's cut) that had been used for test screenings prior to its general release. He proposed a plan to remaster and reissue the newly discovered version, but the studio initially balked, uncertain that there'd be any commercial value in that kind of undertaking. They eventually changed their minds when requests to screen the rediscovered test print poured in, culminating in a two-week, sold-out run at L.A.'s Nuart Theater in the fall of 1991 that pulled in an impressive single-screen gross of over $200,000.[18]

Although both Scott and Warner Bros. were now in agreement that demand existed for a theatrical rerelease of *Blade Runner*, they parted ways over how to ready the film for its return to theaters in a form that was closer to the director's original intentions. The disagreement essentially boiled down to the studio wanting to put the new cut in theaters as quickly as possible, while the director wanted the time, money, and resources to make a cut he was truly proud of. (Complicating matters further was the fact that Scott was in the midst of back-to-back productions of new movies, going from 1991's *Thelma & Louise* to 1992's *1492: Conquest of Paradise*.)[19]

The conflict was understandable given that they were in uncharted territory. While *Lawrence of Arabia* had performed well during its high-profile "director's cut" rerelease in 1989, that film was an Oscar-winning classic that had been a hit in its day. *Blade Runner* was a cult film with a passionate but still relatively small fan base. Rereleasing a box-office disappointment in theaters was rare enough; financing and rereleasing a restored director's cut of said box-office disappointment was practically unheard of.

Scott dug in his heels, however, arguing that Warners wouldn't be able to successfully market the rerelease as being a director's cut without his approval. (Prior to its run at the Nuart, the studio had, in fact, advertised this cut as "The Original Director's Version" without running this wording by Scott. A wider release would demand his cooperation and support.) Warners acquiesced, and Scott was given the go-ahead to assemble a rough cut of his director's cut with the assistance of Arick, who had left the studio to work as an independent consultant for Scott and other filmmakers. While Scott was in the midst of making *1492*, Arick collected existing and archived elements, paying particular attention to locating the unicorn scene that Scott had filmed but had been prevented from including in the theatrical cut. That sequence proved troublesome again as, when the studio was unable to locate the original negative, they used it as an excuse to scrap the director's cut and release a cleaned-up version of the 70mm test print. Scott and Arick only learned of this change as *Blade Runner*'s September 1992 rerelease date drew near and once again stood by their argument that the studio couldn't hype a "Director's Cut" of a version the director hadn't approved.[20]

As the impending release date left Scott with too little time to complete his own assembly of a director's cut, the studio approved an Arick-conceived plan to repurpose an interpositive (the intermediate stage of a film between the original negative and its final release version) of the theatrical cut and adapt it to fulfill some of Scott's specific requests—no narration, no happy ending, and the insertion of the unicorn scene. While this approach wouldn't allow Scott to make all the improvements he wanted, it would result in a version of *Blade Runner* that was close enough to his preferred vision that he felt comfortable approving the "director's cut" label.[21] (The director would have a chance to roll up his sleeves and reconstruct the film to his exact specifications over a decade later with "The Final Cut.")

With *The Director's Cut* subtitle featured prominently in the marketing materials, *Blade Runner* reopened in 58 theaters on September 11, 1992, and collected an impressive $618,586 first weekend gross. The film added almost another 40 theaters during the course of its monthlong run and reached close to $4 million in its final box-office tally with an equally success-ful home video release in March of the following year.[22] It was a strong showing for a movie that had long been deemed a failure and demonstrated the commercial viability of director's cuts both in theaters and on home entertainment formats.

More importantly, however, the striking differences between the theatrical and director's cuts of *Blade Runner* popularized the notion that there could be artistic as well as financial benefits in allowing filmmakers the opportunity to make their preferred version (or at least a version close to it) available to moviegoers. The restored, director-approved version of *Lawrence of Arabia* did not fundamentally change the prevailing opinion of a film that had already attained the status of a classic. *Blade Runner: The Director's Cut* inspired a reevaluation of a film that wasn't as widely loved. In his review of the '92 version, *Entertainment Weekly*'s Owen Gleiberman suggested that the changes made to the film might allow skeptical viewers to finally realize that "*Blade Runner* is a singular and enthralling experience."[23] On the other hand, Roger Ebert wasn't as easily persuaded by the alterations, writing, "Watching the director's cut, I am left with the same over-all opinion of the movie: It looks fabulous, it uses special effects to create a new world of its own, but it is thin in its human story."[24]

In the wake of *Blade Runner*'s revival, Hollywood and filmmakers alike have embraced the trend toward allowing for more director's cuts, none more eagerly than Scott himself. Since 1992, he has released director's cuts of such library titles as *Alien* and *Legend* as well as more recent films like *Kingdom of Heaven* and *American Gangster*. (With the exception of *Alien*, these cuts bypassed theaters and premiered on DVD, as most director's cuts do.) And filmmakers as diverse as James Cameron (*The Abyss*), Guillermo del Toro (*Mimic*), and Richard Donner (*Superman II*) have followed in his stead, taking the opportunity to revisit and reassemble movies for which they didn't necessarily enjoy final-cut privilege the first time around. (Or, in Donner's case, for which they were fired and replaced before the final cut was even completed.) And then there are all the marketing-friendly variations on director's cuts—extended editions, unrated versions and the like, which promise more footage whether or not the director actually wants it in there. Where the theatrical version used to function as the be-all and end-all in a film's existence, today, it's occasionally the first draft of a movie that's regu-larly rewritten.

FILM FIRST FILE #1: FIVE PERSUASIVE DYSTOPIAN FUTURES

One of the lasting appeals of *Blade Runner* is its vivid depiction of a dark, stormy, and thoroughly dystopian Los Angeles—an urban hell teeming with too many people and too few resources. Although the movie's specific vision has not come to pass, it's still a scarily convincing representation of a potential future. Here are five equally persuasive cinematic Cassandras that hopefully continue to remain fiction rather than fact.

Children of Men (Alfonso Cuarón, 2006)

Year: 2027

State of the Planet: Since humankind has lost the power to reproduce, the world's aging population has essentially given up all hope, allowing the world around them to fall into grim disrepair. Despotic dictatorships have seized control of the few stable societies that remain, and immigrants are regularly seized and imprisoned in squalid camps.

Cloud Atlas (Tom Tykwer, Andy Wachowski, Lana Wachowski, 2012)

Year: 2321

State of the Planet: With the majority of Earth's advanced civilizations wiped out following an apocalyptic event referred to as "The Fall," the pockets of humanity that remain have reverted to more primitive ways of life. The Hawaiian Islands, for example, are currently home to various tribes ranging from peaceful farmers to vicious, man-eating warriors.

Idiocracy (Mike Judge, 2006)

Year: 2505

State of the Planet: Centuries of willfully allowing its collective mind to atrophy thanks to modern conveniences and other distractions have transformed humanity into a population of morons and maroons who believe energy drinks are a fine substitute for water when trying to make plants grow. The scariest part of this potential future? The highest-rated TV show, *Ow! My Balls!*, sounds like something that a network might actually broadcast today.

The Running Man (Paul Michael Glaser, 1987)

Year: 2017

State of the Planet: Ever since a worldwide economic collapse rendered jobs scarce, the best way to earn a living is by competing in various high-stakes, high-body-count reality TV shows where people die more often than they get rich. Don't give the producers of *Naked and Afraid* any ideas.

The Terminator (James Cameron, 1984)

Year: 2029

State of the Planet: Under the control of the A.I.-enabled Skynet computer system, the machines have risen up and nuked their makers to kingdom come. Nevertheless, flesh-and-blood survivors band together amidst the rubble to battle the metallic warriors tasked with hunting them down.

FILM FIRST FILE #2: FIVE RADICALLY DIFFERENT DIRECTOR'S CUTS

Even though the changes between the two seem relatively minor, the theatrical and director's cuts of *Blade Runner* play like entirely different movies. The following five director's cuts boast more substantial alterations that also result in substantively different movies.

54 (Mark Christopher, 1998)

Negative test screenings led Miramax to lean on Mark Christopher to reshoot and recut his coming-of-age story set amidst the wild times of the '70s New York hotspot Studio 54. The changes omitted several key storylines, most notably one that emphasized the main character's bisexuality. At a 2008 film festival, Christopher screened his original cut of the movie, which restored that plot point along with 45 additional minutes missing from the theatrical release. That version—currently unavailable on DVD—is reportedly much grittier and more emotionally honest than the sanitized, starry-eyed cut that was released.[25]

Kingdom of Heaven (Ridley Scott, 2005)

Ridley Scott's director's cut of his medieval Crusades epic runs almost an hour longer than the version released in theaters and has the kind of dramatic weight and historical insight into the era that critics complained was missing from the theatrical cut. It's by far one of the most extensively revised films of Scott's career (the tinkering done to *Blade Runner* seems almost minor by comparison), and in its intended form, it's also one of his best.

Léon: The Professional (Luc Besson, 1994)

There was always something a little uncomfortable about the relationship between Jean Reno's hitman and Natalie Portman's 12-year-old orphan he welcomes into his life after her parents are murdered. And the longer version of the movie makes it even *more* uncomfortable by overtly commenting on the sexual attraction between the two, not to mention depicting the assassin bringing his ward along to his "job." These added scenes deeply affect our understanding of the duo's already peculiar bond.

Mimic (Guillermo del Toro, 1997)

Almost fired during the already problematic production of his sophomore film, a giant bug creature feature for Miramax, del Toro had the movie taken away from him and extensively reedited with second-unit footage of scenes he refused to shoot. The version that was eventually released in theaters was more of an action movie with horror overtones. For his director's cut, del Toro jettisoned the majority of the second-unit sequences and worked to shape the existing material he had filmed into the character-driven story he had set out to make.[26]

Superman II: The Richard Donner Cut (Richard Donner, 2006)

Replaced midway through production of the 1980 sequel to his groundbreaking comic book blockbuster, Richard Donner watched as incoming director Richard Lester reshot key sequences and eliminated more dramatic elements in favor of an overall lighter tone. In 2006, Donner had the opportunity to reconstitute his original vision using outtakes, alternate takes, and previously unreleased material. His cut featured an entirely different way by which Lois Lane learns Clark Kent's secret identity as well as a significantly different ending.

Chapter 11

Pulp Fiction (1994)

The Film: Quentin Tarantino's sophomore feature has become so ingrained in popular culture, it's easy to forget what an artistically accomplished movie it is.

In *Down and Dirty Pictures*—Peter Biskind's account of the messy, meteoric rise of the independent film industry in the '80s and '90s—the author describes Quentin Tarantino's 1994 crime picture *Pulp Fiction*[1] as the *Star Wars* of indie cinema.[2] Biskind couches the connection primarily in financial terms, as *Pulp Fiction*'s box-office success had the same seismic impact within the independent film world that *Star Wars* visited upon mainstream Hollywood when it arrived in theaters two decades prior. But the comparison is apt in other ways as well. For one thing, both films cannily seize on their director's formative influences—Golden Age film serials in the case of George Lucas and exploitation fare for Tarantino—and remix them in clever, exciting ways. Both films have also proven hugely influential and stand as certified pop-culture landmarks. And finally, precisely like *Star Wars*, the pure fun of watching *Pulp Fiction* often threatens to overshadow the artistry of the film itself.

And there's a lot of artistry on display in *Pulp Fiction*, starting, of course, with the instantly quotable, strangely poetic dialogue. Tarantino's first completed feature, 1992's heist-gone-wrong drama *Reservoir Dogs*, had offered a taste of his particular flair for wordplay, opening with a lengthy sequence in a diner that features, among other things, a dissection of the "real" meaning of Madonna's hit single "Like a Virgin" as well as an argument over the value of tipping the waitstaff. But the writing in *Pulp Fiction* is richer and more varied, partly due to the shift in premise (a triptych of interlocking stories versus a mostly self-contained single narrative) as well as Tarantino's grander thematic ambitions. Interestingly, the writer/director had conceived the idea for *Pulp Fiction* prior to *Reservoir Dogs*, intending for it to serve as his one-way ticket out of the LA video store where he spent his days watching VHS tapes and dreaming of being on a movie set. (The film that preceded both was the never-released *My Best Friend's Birthday*, a super-low-budget black-and-white 70-minute film that Tarantino directed in the late '80s and that perished in a film lab fire.)[3] But *Dogs* wound up being the script he completed first, and *Pulp* went on the back burner until the latter half of 1992 when, flush with the success of his debut feature, he flew off to Europe for a three-month writing spree aimed at organizing the myriad story points and thematic ideas he had scribbled down into a shootable screenplay.[4] The script he returned with proved far more intricate and contemplative—while still being wildly entertaining—than his vague notion of "an omnibus thing" consisting of familiar crime scenarios.[5] (One casualty of his European sojourn was Roger Avary, a friend and video store colleague who was responsible for dreaming up one of the stories in the film but was gradually frozen out of the writing process as Tarantino's star rose.)[6]

The opening scene—which, as in *Dogs*, takes place in a diner—sets the thematic pace for much of what is to follow, featuring two lovers and small-time crooks Ringo and Yolanda (or, as they address themselves, "Pumpkin" and "Honey Bunny"; by either name, they're played by Tim Roth and Amanda Plummer respectively) engaged in a spirited back-and-forth over how far they'd be willing to go in one of the liquor store robberies they occasionally commit for their livelihood. Both agree that killing someone is out of the question, but Ringo is willing to allow for some wiggle room, saying that in an "us or them" situation, he'd rather it be "them" than "us." Bank robberies are also out, though more due to the severity of the punishment than any moral code. Which leaves coffee shops like the one they're currently in, where, as Ringo argues, there's less likelihood of being put in the position of having to pull a trigger and the wage slaves staffing the place are less likely to want to play hero than a bank employee. And just like that, they've talked themselves into pulling off their latest job right then and there.

This sequence gets at the crux of what *Pulp Fiction* is ultimately about: the age-old conflict between doing right and doing wrong. But this isn't your conventional morality play that pits the virtuous against the craven; Tarantino accepts that his characters are all morally compromised, having chosen lives and professions—assassin, robber, gangster, boxer—in which violence is an intrinsic part of their day-to-day existence. Given that, the movie's guiding question becomes, where is the line that separates necessary evil from *un*necessary evil? When have you broken the laws of your seemingly lawless world to the point where you deserve the consequences that ensue? And, in turn, when is it best to respond to other lawbreakers with mercy rather than punishment?

What Ringo and Yolanda are doing in that opening scene is negotiating the moral code they've chosen to live by, one that's allows for robberies but not murder—at least, not yet. That negotiation plays out over and over again in different forms during the course of the movie. It's there in another early sequence when hitmen Vincent Vega (John Travolta) and Jules Winnfield (Samuel L. Jackson) debate the fate of their colleague Tony Rocky Horror, who was thrown off his balcony by their boss, Marsellus Wallace (Ving Rhames), for the alleged crime of giving Wallace's wife, Mia (Uma Thurman), a foot massage. (Vincent takes the position that a foot massage is "in the same ballpark" as oral sex and thus Tony should have expected ramifications, while Jules argues that they "ain't even the same fuckin' sport" and Tony did nothing wrong.) It's there in the first story, "Vincent Vega and Marsellus Wallace's Wife," when Vincent—having been tasked with taking Mia to dinner—retreats to the bathroom after their sexual tension-tinged night out and discusses the delicate situation with his own reflection, advising the man in the mirror that the only proper and loyal thing to do is have one drink and then get the hell out of Dodge. It's there in the second story (the one that Avary originally created[7]), "The Gold Watch," when pugilist Butch Coolidge (Bruce Willis) has to decide in a split second whether to abandon or rescue his nemesis and would-be executioner Marsellus—the man who convinced him to take a dive during a big fight and is now hunting him down after Butch's last-minute change of heart and knockout victory—in the sex dungeon below a pawnshop.

And finally, it's there in the third story, "The Bonnie Situation," when Vincent and Jules are forced to seek refuge at a friend's house to clean up a particularly nasty mess, and while Vincent wants to take what they need from their unwilling accomplice, Jules insists on following established social decorums—decorums like not getting blood all over your host's bathroom towels. Through his characters and the wild, improbable situations they get caught up in, Tarantino is engaging in a serious dialogue about the moral compasses we build for ourselves and the ways in which we do and don't follow them. And don't think for a moment that the writer/director is a benevolent creative God; during the course of the movie, he punishes the wicked (RIP Vincent, shot to death while emerging from the bathroom) and rewards the ... well, *less* wicked (for helping Marsellus, Butch is given his life back, although his "LA privileges" are revoked) based on their respective actions and choices.

Given the nature of the material, *Pulp Fiction* is a more expansive film than *Reservoir Dogs*, and a more playful one as well. Set primarily in a single location, *Dogs* was an exercise in sustained tension that required Tarantino to keep tightening the screws as the story progressed; even the comic beats were underscored by a tinge of menace. For all the violence and danger on display in *Pulp*, it's not a particularly taut, edge-of-your-seat viewing experience. The overall mood is lighter and the rhythm slower, as Tarantino allows the pace to be dictated by the characters rather than the machinations of a master plot. This is a movie that values behavior over incident, which gives Tarantino the room to linger over details that a more tightly wound narrative would be forced to skim through in order to move along to the next story point. In a story-first version of *Pulp Fiction*, we likely wouldn't spend quite so much time at Jack Rabbit Slim's, the '50s-themed diner where Vincent takes Mia on their nondate date. And the entire "Bonnie Situation" that Jules and Vincent find themselves in after the latter's gun goes off in a poor kid's face, turning their car into an abattoir, would be resolved more quickly in the interests of speeding the hitmen along to the diner for the climactic encounter with Pumpkin and Honey Bunny. Tarantino's approach allows him to luxuriate in these setting and situations, presenting viewers with a world that's as stylized yet still lived-in as the ones vintage pulp writers described on the page.

It's a sign of just how thoroughly *Pulp Fiction*, like *Star Wars* before it, dominated pop culture upon its initial release that our memories of it are as tied up with the wave of imitators, homages, and spoofs it inspired as they are with the movie itself. The mid-'90s are littered with quirky crime movies straining to capture the peculiar alchemy that Tarantino seemed to achieve so effortlessly, just as the late '70s and early '80s were packed with sci-fi spectacles longing to be the next *Star Wars*. And because both have been referenced so often over the years—not just in other movies but also television shows, novels, essays, viral videos. and just about every other form of media imaginable—it can be easy to forget what seemed special about them in the first place. Which is why, in each case, going back to the source is instructive and invigorating. Tarantino would go on to make more emotional movies (*Jackie Brown*), more provocative movies (*Django Unchained*), and more stylistically daring movies (the *Kill Bill* pictures) than *Pulp Fiction*, but this arguably remains his most consistently surprising work—a meditation on morality slipped between the pulpy pages of crime fiction.

The First: By becoming the first independent movie to cross the $100 million mark at the domestic box office, *Pulp Fiction* redefined the potential of indie film on a commercial—and conceptual—level.

Although Quentin Tarantino is generally cited as one of the leading independent filmmakers of the past two decades, one could make the argument that only one of his features qualifies as a "true" indie. That would be *Reservoir Dogs*, which came together by following what in the early '90s was the traditional financing and distribution model for independent productions. First, Tarantino wrote the script on his own dime and started talking it up to anyone and everyone who might listen until he got a nibble of interest.

The nibbler in question was Lawrence Bender, a one-time tango dancer-turned-film producer with two low-budget credits to his name—the drama *Tale of Two Sisters* and the thriller *Intruder*. Through his own connections, Bender moved the script up the industry food chain to actor Harvey Keitel, who liked it immediately and, after agreeing to star in the movie, used his modest amount of clout to help the production raise its $1.5 million budget and, more importantly, secure the director's chair for Tarantino.[8] The writer/director's indie cred was further enhanced after he attended the Sundance Institute's annual Directors Lab in 1991, where he workshopped the script with the aid of instructors Terry Gilliam and Monte Hellman.[9] *Reservoir Dogs* returned to Park City in January 1992 as part of that year's Sundance Film Festival, where it electrified audiences and critics, although distributors proved slower to respond due to the film's intense violence—most notably the infamous ear-slicing scene, memorably scored to Stealers Wheel's "Stuck in the Middle with You."[10]

Eventually, Sundance mainstay Miramax Films and its notoriously tough-to-please head Harvey Weinstein welcomed Tarantino's film under its banner even though Weinstein strongly advised the director to drop the bit of business with the ear, insisting that it would hinder the movie's appeal, not to mention its release pattern. As he's said to have urged Tarantino, " 'Without that scene, I could open this movie in three hundred theaters. As opposed to one! Thirty seconds would change the movie in the American marketplace.' "[11] But the ear stayed in—make that, off—and, as Weinstein warned, the movie performed like an average indie feature, never going beyond limited release and finishing its theatrical run with under $3 million.[12]

If *Dogs* didn't perform up to Tarantino's expectations, the movie's acclaim did accomplish what he had really desired all along: it elevated him from the fringes of the movie business into the heart of the industry where the money was. And money very quickly came his way, as TriStar Pictures paid him $900,000 to write and potentially direct his follow-up movie, *Pulp Fiction*, for them. In contrast to his previous experience, Tarantino had a paycheck and potential home for *Pulp* . . . except that when he turned the script in, TriStar didn't want it. In fact, none of the major Hollywood studios wanted it, put off by its complicated structure as well as Tarantino's continued predilection for over-the-top violence. Once again, Harvey Weinstein came to the rescue, deciding to bring the movie into the Miramax fold after reading the 159-page script on a cross-country plane ride.[13]

But Miramax wouldn't just be releasing Tarantino's film this time—they'd be funding it, a somewhat rare occurrence for a company that generally focused on acquiring completed films for distribution as opposed to paying to make them. (Potentially complicating matters further was Miramax's recent sale to the Walt Disney Company, which almost certainly would have concerns about associating its brand with a movie like *Pulp Fiction*. Fortunately, the contract that Weinstein signed with Disney ensured that he and his brother Bob were able to maintain their autonomy within the larger corporation, thus rendering that a moot point.)[14]

Miramax set *Pulp*'s budget at $8.5 million, and while they gave Tarantino a long creative leash, Weinstein did bring his influence to bear in the casting department. While *Reservoir Dogs* had an impressive cast that ranged from veterans like Keitel and Lawrence Tierney to newcomers like Tim Roth and Steven Buscemi, none of those actors were bankable names. Based on the heat surrounding Tarantino and the commercial potential of his script, Weinstein had the opportunity to get a big-time movie star into *Pulp Fiction*[15]—a coup for the once-tiny company he and his brother founded two decades prior in Buffalo, New York.

As it turned out, Tarantino already had a movie star in mind for the lead role of Vincent Vega—Travolta, the iconic leading man of *Grease* and *Saturday Night Fever* fame. But measured in Hollywood time, those movies were hits in the medieval era, and Travolta's once-hot career had been ice cold for years. Weinstein himself rolled his eyes at the thought of handing the part to a has-been especially when he had a current star—Bruce Willis, who joined Hollywood's A-list with 1988's *Die Hard* and had mostly remained there despite duds like *Hudson Hawk*—champing at the bit to play Vincent. (Daniel Day-Lewis was a strong contender for the part as well.)[16] Having Willis front and center would immediately mark *Pulp Fiction* as a mainstream movie. But, just as he did with the ear mutilation in *Reservoir Dogs*, Tarantino refused to change his mind, even going so far as to have Travolta's casting written into a list of his terms if he were to make the movie with Miramax, leaving Weinstein with little choice but to give in with a resigned " 'O.K., fuck it.' "[17] (And, as it turned out, the Miramax chief wound up getting his A-list star anyway as Willis agreed to take the smaller role of Butch the boxer.)

Any reservations Weinstein might have had about the commerciality of *Pulp Fiction*—as well as Travolta's presence in the movie—fell away when he saw the finished product. The rapturous response that greeted the film's premiere at the 1994 Cannes Film Festival, where it won the Palme d'Or, further suggested that he had a sizable hit on his hands. Rather than pursue the traditional pattern of a limited release followed by a national rollout, Weinstein decided to put *Pulp Fiction* in over 1,000 theaters across the country starting on opening day, October 14, 1994. Tarantino would be going head-to-head with a representative of mainstream studio filmmaking, Sylvester Stallone, whose latest action blockbuster *The Specialist* had opened in first place the week prior and was playing on a thousand more screens. Going into the matchup, few predicted that the once and future Rocky Balboa would lose the bout, but *Pulp Fiction* proved to be the underdog that took down the underdog, nabbing the top slot with $9.3 million.[18] And, as box office charts show, where *The Specialist* faded after banking $57 million, *Pulp Fiction* kept playing and playing, eventually earning $107.9 million in the United States and another $100 million overseas. For the first time, an independent feature had raked in a sum typically associated with a big-budget blockbuster.

Of course, there's still the question of whether or not *Pulp Fiction* truly qualifies as an indie in the first place. Longtime independent film industry figure John Pierson, for one, disputed the classification, pointing out that *Pulp* had initially been written for a major studio and then made and released by a company associated with *another* major studio. And even though the budget was small by Hollywood standards, $8.5 million far exceeded the cost of most independent fare. "You have to bend over backward and jump through hoops to define *Pulp Fiction* as independent," argued Pierson, who went on to conclude that, thanks in part to Tarantino, "The definition of 'independent' is much more elusive than a decade ago."[19] Empirically, labeling *Pulp Fiction* as a "true" indie—at least in the *sex, lies and videotape* and *Reservoir Dogs* sense of the term—does seem to be a stretch. On the other hand, the movie's rebellious spirit and upending of traditional cinematic conventions is very much in keeping with the notion that independent film chiefly represents an alternative to the Hollywood mainstream. That's the angle Miramax, Tarantino, and the media itself chose to run with, as *Pulp Fiction* was frequently positioned as being a cure for the common blockbuster. "Independent" was no longer just a description of how a film was made—it became a marketing hook.

For their parts, Tarantino and the Weinstein brothers didn't toss and turn at night wondering how indie *Pulp Fiction* was. Since *Pulp*, all of Tarantino's films (for which the budgets have ranged from $12 million to $100 million) have been backed and released by the Weinsteins—both at Miramax and, after their departure from that company, through their current outfit, The Weinstein Company—while the Weinsteins moved away from just acquiring small movies for distribution toward funding more ambitious (i.e., expensive) fare geared toward making a sizable dent at the box office as well as in the annual awards race. Two years after *Pulp Fiction*, Miramax scored another commercial hit and won its first-ever Best Picture Oscar with *The English Patient*, a $30 million period love story with international stars like Ralph Fiennes and Kristin Scott Thomas that barely qualified as an independent film, even by *Pulp Fiction* standards.

Because nothing breeds imitation like financial success, other companies soon adopted the Miramax model, with major studios either acquiring or creating so-called specialty labels that would make and/or distribute smaller-budgeted "independent" fare hoping to reap *Pulp*-sized rewards.[20] Effectively, the post-Tarantino landscape saw the rise of two different classes of indie films: modestly budgeted features starring recognizable faces that are put out into the world by studio-affiliated companies and no-budget pictures starring nobodies that are picked up by smaller distributors or take other paths to find an audience—a situation that continues today, although the divide separating the two camps has narrowed somewhat as the economics of the industry continue to evolve. The fact that Tarantino almost single-handedly brought about this sea change is what Biskind was really referring to when he compared *Pulp Fiction* to *Star Wars*. Both movies were intended as artistic statements for their respective directors, but have become better known for their far-reaching and long-lasting commercial impact.

FILM FIRST FILE #1: FIVE KEY GENRES THAT INFLUENCED QUENTIN TARANTINO

Before (and after) he became a filmmaker, Quentin Tarantino was (and is) acknowledged as one of the biggest film buffs around, with a voracious appetite for consuming all manner of movies. Small wonder that his own films can be viewed as kaleidoscopic acts of homage, with multiple influences fused into a unique whole. While a full accounting of Tarantino's influences could run for pages, here's an overview of just five of the dominant genres that have clearly shaped his own work.

Blaxploitation

As Seen in: *Pulp Fiction, Jackie Brown, Django Unchained*
One of the hallmarks of Tarantino's films is an affinity for African American culture, particularly the action films of the '70s starring black actors like Pam Grier, Jim Brown, and Richard Roundtree. The casting of Grier makes *Jackie Brown* Tarantino's most direct link to blaxploitation cinema, but *Pulp Fiction*'s Jules has the attitude (and hair) of a '70s *Superfly* veteran trapped in '90s America, while *Django Unchained*—like the best blaxploitation vehicles such as *Shaft* and *Coffy*—is a bracing take on racial politics filtered through an action-movie lens.

Exploitation

As Seen in: *Kill Bill Vol. 1* and *Vol. 2, Death Proof*
They may not get much respect from critics, but for Tarantino, B movies are often A-plus movies. The writer/director's undying affection for trashy, cheap, and cheesy horror films, revenge pictures, crime yarns, and other grindhouse and drive-in favorites gets its biggest exposure in the pureed blend of exploitation that are the two *Kill Bill* films as well as *Death Proof*, a bit of vehicular mayhem that made up his half of the latter-day *Grindhouse* epic he conceived with cohort Robert Rodriguez.

Musicals

As Seen in: *Reservoir Dogs, Pulp Fiction, Jackie Brown*
Although he's never made a conventional movie musical, few directors understand and employ the power of song as effectively as Tarantino. His

soundtracks are expertly curated, and each individual tune is well chosen to complement or comment on the on-screen action. The dance sequence with John Travolta and Uma Thurman may be the most iconic scene from *Pulp Fiction*, while *Jackie Brown*'s opening scene manages to turn the simple act of walking through an airport into a kind of ballet through the driving beat of "Across 110th Street." And the ear-slicing scene in *Reservoir Dogs* is made all the more intense by the little soft-shoe that Michael Madsen performs before getting down to business with his razor.

Hong Kong Cinema

As Seen in: *Reservoir Dogs, Kill Bill Vol. 1* and *Vol. 2*

Tarantino was still a video store clerk during the Hong Kong action-movie revolution that occurred in the late '80s and early '90s, when directors like Ringo Lam and John Woo made movies that traveled far beyond the former colony's borders. And, indeed, Tarantino borrowed a lot (some would say too much) from Lam's 1987 film *City on Fire* for his own breakthrough debut feature, *Reservoir Dogs*. A decade later, Tarantino would have the chance to shoot in the region while making his overtly Hong Kong–inspired *Kill Bill* movies, for which he employed some of the industry's top talents including famed action choreographer Yuen Woo-ping.

Spaghetti Westerns

As Seen in: *Inglourious Basterds, Django Unchained*

With its Old West setting and gunslinger hero (not to mention the shout-out to Sergio Corbucci's 1966 feature *Django* in the title and opening credits), *Django Unchained* is an obvious homage to the Italian-made westerns of the mid-'60s. But the spaghetti western touch is also felt in Tarantino's World War II movie, *Inglourious Basterds*, which resembles a Sergio Leone feature in both its form (lots of tight close-ups and expansive shots of the landscape) and content (more than one dramatically charged standoff).

FILM FIRST FILE #2: THE MOST SUCCESSFUL 1990s INDEPENDENT FILM COMPANIES

The success of *Pulp Fiction* transformed both Miramax and independent film itself into a profitable enterprise during the '90s—profitable enough to launch a number of distributors eager to profit from the suddenly fashionable indie movie realm. Here are that heady decade's biggest names in independent film and whether they are still around in today's wildly different indie marketplace.

Artisan Entertainment

Origin Story: Artisan launched in 1998 as the latest iteration of LIVE Entertainment, which itself grew out of a home video distribution company founded in the early '80s. (LIVE was also the company that funded Quentin Tarantino's first movie, *Reservoir Dogs*, in 1992).

Biggest '90s Hit: *The Blair Witch Project* (1999): $140.5 million

Other Notable '90s Releases: *Pi* (1998); *Belly* (1998)

Where Are They Now: Despite being flush with cash from the phenomenal success of *The Blair Witch Project*, Artisan struggled to stay afloat after the '90s indie boom drew to a close. The company and its catalogue were both purchased by Lions Gate Entertainment in 2003.

Fine Line Features

Origin Story: The indie-centric arm of New Line Cinema was founded in 1990 and tasked with pursuing the kinds of low-budget American and foreign films that its parent company—which had been around since the mid-'70s—used to traffic in before it found mainstream success in the '80s thanks to movies like the *Nightmare on Elm Street Series*.

Biggest '90s Hit: *Shine* (1996): $35.8 million

Other Notable '90s Releases: *Short Cuts* (1993); *Hoop Dreams* (1994); *The Sweet Hereafter* (1997)

Where Are They Now: Fine Line survived New Line's acquisition by Time Warner in the mid-'90s, but its release slate steadily dwindled in the early '00s. and it was eventually replaced by Picturehouse—an indie-oriented joint venture between Warner's New Line and HBO Films divisions—in 2005.

Fox Searchlight

Origin Story: Created in 1994, Searchlight hit the ground running with the breakout Sundance hit *The Brothers McMullen* in 1995 and never looked back.

Biggest '90s Hit: *The Full Monty* (1997): $45.9 million

Other Notable '90s Releases: *Stealing Beauty* (1996); *The Ice Storm* (1997); *Boys Don't Cry* (1999)

Where Are They Now: Still one of the leading indie and foreign film distributors around and a perennial Oscar heavyweight that took home the Best Picture prize in 2008 with Danny Boyle's *Slumdog Millionaire*.

Lionsgate Films

Origin Story: In 1997, the start-up entertainment company Lions Gate Entertainment acquired the Montreal-based production company Cinépix Film Properties and renamed it Lions Gate Films (later Lionsgate) the following year.

Biggest '90s Hit: *Dogma* (1999): $30.6 million

Other Notable '90s Releases: *Buffalo '66* (1998); *Gods and Monsters* (1998); *Mr. Death* (1999)

Where Are They Now: While still technically an independent in that it's not controlled by any larger corporate entity, Lionsgate has become a major studio with some of the biggest franchises around, including *The Hunger Games*.

Miramax

Origin Story: Created by the Weinstein Brothers in the late '70s—and named after their mom (Mira) and dad (Max)—the operation started small but became *the* name in independent film in the '90s in large part by allying itself with Quentin Tarantino.

Biggest '90s Hit: *Good Will Hunting* (1997): $138.4 million

Other Notable '90s Releases: *The Crying Game* (1992); *The Piano* (1993); *The English Patient* (1996)

Where Are They Now: Sold to Disney in 1993, the Weinsteins continued to run the place mostly their way until tensions with the studio eventually led to them parting ways in 2005. Today, they operate The Weinstein Company, while Miramax's ownership has changed hands several times and lately functions as a library of films instead of a producer and acquirer of new content.

October Films

Origin Story: Indie film stalwart Bingham Ray cofounded October in 1991 specifically to ensure that one of his passion projects, Mike Leigh's *Life Is Sweet*, would receive American distribution.

Biggest '90s Hit: *The Apostle* (1997): $19.8 million

Other Notable '90s Releases: *Cronos* (1993); *Breaking the Waves* (1996); *Lost Highway* (1997)

Where Are They Now: Within a five-year span, October went through a dizzying series of transformations: acquired by Universal in 1997, sold to Barry Diller in 1999 and renamed USA Films, purchased by the French media conglomerate Vivendi in 2002 and merged with another company, Good Machine, to become part of Focus Features—the specialty arm owned by Universal.

Sony Pictures Classics

Origin Story: Sony Pictures Entertainment launched this specialty division in 1991 with a particular emphasis on world cinema.

Biggest '90s Hit: *Howards End* (1992): $25.9 million

Other Notable '90s Releases: *Crumb* (1994); *Lone Star* (1996); *The Opposite of Sex* (1998)

Where Are They Now: Sony Pictures Classics celebrated its 20th anniversary in 2011 and continues to be one of the leading American distributors of foreign films, enjoying its biggest-ever hit in 2000 with Ang Lee's *Crouching Tiger, Hidden Dragon.*

Chapter 12

Showgirls (1995)

The Film: The vibrant afterlife enjoyed by Paul Verhoeven's much-derided adventure in the skin trade demonstrates that sometimes, it's good to be bad.

There are ordinary bad movies, and then there are epic fails like *Show-girls*,[1] Paul Verhoeven's notorious 1995 Las Vegas stripper epic, which survived a slew of disastrous reviews, underwhelming box-office receipts, and numerous years as a walking punch line to emerge, in some quarters at least, as a well-liked and even vaguely respected act of cinematic provocation. Granted, a significant portion of the people now defending its honor might still do so without awarding it the status of being a "good movie"—a label that generally refers to a film that offers fine performances, a substantive screenplay, and a high level of artistry behind the camera. *Showgirls* offers very few of these things; the performances are laughable (some intentionally so, others not); the screenplay, by Joe Eszterhas, is tone-deaf; and Verhoeven's direction is functional without being especially distinguished. Despite—or maybe because of—these lapses, the movie is absurdly entertaining . . . with a strong emphasis on the "absurd." *Showgirls* is a daffy witch's brew of questionable decisions and wildly strange execution, but its sheer oddity is also its greatest attribute. There's no other movie out there quite like it, and that's one of the reasons why it has built and maintains a loyal fan base over the years, one that adores the film for many of the same excesses that others once trashed.

This core group of fans has also helped *Showgirls* undergo a unique metamorphosis since its initial theatrical release. No longer simply dismissed as an out-and-out bad film, the now-common perception is that *Showgirls* belongs to the "so bad it's good" school of cult favorites, a seemingly counterintuitive description applied to films where the inadvertent and/or purposeful lapses in quality amp up the entertainment value. It's a category that includes such titles as *The Rocky Horror Picture Show*, *Road House*, and *The Room*, all films that, like *Showgirls*, were widely mocked and rejected when they first landed on movie theater screens. Membership in this exclusive club doesn't happen overnight; it can frequently take years after the film in question has slunk out of theaters and into semiobscurity, during which time it's potentially rediscovered and shared amongst like-minded viewers, who gradually convert others to their cause. It's no accident that many "so bad they're good" movies enjoy an afterlife as midnight movie staples, where the festive atmosphere enveloping the screenings make it that much easier for the established cult to recruit new members. Watched in isolation, *The Rocky Horror Picture Show* isn't especially impressive. Seen after midnight in a packed theater filled with people decked out in costumes and talking back to the screen, it provides a special kind of thrill.

Another thing many of these films have in common is that they have come to be embraced as comedies, even if they weren't intended that way in the beginning. (*Rocky Horror* has obvious comic elements in it; *The Room*, on the other hand, seemingly wanted audiences to take it seriously, but seriously failed at that.) And indeed, one of the sticking points the first wave of critics had with *Showgirls* was how much of the humor—if any—was intentional. Part of the problem is that many of the prerelease stories about the movie focused on its status as a kind of guinea pig for testing the mainstream viability of the NC-17 rating, which the Motion Pictures Association of America's ratings board had created in 1990 to award to films with extensive and graphic sexual content.[2] MGM had produced the film knowing full well that it would be rated NC-17 and voiced excitement at the prospect of altering the public and industry perception of a rating that was still controversial. Being the ambassador of a potential sea change in the way studio-backed productions approached sex on-screen placed a fair amount of weight on *Showgirls*, weight that Verhoeven himself didn't do much to dispel, describing the movie as "audacious" and "provocative" in interviews.[3] Words like that undoubtedly geared viewers to expect a more serious and grounding, gritty treatment of the Las Vegas stripping scene, one that would provide titillation-for-thought.

What they saw instead was a movie that was distinctly a comedy, albeit one where not everybody appeared to be in on the joke. The chief victim in that respect is the movie's leading lady, Elizabeth Berkley, who delivers a performance that's either wholly inept or a brilliantly sustained piece of subversive anti-art. Berkley plays Nomi, a legend in her own mind who makes the pilgrimage to Vegas not just hoping but *expecting* to find fame and fortune. But the path to stardom proves more challenging than expected, pitting her against thieving Elvis impersonators, sleazy strip club owners whose commission includes the occasional blow job, and supremely bitchy showgirls, including Queen Bee Cristal Connors (Gina Gershon, who, unlike Berkley, does seem to recognize the movie's mile-wide silly streak). But Nomi's biggest enemy may be her own personality, which could generously be described as "obnoxious" ... and, less generously, as "certifiable." She moves through life like she moves through her dance routines: violently and with barely concealed menace. Nomi is the inverse of the conventional Horatio Alger hero; rather than move upwards in the world through honesty and humbleness, her bad attitude is the key to her success. The nastier she is, the more people (men specifically) seem to want to help her ... or just *want* her.

Much like its "heroine," the humor in *Showgirls* is blunt and to the point, with lines like "Must be weird, not having anybody cum on you" and "I like nice tits. I always have. How about you?" effectively summarizing Eszterhas's particular brand of wit. And then there are the bits of dialogue and character beats that may not have even been intended to provoke guffaws, but do anyway thanks to the cast's performance choices. Certainly, Berkley's histrionics provide a steady stream of laughs, largely because she appears to be playing the role so earnestly. (Earnestness is often another unifying element in "so bad they're good" movies, stretching back to the days of Ed Wood and his bad movie classics like 1953's *Glen or Glenda* and 1959's *Plan 9 From Outer Space*, where the humor inspired by the ineptness of the execution is enhanced by the seriousness of the movie's intent.) As *Showgirls*' main attraction, the actress bore the brunt of the initial wave of negative feedback, although Verhoeven didn't escape censure for apparently leaving his leading lady out to dry. The director was also chastised for the movie's pronounced lack of sex appeal, despite the amount of naked flesh on display. In his two-star review, Roger Ebert spoke for the critical majority when he wrote: "[*Showgirls*] contains so much nudity that the sexy parts are when the girls put on their clothes. It contains no true eroticism, however ... Eroticism requires a mental connection between two people, while masturbation requires only the other person's image."[4]

The disappointment in the movie's relative tameness is understandable given its place in the debate over the future of the NC-17 rating, as well as the titillating ad campaign mounted by MGM, which teased an erotic experience that would outdo the last Eszterhas/Verhoeven collaboration, the 1992 sexually charged thriller *Basic Instinct*.[5] And frankly, *Showgirls* hasn't exactly gotten any sexier with age. When the sex and nudity aren't being treated so matter-of-factly as to be part of the Vegas landscape, they serve as an extension of the movie's blunt-force humor, most notably in Nomi's two encounters with a sleazy casino entertainment director played by Kyle MacLachlan—the first an absurd striptease and the second a demented scene of aquatic lovemaking.

At the same time, though, the passage of time has allowed viewers to more fully see how *Showgirls* fits into the context of Verhoeven's English-language filmography, which in turn helps shed light on his approach to sexuality in the movie. The majority of the director's Hollywood films—from his very first studio vehicle, 1987's *Robocop*, to his last great movie, 1997's *Starship Troopers*—are correctly recognized as satires of specific aspects of American society, from *Robocop*'s send-up of corporate greed and the drive to privatize public services to *Troopers*' parodic depiction of militaristic jingoism. The driving satirical idea behind *Showgirls*, which Eszterhas even makes explicit in the script, is that the distinctly American capitalistic pursuit of fame and/or fortune functions as a form of prostitution. "Sooner or later, you're gonna have to sell it," a man tells Nomi on her first night in Vegas after she shoots down his clumsy proposition, and it's a refrain she'll hear throughout the rest of the movie. What she quickly realizes is that her body—and the body of every other woman in the city—is a commodity, a *currency*, first and foremost. It's what she has to barter with, and since that is its primary purpose, it's somehow only natural that the movie's presentation of the female form is disconnected from any feelings of eroticism. If anything, actual sexuality would seem out of place in an environment that more closely resembles a meat market, where bodies are bought and sold with little regard for the people inhabiting them.

When viewed through this prism, *Showgirls* emerges as less of an out-and-out disaster and more of a deeply flawed but also strangely admirable attempt at tweaking the traditional rags-to-riches, up-by-their-bootstraps narrative of capitalist success. And while the film's lack of subtlety is undeniable, that may be one of its better attributes. Aside from serving as a steady source of humor, the directness of Eszterhas's screenplay complements the characters and the setting. Nomi, for one, doesn't have the time or the interest to traffic in nuance; she's a creature of instant gratification, much like the other men and women in her orbit. The merits of *Showgirls* are starting to find defenders beyond the "so bad it's good" crowd, with some noted film experts (including critic Jonathan Rosenbaum and filmmaker Jim Jarmusch) expressing their esteem for Verhoeven's film without shame.[6] Any movie that provokes those kinds of impassioned second opinions—not to mention plenty of entertainment value—can't be all bad.

The First: *Showgirls* was intended to be the first mainstream movie to legitimize the NC-17 rating within Hollywood. Instead, it wound up making it irrelevant.

The critical shellacking *Showgirls* endured wasn't simply the result of its perceived lack of quality. Underlying many of the negative notices was a sense of profound disappointment that *this* was the movie that would serve as the trial balloon for the mainstream future of the NC-17 rating, which had been languishing in semiobscurity since its creation five years earlier.

Critics were particularly concerned about the fate of the new rating, since they had been arguing in favor of it—or a category like it—for some two decades. The rallying cry began in the 1970s, following the implementation of the new national ratings system devised by the Motion Picture Association of America's Classification and Rating Administration (originally known as Code and Rating Administration) or CARA in 1968.[7]

Prior to the industry-wide upheavals of the early '60s, the MPAA had strictly monitored and dictated the content of mainstream studio films through the infamous Production Code, introduced in the 1930s as a way to appease outside regulators and retain control over its wares. But the power of the Code had waned significantly over the decades as new generations of moviegoers sought out more challenging and risqué fare and the increasing lack of standardization was beginning to affect the way movies were distributed, with local communities and exhibitors taking a stronger role in deciding which films could and could not be shown in their theaters. To help recentralize control under the MPAA, CARA created a four-tiered classification system that paid particular attention to a movie's suitability for younger viewers, starting with the all-ages appropriate G and then progressing on to PG (initially M and then GP), R, and, finally, X—a rating that expressly forbad the attendance of moviegoers under 16, an age limit that was eventually elevated to 18.[8] (A fifth rating, PG-13, would be created in 1984 as a reaction to movies like *Indiana Jones and the Temple of Doom*, which were deemed too dark and violent for the PG-targeted audience.)[9]

Although CARA's rating system successfully established an accepted nationwide industry standard that remains in effect to this day, it wound up reinforcing—rather than solving—a problem that filmmakers had faced since the days of the Production Code: namely, how to make films with serious adult content (particularly in regard to sex) with the guarantee that they would play in theaters. The X rating was supposed to cover films of that type, but it quickly became perceived as more of a scarlet letter than a badge of honor, an impression that the MPAA did little to countermand. By the mid-'70s, the X rating had been adopted by the ascendant pornography industry, and the accompanying notoriety mostly closed it off to the mainstream movie studios,[10] occasional exceptions like Columbia's decision to release the European soft-core film *Emmanuelle* notwithstanding.[11] And while some filmmakers—such as William Friedkin with *Cruising*[12] or Brian De Palma with *Scarface*[13]—would deliberately try to test the limits of what separated an R-rated film from an X-rated film, the studios backing them would inevitably order the picture to be fine-tuned until it earned the former rating rather than the latter.

The debate over the rating system's strangulation of a viable adult cinema separate from pornography intensified in the 1990s, as both reviewers and filmmakers grew more vocal in their demands for a new category that would stand apart from the dreaded X rating. The MPAA finally acquiesced and in

September 1990 introduced the NC-17 label, which would restrict a film's audience to viewers over 17.[14] The first movie to receive the new rating was *Henry & June*, director Philip Kaufman's erotic biographical drama that depicted the unconventional romance between authors Henry Miller and Anaïs Nin, as well as Miller's spouse. Released by Universal Pictures in October—only a few weeks after the creation of the NC-17—the movie arrived in theaters riding a wave of hype due to its rating . . . and promptly sank like a stone, largely due to the fact that audiences apparently weren't interested in watching a 136-minute art film about a pair of long-dead authors, the promise of mature adult content or no.[15] (It didn't help that some still saw the X stigma attached to the new rating; Blockbuster Video, for one, announced that it wouldn't stock NC-17 films just as it declined to carry X-rated titles.)[16] Clearly, if the NC-17 was going to avoid becoming another X, it would have to be applied to a film that mainstream moviegoers might actually *want* to see.

That's where Paul Verhoeven and Joe Eszterhas came in. In the early '90s, both men were situated well atop Hollywood's A-list, with such successful solo credits as *RoboCop*, *Jagged Edge*, and *Total Recall*. And their joint effort, *Basic Instinct*, became an instant smash hit that made a star out of Sharon Stone, who famously flashed her nether regions on camera in one of many just-*this*-shy-of-NC-17 scenes that seemed designed to get the ratings board hot and bothered. Having already skated the line separating an R from an NC-17, the duo decided to head fully into NC-17 territory with their follow-up project, *Showgirls*, which MGM/UA agreed to make and distribute fully aware of their intentions.[17] Beyond being the highest-budgeted NC-17 film to date (at a cost of some $40 million), Verhoeven's movie was also going to be the first to receive a wide opening weekend release, playing in 1,388 theaters[18] across the country, compared to the more contained release pattern of its predecessor, *Henry & June*. That strategy was in large part formed by the material; unlike the more serious-minded *Henry & June*, *Showgirls* was going to be a glossy, populist affair filled with well-known actors (MacLachlan was recognizable from his stint on *Twin Peaks*, while Berkley had a long-running role on the popular teen comedy *Saved by the Bell*), as well as lots of sex, violence, and humor that would draw people in regardless of the rating. As one of the studio's marketing executives said in an interview, "I think the material is incredibly provocative and energetic. It stands on its own. The rating is making it topical, but people won't just see a film because it's NC-17 rated."[19]

As it turned out, not many people saw it at all. Despite the rating-attendant media hype and a heavy marketing campaign that included commercials on national network television during the 10 p.m. hour, print ads in prominent newspapers and even outdoor billboards,[20] *Showgirls* opened to an anemic $8 million first weekend gross and watched its intake plunge from there, finishing its domestic run with barely $20 million stuffed into its sequined coffers.[21] (A dispiriting number, to be sure, but the film can at least boast that it remains the highest-grossing NC-17-rated film of all time.) The tepid commercial reaction combined with the largely negative critical notices gave the whole endeavor the feel of a missed opportunity, a sentiment echoed in the closing line of Roger Ebert's pan: "*Showgirls* is such a waste of a perfectly good NC-17 rating."[22]

Harsh words, but they weren't incorrect from an industry standpoint. Mainstream Hollywood regarded *Showgirls'* poor showing as confirmation that there was little value in the NC-17 rating, effectively putting them out of that business for good. Since 1995, no major studio has released a film that has a rating higher than an R, although specialized arms of larger companies—along with independently operated small distributors—have occasionally tested the commercial waters with NC-17 releases. (Some of these companies have also sought to avoid the stigma of that rating by releasing films unrated, an approach that has its own limitations and frequently little commercial reward.) The Universal-affiliated Focus Features, for example, released Ang Lee's *Lust, Caution* in 2007, while 20th Century Fox's boutique label Fox Searchlight distributed Steve McQueen's *Shame* in 2011, both of which went out to theaters bearing the NC-17 rating. But each was also then confined to a limited release pattern that booked them primarily into art houses and specialty screens, and their minuscule grosses reflect that. No distributor, large or small, has yet attempted the wide release of another NC-17 feature film. The MPAA may have combined a different set of letters and numbers to create this rating, but for now, at least, NC-17 continues to spell X.

FILM FIRST FILE #1: THE BEST MIDNIGHT MOVIE PARTIES

Although *Showgirls* tanked during its first run in theaters, Paul Verhoeven's film has enjoyed a long afterlife as a midnight movie favorite. But those late-night screenings aren't watched in silent reverence; instead, the movie unspools in a festive atmosphere, where audience participation—in the form of donning costumes inspired by the movie and talking back to the screen—is accepted and encouraged. If you're looking for a great after-hours party, find your nearest midnight screening of *Showgirls* or one of these other four movies.

The Rocky Horror Picture Show (Jim Sharman, 1975)

As the founding member and still reigning champion of the midnight movie circuit, attendance at a *Rocky Horror Picture Show* shindig is practically a rite of passage for movie nerds and nerds in general. In addition to an audience that arrives decked out in fishnets and leather to experience the movie version of the cult stage musical, screenings are often accompanied by an in-theater reenactment of the action happening on-screen performed by a cast of volunteers who know every camp-drenched line and dance move by heart.

The Big Lebowski (Joel and Ethan Coen, 1998)

A unique fusion of film *noir*, stoner comedy, and bowling-centric sports movie, *The Big Lebowski* has acquired such a devoted following that in addition to regular midnight screenings, an annual party known as "Lebowski Fest" has sprung up in various cities around the United States, including New York, Chicago, and Louisville. Activities include bowling competitions, live music (sometimes performed by actors from the movie), and, of course, a screening of the movie that started it all.

Once More, with Feeling (Joss Whedon, 2001)

The musical episode of Joss Whedon's beloved TV series *Buffy, the Vampire Slayer* graduated from the small screen to the big screen following its original 2001 airing on the now-defunct UPN network. Devoted Whedonites (who are among the most passionate fan bases around) gave the 42-minute episode the full *Rocky Horror* treatment, including costumes, reenactments, and homemade props. Unfortunately, the party came to a sudden halt when the studio behind the series stopped licensing the episode for public showings, although unlicensed, unendorsed screenings are still a regularity on the comic book convention circuit.

The Room (Tommy Wiseau, 2003)

Upon its release, Tommy Wiseau's bizarrely inept drama immediately entered the rarefied atmosphere of such bad movie classics as Ed Wood's *Plan 9 from Outer Space*. And while DVDs of the movie are readily available, the best way to experience it is on a big screen at midnight, surrounded by fans hurling insults (and, occasionally, plasticware) at the inanity happening on-screen.

FILM FIRST FILE #2: THE TOP TEN HIGHEST-GROSSING NC-17 RATED FILMS[23]

1. *Showgirls* (Paul Verhoeven, 1995): $20.3 million
2. *Henry & June* (Philip Kaufman, 1990): $11.5 million
3. *The Cook, the Thief, His Wife and Her Lover* (Peter Greenaway, 1989): $7.7 million[24]
4. *Bad Education* (Pedro Almodóvar, 2004): $5.2 million

5. *Lust, Caution* (Ang Lee, 2007): $4.6 million

6. *Tie Me Up! Tie Me Down!* (Pedro Almodóvar, 1990): $4 million

7. *Shame* (Steve McQueen, 2011): $3.9 million

8. *The Dreamers* (Director: Bernardo Bertolucci, 2003): $2.5 million

9. *Crash* (Director: David Cronenberg, 1996): $2 million

10. *Bad Lieutenant* (Director: Abel Ferrara, 1992): $2 million

Chapter 13

Toy Story (1995)

The Film: The computer-animated feature that put Pixar on the map
still encapsulates its mission statement as a studio: Technology
must always serve the story and characters, not the other way
around.

Pixar has been the top dog in the realm of family-friendly computer animation for so long, it's hard to remember a time when the sight of the Emery-
ville, California–based studio's name above the title didn't guarantee
commercial and/or critical success. But the mood around Hollywood was
radically different on November 22, 1995, the day that *Toy Story*[1]—Pixar's
first full-length film and the first full-length computer-animated cartoon in
movie history—arrived in theaters after a problem-plagued production process. Even with the considerable marketing might of the Walt Disney Company, which had struck a deal with the independently owned and operated
Pixar to release three features, behind it, a triumphant reception for the fledgling studio's big experiment was far from assured.

For starters, unlike the recent run of Disney-made animated blockbusters
that began with *The Little Mermaid* and culminated in the enormous success
of *The Lion King*, *Toy Story* wasn't a musical, a fact that had worried the
Mouse House's brand-conscious executives from the beginning.[2] Also unlike
those earlier movies, it didn't feature a stalwart, youthful hero (be it Ariel or
Aladdin or Simba) occupying center stage, instead putting forth a likable but
flawed protagonist who commits several less-than-admirable actions during
the course of the movie. And last, but certainly not least, there was the computer animation question; up until that point, audiences had proven receptive
to the still-young medium when it was employed in short cartoons—like
Pixar's own Oscar-winning 1988 short *Tin Toy*—as well as part of the

special-effects arsenal of live-action films, such as *Tron* and *Terminator 2: Judgment Day*. Whether they'd want to watch 80 minutes of cartoon characters generated within the computer rather than by hand was less apparent.

In hindsight, all of these concerns sound unnecessary, if not absurd. Yes, *Toy Story* lacks grandly choreographed musical numbers like those seen in Disney's *Beauty and the Beast*, but they aren't at all missed. Furthermore, the protagonist's failings actually make him *more* relatable to young viewers rather than less. And finally, the computer animation is immediately inviting as it is rendered with all the care and artistry of a hand-drawn production. Even though it wasn't a Disney-generated project, *Toy Story* is a Walt Disney movie through and through, one that boldly sets out to expand the language of animation, but through character and narrative rather than at its expense. Prompted to describe what sets Pixar's approach to computer animation apart from other companies in the same field, John Lasseter—one of the company's driving creative forces and *Toy Story*'s director—said simply, "We create characters."[3] That's a sentiment that Walt Disney himself would probably echo.

Lasseter's statement may sound like humblebragging, but it happens to be true: *Toy Story*'s chief asset are the terrific toy characters brought to vivid life by the vocal performers and the animators, who imbue the faces of these pieces of computer-generated plastic with more emotional range than many flesh-and-blood performers. That's particularly the case with the movie's central odd couple, the rootin'-tootin' cowboy, Woody (voiced by Tom Hanks), and the space-age explorer, Buzz Lightyear (Tim Allen). The property of a rambunctious tyke named Andy, Woody basks in the glow of being his owner's favorite plaything, a status that gives him no small amount of authority over all his fellow plastic, factory-assembled creations. Although he's careful not to abuse this power, it's clear he enjoys being in charge, which is one of the reasons why he's knocked for a loop when birthday present Buzz enters the picture and replaces Woody in both Andy and the other toys' affections. So he reacts like almost any jealousy-consumed soul would: by knocking Buzz out of a window. He's quickly repaid for this rash action by winding up in the outside world himself, far from the comforts of Andy's bedroom and with only his frenemy for company.

Toy Story's narrative unfolds so seamlessly, it's surprising to learn just how many false starts and dead ends Lasseter and the rest of the creative team—which includes ground-floor level Pixar employees Pete Docter, Joe Ranft, and Andrew Stanton, as well as screenwriters Joss Whedon, Joel Cohen, and Alec Sokolow—encountered on their way to constructing the movie's beautifully built three-act structure. In Lasseter's original pitch to Disney in the spring of 1991, *Toy Story* started out as a road movie that found Tinny, the diminutive toy star of Pixar's *Tin Toy* short, getting lost by his child owner in the course of a family road trip and experiencing a series of adventures en route to finding a new home, while befriending a cowboy-hatted ventriloquist's dummy along the way.[4] When the filmmaker faced studio executives again in the fall with another treatment, the road movie idea was jettisoned, and the story instead focused on the personality clash between two toys—the current favorite and the usurper. In this scenario, the cowboy dummy became the early version of Woody, while Tinny had the Buzz Lightyear role of the new toy on the block,[5] a role he held until it was decided that a one-man band made out of tin wasn't exactly the kind of plaything '90s kids would covet, especially when placed alongside a tricked-out space warrior.[6]

Even with the central conflict established, the filmmakers struggled to find the right tone for *Toy Story*, which they wanted to be savvier and more adult in its sense of humor than the typical Disney fare, but not at the expense of the young audience. Their attempts to find the right balance was reflected in the evolution of Woody from draft to draft. From the beginning, the cowboy was written with more of an edge than the guileless, earnest heroes of *Aladdin* and *The Little Mermaid*, but early passes at the character rendered him downright unlikable. A short test reel from 1992, for example, finds Woody (still bearing traces of the ventriloquist dummy design) tricking Buzz into leaping headfirst into a wall, so that he falls behind a bureau and out of sight. And in a rough assemblage of story reels that Pixar screened for Disney in 1993, the character came off like—as Whedon diplomatically put it—"a thundering [*sic*] a — — —."[7] Indeed, that screening went so poorly, the film was very close to being junked entirely. The Pixar team had mere months to tear up almost everything they had spent the past two years working on and essentially start over from scratch.[8]

As disheartening as that must have been at the time, having to literally go back to the drawing board was perhaps the best thing that could have happened to Lasseter and his team, because in doing so, they finally found Woody and Buzz's real voices. Instead of straining to mimic the snappy bickering of odd couple buddy movies aimed more at grown-ups, the writers clearly awakened to the idea that the two have a relationship that's grounded in a dynamic that viewers of all ages could relate to: siblinghood. At heart, *Toy Story* is the tale of an only child whose parent suddenly brings another kid home one day and that new arrival winds up stealing all of the attention, thus stirring up feelings of resentment, anger, and neglect. Woody's behavior toward Buzz may not necessarily be heroic (at least, not at first), but it is relatable, as is his "brother's" casual bucking of the house rules in the name of establishing his own identity.

The sense of kinship we feel for these children's playthings is a key source of the movie's lasting appeal and, at the time, no doubt helped audiences over the hurdle of watching an animation style they were unaccustomed to. (Woody and Buzz's all-too-human personalities certainly make up for some of the limitations of the still-young technology, most notably the characters' occasionally stiff movements and static facial features. Of course, we are talking about plastic toys here, so static facial features come with the territory.) Having learned from their mistakes during *Toy Story*'s development process, all of the studio's subsequent films have hewed closely to the same character-centric model. Pick a Pixar movie, any Pixar movie and what typically springs to mind first are the memorable humans, animals, robots, cars, and toys you encountered in them, from befuddled Dory and adventurous Carl to unflappable Sully and iron-willed Elastigirl. *Toy Story* may have single-handedly ushered in a sea change in the art and technology of animation, but its enduring legacy are the classic characters it gifted us with.

The First: Still perceived as a novelty at the time of the movie's release, *Toy Story* almost single-handedly made computer animation the cartoon industry norm.

For John Lasseter, *Toy Story*'s 1995 theatrical release marked the end of an almost 15-year mission to prove the artistic value of computer animation to an industry that was still dubious about its potential. Lasseter understood where so many of his colleagues were coming from; after all, he had grown up worshipping the hand-drawn entertainments created by Walt Disney and his core crew, the so-called Nine Old Men. Studying pen-and-ink animation at the California Institute of the Arts only increased his admiration for the medium, and in the early '80s he wound up with what must have been his dream job: a place on the animation staff at Disney. At the time, though, the studio was going through a creative lull, and the aspirational artist found himself primarily assigned to uninspired productions like *Mickey's Christmas Carol*. It was while making the latter short in 1981 that Lasseter happened to see test footage for a live-action vehicle that Disney was financing, *Tron*, the story of a video-game developer zapped into a digital world. What hooked his attention in particular was the movie's extensive use of three-dimensional computer animation in several key sequences, most notably a dazzling race between two "light cycles"—sleek motorbikes that zipped along a racing grid emitting a trail of light behind them.[9]

Lasseter was immediately taken with the aesthetic of this type of animation, which to him possessed a solid, tactile quality that was difficult to replicate by hand.[10] He tried to sell his superiors in Disney's animation department on adapting the technology, putting together a 30-second test reel that placed traditionally animated characters in digitally rendered settings. At the same time, he developed a pitch for a fully computer-animated feature based on the Thomas Disch children's story *The Brave Little Toaster*, taken with the idea of bringing inanimate objects to life—and granting them personalities—through a keyboard rather than a pen.[11] (This was the key difference between what *Tron*'s makers had done with the technology and what

Lasseter hoped to achieve; *Tron* employed computer animation for spectacle and world-building, while he wanted to apply it directly to characters.)

Despite his enthusiasm, Disney never warmed up to the idea, and Lasseter's vision of a full-length computer-animated film remained locked in his head. In 1983, he was let go from Disney and soon found a berth amongst the digital wizards at The Graphics Group, the computer division of George Lucas's production company, Lucasfilm. Not long after joining, Lasseter served as the lead animator on the group's short cartoon *The Adventures of André and Wally B.*[12] Despite running only two minutes, this cartoon encapsulates the approach Lasseter wanted to take with computer animation—namely, it was character based and told a straightforward story with plenty of humor. Ownership of The Graphics Group changed hands in 1986 when Lucas sold it to Apple founder Steve Jobs and the group adopted the name Pixar.[13] Through all of these changes, Lasseter's plan never wavered: he intended for the company to make a feature-length cartoon animated entirely on the computer[14] and worked toward that goal over the next decade through a series of well-received shorts—starting with 1986's *Luxo Jr.* (whose hero, an overeager desktop lamp, still serves as Pixar's mascot) and culminating in the Oscar-winning *Tin Toy*—that established the company's creative bona fides and highlighted the advances made in Pixar's chosen medium.

Now that his former employers at Disney were able to witness Lasseter's skills in action, they made a full-court press to bring him back into the fold. In the years since his firing, the company had dipped its toe into the realm of computer animation, working with Pixar to design a propriety software system known as the Computer Animation Production System or CAPS, whereby sketches would be inked and painted on the computer rather than by hand, allowing the camera to be used in grander ways.[15] (The famous ballroom sequence in *Beauty and the Beast*, for example, where the camera floats around the titular characters as they share a dance, was made possible by CAPS.) But they hadn't yet taken the plunge into an entirely computer-generated feature, which is where Lasseter and his creative team at Pixar would come in. A three-picture deal was struck between the companies in 1991,[16] and the arduous four-year journey to bring *Toy Story* to the screen commenced.

In the run-up to *Toy Story*'s theatrical release, there was some concern over how receptive audiences would be to sitting through 80 minutes of an animation method that they had only been exposed to in short bursts up until that point. As it turned out, almost nobody batted an eye. In his four-star review, Roger Ebert commented that *Toy Story* "achieves a three-dimensional reality and freedom of movement that is liberating and new," going on to add later, "Watching the film, I felt I was in at the dawn of a new era of movie animation, which draws on the best of cartoons and reality, creating a world somewhere in between, where space not only bends but snaps, crackles and pops."[17] Hooked by Woody and Buzz's exploits, moviegoers made repeat trips to *Toy Story*, powering the movie to an almost

$200 million gross, well beyond that year's traditional hand-drawn animated offering from Disney, *Pocahontas*.

That trend would repeat itself over the next few years. In 1998, Pixar's sophomore feature, *A Bug's Life*, outgrossed Disney's *Mulan*, and 1999's *Toy Story 2* leapfrogged past *Tarzan*. Naturally, Pixar's mastery of story and character had a great deal to do with its continued success, but both within the industry and amongst audiences there was a very real sense that, as Roger Ebert expressed, computer animation represented the industry's future. A sea change occurred in 2001 when Disney's chief rival, Dream-Works Animation—which had just enjoyed an enormous hit with the computer-animated fairy tale spoof *Shrek* after releasing two commercially disappointing traditionally animated features—announced that they would be abandoning hand-drawn animation entirely in favor computer-generated productions.[18] After struggling through its own series of hand-drawn disappointments, the Mouse House had adopted similar measures by 2005,[19] when computer animation became its main stock in trade, occasional anomalies like 2009's traditionally animated *The Princess and the Frog* notwithstanding. (Funnily enough, the latter movie was a passion project for Lasseter, who by that time had been named one of the heads of Disney's animated division after the company purchased Pixar in 2006.)[20] Meanwhile, upstart animation studios like Blue Sky started making their computer-animated cartoon features. Clearly, *Toy Story* has had an impact beyond its creator's wildest dreams—it turned what had previously been a novelty toy into one every animation house wanted to play with.

FILM FIRST FILE #1: INSIDE PIXAR'S BRAIN TRUST

One of the many innovations that sets Pixar apart from other animation houses is its famous (and famously secretive) brain trust—a handful of top-level executives and key creative personnel who closely consult on every movie currently going through its pipeline. Although writers and directors are given space to work, the brain trust reserves the right to implement significant editorial and staff changes. It's an approach that has often resulted in sharper, more rigorous storytelling . . . while occasionally inspiring some bruised feelings along the way as well. Although it's rare for Pixar to publicly discuss the brain trust or which individuals have been or currently are a part of it, here are some of the past and present employees who are known to have been part of it.

Brad Bird

Who He Is: After spending his formative years in television animation, Bird made a big impression with his first animated feature, 1999's *The Iron*

Giant. Although it was a failure at the box office, the movie won Bird a devoted following amongst animation fans, and Pixar eagerly brought him into the fold as the director (he helmed 2004's *The Incredibles* and 2007's *Ratatouille* for the studio) and creative consultant.

Still Part of the Trust? Having made the leap to live-action filmmaking with 2011's *Mission: Impossible—Ghost Protocol*, it's unclear how closely Bird remains associated with the studio.

Brenda Chapman

Who She Is: Rising through the ranks of animators at both Disney and DreamWorks, Chapman joined Pixar in 2003 and was set to become the studio's first female director with the 2012 mother/daughter fairy tale *Brave*, until she was replaced during the film's production.

Still Part of the Trust? Following the *Brave* brouhaha, Chapman departed Pixar in the summer of 2012.

Pete Docter

Who He Is: One of Pixar's earliest employees and a founding member of its brain trust, Docter has worked in some capacity on almost every one of the studio's movies and directed both *Monsters Inc.* and *Up*, the latter of which won the Oscar for Best Animated Feature.

Still Part of the Trust? Currently directing his third feature film for the studio, Docter appears to be a Pixar lifer and is likely still a key member of the brain trust.

John Lasseter

Who He Is: Pixar's chief creative force for many years, Lasseter directed the studio's first three films (*Toy Story*, *A Bug's Life*, and *Toy Story 2*) as well as one of its most marketable franchises, *Cars* and *Cars 2*.

Still Part of the Trust? While Lasseter undoubtedly continues to have a great deal of input into Pixar's output, the fact that he's also now overseeing all of Walt Disney's animated offerings means that his attention is necessarily divided.

Joe Ranft

Who He Is: Friends with John Lasseter since their days as animation students at CalArts, Ranft joined Pixar in 1992 and played an instrumental role in bringing *Toy Story* to life and was a close creative collaborator on *A Bug's Life* and *Cars* as well.

Still Part of the Trust? Ranft perished in a car accident in 2005.

Andrew Stanton

Who He Is: Along with Docter, Lasseter, and Ranft, Stanton was one of the original members of Pixar's brain trust, having been a part of the company since 1990. He has directed two Pixar features, *Finding Nemo* and *Wall-E*, both of which won Oscars for Best Animated Feature.

Still Part of the Trust? Stanton took a leave of absence from Pixar to direct the 2012 live-action feature *John Carter*. He subsequently returned to the studio (and potentially it's brain trust) to develop a sequel to *Finding Nemo*.

Lee Unkrich

Who He Is: A Pixar mainstay since the first *Toy Story*, Unkrich has worked as an editor or codirector on several of the studio's biggest hits and got his first crack at directing with *Toy Story 3*.

Still Part of the Trust? As long as he remains at Pixar—which will likely be a long, long time—he's all but guaranteed a seat on the brain trust.

FILM FIRST FILE #2: THE COMPANIES THAT WOULD BE PIXAR

Pixar may have single-handedly launched the age of computer-animated cartoon features, but they're not the only game in town anymore. Here are the five most prominent American computer animation houses and how they stack up against their rival.

Blue Sky Studios

Who They Are: Originally founded in 1986 by former employees of the Mathematical Applications Group Inc. (or MAGI), Blue Sky spent the first decade and a half of its existence making short cartoons and commercials, as well as providing visual effects, before moving into features. Based in Connecticut, they distribute their movies through a partnership with 20th Century Fox.

First Computer-Animated Feature: *Ice Age* (2002)

How They Compare to Pixar: Blue Sky is somewhat akin to the little brother—often overlooked but still be a force to be reckoned with. The *Ice Age* franchise in particular has proven extraordinarily profitable for them and essentially stands as their *Toy Story*. Unlike Pixar, however, Blue Sky hasn't had as much success beyond their signature series.

DreamWorks Animation

Who They Are: Part of the much-ballyhooed DreamWorks SKG studio that was founded by Steven Spielberg, Jeffrey Katzenberg, and David Geffen in 1994, the animation division—which started off in traditional hand-drawn animation before switching over to computer animation—went solo a decade later (with Katzenberg still at the helm) producing features that have been distributed by other studios, including Paramount and 20th Century Fox.

First Computer-Animated Feature: *Antz* (1998)

How They Compare to Pixar: Easily Pixar's fiercest competitor, Dream-Works is the studio that has proven most capable of matching them in box-office grosses, critical acclaim, and awards attention.

Illumination Entertainment

Who They Are: Formed in 2007 as a joint venture of sorts with Universal Studios, Illumination is the newest computer animation house on the block, but has already made a big splash in the family movie market.

First Computer-Animated Feature: *Despicable Me* (2010)

How They Compare to Pixar: Quality-wise, Illumination's films have fallen short of the high bar set by Pixar, but they have been huge hits at the box office thanks in large part to clever marketing and smart release dates.

Sony Pictures Animation

Who They Are: Created in 2002, the animation arm of the multimedia conglomerate mixes full-length computer-animated cartoons with live-action/cartoon hybrids like *The Smurfs*.

First Computer-Animated Feature: *Open Season* (2006)

How They Compare to Pixar: Sony Pictures Animation is still in search of that defining breakout hit like *Ice Age* for Blue Sky, or *Shrek* for Dream-Works. It's had some successes, like the *Cloudy with a Chance of Meatballs* films, but nothing approaching the level of *Toy Story* or even *Cars*.

Walt Disney Animation Studios

Who They Are: Hollywood's most prestigious animation studio (and Pixar's parent corporation), originally founded in 1923.

First Computer Animated Feature: *Dinosaur* (2000)

How They Compare to Pixar: Pixar may owe its existence to Disney, but the Mouse House has been playing catch-up ever since *Toy Story* hit theaters. Recently, however, they've been on a roll with a series of computer animated films like *Tangled* and *Frozen* that equal (and in some cases surpass) certain Pixar projects.

Chapter 14

Psycho (1998)

The Film: Perhaps Gus Van Sant's most significant accomplishment with his shot-for-shot remake of Alfred Hitchcock's *Psycho* was convincing Hollywood to fund an experimental art project dressed up as a feature film.

It's not difficult to understand why Universal Pictures would greenlight a contemporary remake of *Psycho*,[1] the 1960 horror film directed by Alfred Hitchcock about a very disturbed young man with some deep-seated mommy issues. A classic of its genre with numerous elements—among them an infamous shower scene, lines like "We all go a little mad sometimes," and the isolated lodge called the Bates Motel, which serves as the central setting—that have long since entered the realm of pop-culture iconography, *Psycho* is both a revered film *and* a recognizable brand name. The latter attribute is something that the studio had already exploited to its advantage by releasing a pair of sequels in 1983 and 1986 respectively, with the star of the original film, Anthony Perkins, reprising his role as Norman Bates, the owner of the eponymous motel and the titular psycho. (Perkins also played Bates in a fourth, made-for-TV *Psycho* film; needless to say, Hitchcock himself wasn't involved in any of these continuations, having passed away in 1980.) The actor's death in 1992 effectively put an end to the *Psycho* franchise, at least in its original incarnation.

But in Hollywood, few profitable film series remain dead and buried for very long, so it's hard to imagine the idea of relaunching *Psycho* not being a topic of conversation within the halls of Universal. And eventually, the studio was approached by someone eager to do it: Gus Van Sant, the independent-minded director of such acclaimed art house films as *Drugstore Cowboy* and *My Own Private Idaho*. Going with a filmmaker like Van Sant seemed like a win-win for Universal; not only would they have a new *Psycho* to peddle to audiences, but the critical respect that he commanded might help offset accusations that a remake was being driven purely by profit rather than by art.

But Van Sant had a very specific pitch for *Psycho*, one that he had hit upon after years of enduring studio meetings during which they had handed him lists of potential projects that always included a remake or two. Thanks to those experiences, he had already decided that if he was ever going to helm a remake, he wanted it to be what he considered a true remake: a film that featured different actors and potentially a different time period, but used the same script and replicated the same shots from its predecessor.[2] So while Norman Bates, his victim Marion Crane (played by Janet Leigh in Hitchcock's film), and the other characters populating the story would be portrayed by new performers, they'd be speaking the identical lines penned by Hitchcock's screenwriter Joseph Stefano some three decades ago, minus a few updates to reflect the present-day setting. It was an approach closer to theater than cinema, as restagings of plays always follow the same text whereas remakes of movies are expected to be ground-up reinventions of the earlier film.[3] That was the kind of remake Universal expected, and the studio initially balked at Van Sant's offbeat pitch. The director kept suggesting the idea, and they kept turning him down ... that is, until 1997 when Van Sant directed *Good Will Hunting*, a movie that received his typically positive reviews, but performed atypically (for him) at the box office, grossing almost $140 million and receiving multiple Oscar nominations, including Best Picture. *Good Will Hunting* gave Van Sant new clout within the industry, and he used it to convince Universal that if anyone was going to take a stab at a new version of *Psycho*, it should be him.

Van Sant's desire to remake *Psycho* in this specific way was motivated by two factors. First, as a great admirer of Hitchcock in general and *Psycho* in particular (in fact, almost two decades prior to his full-length remake, he recreated the movie's most famous sequence—the shower scene in which Marion is stabbed to death by a cross-dressing Norman—for a comedy short he directed for a San Francisco-based theater company),[4] he was disappointed to learn that fewer and fewer contemporary moviegoers were making an effort to see it. In his experience, younger viewers especially might be vaguely aware of the title and key sequences, but had rarely watched the film in its entirety, put off by such era-dating elements as the unfamiliar cast and the black-and-white photography.[5] In short, through no fault of its own, the movie was on its way to becoming a museum piece, relevant only to scholars and serious film buffs, despite still being a thoroughly accessible picture. As Van Sant himself put it, "There's nothing wrong [with *Psycho*], except nobody goes to it."[6] By replacing black and white with color and the original stars with actors, audiences of 1998 would recognize (among them, Vince Vaughn as Norman Bates; Anne Heche as Marion Crane; and

William H. Macy as the private eye, Frank Arbogast), the director hoped to
remove what he perceived to be the two main obstacles limiting *Psycho*'s
appeal. Meanwhile, preserving Stefano's screenplay and Hitchcock's choice
of shots would theoretically allow them to experience the same movie that
had thrilled previous generations of moviegoers, Van Sant among them.

Van Sant's second motivation for remaking *Psycho* shot-by-shot had
less to do with the audience's experience than his own curiosity. Hollywood
had been churning out remakes of older films for much of its history
(indeed, Hitchcock himself had remade one of his own movies; 1956's Jimmy
Stewart/Doris Day thriller *The Man Who Knew Too Much* was an update of
1934's *The Man Who Knew Too Much*, starring Peter Lorre and Leslie
Banks), but nobody had ever set out to so specifically recreate the same film.
The traditional assumption was that a new version would by necessity differ
from what had come before, due to such variables as advances in filmmaking
and the desire of the incoming director, writer, actors, and assorted crafts-
people to put their own stamp on the material. But Van Sant's thought
process instead ran like so: "What would happen if you followed in the footsteps of any film? We could have remade *Fargo*, which is only 2 years ago,
and what would that be like if you followed it every single line and cut?
Would it be *Fargo* or would it be something different? My question was . . .
would it actually be *Psycho* if you took every single piece and connected it
together? Would it in fact be the same film?"[7] Fascinated by this hypothesis,
Psycho represented more than just another filmmaking assignment for Van
Sant—it was an artistic experiment funded on a major studio's dime and with
the blessing of the Hitchcock estate. (The director's daughter Pat, who had a
small role in the original film, made a point of visiting the set of the remake
and spoke about how flattered her father would have been.)[8]

When the dust settled from *Psycho*'s controversial production and release,
it appeared that Van Sant had largely failed to meet both of his goals. To
begin with, the wide audience of *Psycho* newbies he hoped to reach never
materialized; following an anemic $10 million opening weekend, *Psycho*
finished its run with a little over $20 million, well behind its predecessor's
$32 million final gross (which, adjusted for inflation, would be closer to
$250 million). Van Sant in part blamed the movie's failure on its marketing
campaign, which he felt promised a gorier experience than either version of
Psycho was intended to be.[9] Of course, what the director failed to take into
account was that the taste of the younger audience he hoped to reach ran
toward more visceral horror fare—hence the success of franchises like *Friday
the 13th* that were far less artful than *Psycho* but a heck of a lot bloodier.
The resoundingly negative reviews couldn't have helped either; from the
beginning, critics were skeptical of Van Sant's experiment, and many of the
reviews took him to task for daring to imitate the Master of Suspense.
Even the kinder pans, like J. Hoberman's review in the *Village Voice*,
described the movie as being little more than "a superfluous and inferior

version."[10] Instead of introducing Hitchcock's movie to a new audience, Van Sant's *Psycho* only seemed to interest those people who were familiar with the original and showed up for this one with their minds mostly made up.

On the commentary track included on the film's DVD release, Van Sant can be heard blaming himself for the movie's second failing. Having set out to answer the question of whether his version would be the same film as Hitchcock's were he to follow every line, shot, and edit, he ultimately found that, "It wasn't the same film. Because of all the stuff that we do to make the film, [we] completely changed it." And those changes weren't necessarily for the better. Viewed on its own terms, the 1998 *Psycho* is a problematic movie; there's a pronounced lack of atmosphere; the murders themselves aren't especially tense or frightening (even though you know what's coming, Hitchcock's shower sequence is still unnerving today); and, most damagingly of all, there's a gaping void at the center of the movie where a fascinating and disturbing psycho should be. Vaughn himself had admitted to being nervous about stepping into a role that had been so thoroughly defined by Perkins—nervous enough that he felt "overwhelmed" his first day on set, which necessitated reshooting a few sequences the following day.[11] Based on the performance he delivers during the rest of the movie, that nervousness never really went away. Where Perkins had a very specific idea of who Norman was and performed the role accordingly, Vaughn seems unable to make up his mind, and that indecisiveness costs the movie greatly.

More than anything, however, what really impacts the experience of watching Van Sant's *Psycho* is the knowledge that you're observing a replication of a previous work of art. Thus, the impetus is to look for the differences between the original and its copy, rather than treating them both as stand-alone pieces. Considering how instructive some of those differences are, though, it's difficult to classify Van Sant's experiment with *Psycho* as a total failure. Certainly, from a performance standpoint, the new version offers an interesting lesson in how two actors can create entirely different characters while saying the same lines of dialogue. Although Vaughn is merely a pale shadow of Perkins, his costar Heche plays a version of Marion who is very distinct from Leigh's interpretation. She's more self-confident and assertive than her predecessor, and there's a touch of mockery, of *cruelty* in her performance that Leigh never achieved. Julianne Moore and Viggo Mortensen—who play Marion's sister, Lila (originally played by Vera Miles), and lover, Sam (John Gavin), respectively—give their roles an equally thorough makeover, with Moore bringing a barely simmering rage to Lila, while Mortensen oozes a roguish charm that's absent from Gavin's square-jawed take on Marion's boyfriend. It's worth noting that Van Sant specifically instructed the actors to avoid mimicry; only Macy and James Remar—who has a small role as a highway cop Marion briefly crosses paths with—seem to be taking direct cues from their predecessors.[12]

Interestingly, Van Sant adopted the no-mimicry advice behind the camera as well. Although the majority of the camera setups in his *Psycho* are direct re-creations of the earlier film, he makes room for extra shots and storytelling beats (like a short scene in which Lila surreptitiously explores Norman's childhood bedroom, finding a collection of toy soldiers as well as a porn magazine, items that juxtapose his childish and adult pleasures) and takes advantage of improvements in filmmaking technology to shoot specific sequences in a way Hitchcock wasn't able to. For example, the opening scene of the camera floating through the Phoenix skyline before settling on Marion and Sam in bed together was accomplished via a helicopter shot—something Hitchcock was unable to do in the 1960 film.[13] The shower scene carries Van Sant's distinct stamp as well; in his staging, the camera pushes in on Marion's attacker sneaking up on her; her corpse has visible stab wounds; and, in the midst of the attack, Van Sant inserts two seemingly random shots of clouds passing overhead. Even the mood of the two films is different; the black-and-white photography, coupled with the Gothic look of Norman's house, lends the original *Psycho* a more overtly horrific touch that's somewhat akin to one of those vintage '30s Universal-produced monster movies like *Frankenstein*. In contrast, the design of both the Bates homestead and the motel—which is frequently bathed in a fluorescent glow—is deliberately generic in the 1998 version, which complements Van Sant's apparent interest in depicting the banality of evil, a theme also present in his award-winning 2003 feature *Elephant*. These alterations result in a *Psycho* that's less frightening than its predecessor, but in a strange way, one that's also more realistic. It also speaks to the lasting lesson imparted by Van Sant's brave (or, if you prefer, foolhardy) experiment: sometimes you have to make the same movie to make a different movie.

The First: Gus Van Sant's *Psycho* presaged the dawn of a remake culture within Hollywood that started with horror movies and subsequently spread outwards.

The '90s were by and large a fallow period for American horror cinema, following a sustained 20-year period of great creativity and even greater success stories. Starting with 1968's no-budget zombie classic *Night of the Living Dead* and continuing on with 1972's *The Last House on the Left*, 1978's *Halloween*, and 1981's *The Evil Dead*, the genre was revitalized by new directors frequently working on their own with limited resources, yet managing to find creative ways to scare the bejesus out of people. Even when studios got into the act in the '80s—as New Line did with its *Nightmare on Elm Street* series or Universal by funding risky films like *Phantasm II* and *The Serpent and the Rainbow*—the initial results were often positive. But as franchise fever set in during that era, brand names like *Elm Street*, *Friday the 13th*, and *Child's Play* became more valuable than potentially one-off ideas, and sequel after sequel was churned out until each series lost its appeal and its audience. By the early '90s, the industry had burned through most of its established series and had few original ideas left. It's telling that one of the decade's biggest horror hits, 1996's *Scream*, was a film that poked fun at the genre's familiar conventions in the guise of telling a new story. That movie featured as much recycling as any uninspired horror sequel, but at least it was aware of it.

The announcement of Gus Van Sant's *Psycho* remake in 1998 was taken as a sign that Hollywood had really and truly run out of original ideas when it came to horror movies and instead was forced to plunder past glories. In a way, though, Van Sant's pitch *was* original, and not just for its shot-for-shot conceit. Up until that point, the preferred way to continue a popular horror brand was via a sequel; witness *Psycho II-IV*, *The Texas Chainsaw Massacre* 2-4, and even *Critters* 2-4. Though the plots were frequently identical enough to function as de facto remakes, these movies were technically continuations, with the same killer or killers offing different victims. (Some exceptions to this loose rule included John Carpenter's remake of *The Thing*, David Cronenberg's superb take on *The Fly*, and a forgettable 1988 version of *The Blob*.) Rather than continuing *Psycho* with the son, daughter, or cousin of Norman Bates, Van Sant wanted to make the Hitchcock film again, despite the perception that it was untouchable. Had the movie been a hit, complaints about remaking a classic would likely have been shrugged off, but its poor box-office performance coupled with the stridently negative reviews scared studios off from continuing to raid the horror genre's past . . . for a little while, anyway.

Remakes gained a foothold again in the early '00s, initially thanks to the popularity of English-language versions of international horror movies, most notably Gore Verbinski's 2002 smash hit *The Ring*—an adaptation of the 1998 Japanese film *Ringu*, a cornerstone of what was being called J-horror. The movie that really opened the floodgates for updated versions of American-made scary movies, though, was the 2003 relaunch of *The Texas Chainsaw Massacre*, the first direct remake of Tobe Hooper's 1974 original. Unlike *Psycho*, the new *Chainsaw Massacre* wasn't a shot-for-shot re-creation of its predecessor, although certain iconic moments are carefully preserved with even more reverence than Van Sant displayed in restaging Hitchcock's film. Also unlike *Psycho*, it was a major success, grossing some $80 million. With audiences of young and veteran horror fans signaling that they were now ready to see the scary movies of yesteryear revived in the present day, multiplexes were promptly flooded with remakes of such familiar titles as *Dawn of the Dead*, *The Amityville Horror*, *The Hitcher*, *Prom Night*, *Halloween*, and, eventually, even *A Nightmare on Elm Street* and *Friday the 13th*—two of the defining horror franchises of the '80s. Not all of these remakes met with the same commercial success enjoyed by *The Texas Chainsaw Massacre* (and with a few notable exceptions, the reviews were mostly unkind), but most surpassed *Psycho*'s unimpressive take.

Wary of the lambasting Van Sant took for reproducing Hitchcock's film so closely, the new wave of horror remakes instead followed *The Texas*

Chainsaw Massacre's lead and recycled the same premise and characters from their respective sources, but altered the visual style, key story points, and even manners of death. And yet in interviews the filmmakers behind these movies tended to emphasize how they also set out to remain "faithful" to the original movie—a goal that was often met by replicating specific scenes and moments in often shot-for-shot fashion. One of the more egregious examples of this was John Moore's 2006 remake of Richard Donner's 1976 hit *The Omen* (primarily made to take advantage of the 06/06/06 release date),[14] which apes the original so closely, it's essentially the same movie. In a way, this remake represents the film Van Sant speculated he might make by trying to follow "every single line and cut"[15] of the 1960 *Psycho*, in which case he should be happy that his experiment failed. Despite the overwhelmingly negative critical reaction, *The Omen* still managed to more than double *Psycho*'s gross, earning $54 million. Only eight years separated the two remakes, and yet by 2006, audiences seemed less perturbed by the prospect of paying to see a close reproduction of a popular older film.

The shift in attitude can be chalked up in large part to the way remakes had become an entrenched part of the movie landscape by the mid-'00s outside of the horror genre. Amidst soaring coasts and up-and-down attendance levels, the major Hollywood studios became heavily dependent on established brand names as they planned out their production schedules. Thus, franchises that seemed finished were resurrected with new sequels (think *The Terminator* and *Indiana Jones*), while others started over from the beginning (the James Bond series, as well as the Batman films) with new origin stories that were described as reboots rather than remakes. And then there were more traditional remakes like *The Karate Kid* and *Footloose*, the latter of which was packed with visual references to its predecessor, sometimes jokingly and sometimes seriously.

The trend even extended to television; *Battlestar Galactica*, *The Bionic Woman*, *Dragnet*, and *Hawaii Five-0* were just some of the familiar TV shows that returned to the airwaves in new incarnations between 2000 and 2010. In fact, even the *Psycho* franchise spawned a small-screen offshoot, the A&E series *Bates Motel*, a present-day prequel to and reimagining of the film that focuses on the formative years of Norman Bates and his still-living mother, Norma. As easy as it is to blame Hollywood for the current remake culture, the fault also lies with consumers who continue to demonstrate an appetite for seeing old brands repurposed and resold in new packaging. (Although it's worth noting that audiences have refused to take the bait on a number of remakes, as commercial disappointments like the new *Footloose* attest.) In hindsight, Van Sant was ahead of his time by seeing the value in remaking *Psycho* in 1998. It was a prelude to an age during which Hollywood and moviegoers alike didn't want to learn from the past so much as repeat it.

FILM FIRST FILE #1: DIRECTORS WHO HAVE REMADE THEIR OWN MOVIES

It's a regular occurrence for directors to remake the work of others—rarer are the cases where directors remake their own films. Here are five film-makers who have had a second chance to help their movies make a first impression.

Ole Bornedal

Original Film: *Nattevagten* (1994)
Remake: *Nightwatch* (1997)
Bornedal's thriller about a law student who nabs a night watchman gig in a medical facility while a serial killer is on the loose proved a hit in its native Denmark, so when Miramax's genre arm, Dimension, acquired the remake rights, they retained him as director. Despite a cast that included Ewan McGregor, Josh Brolin, and Nick Nolte and a script penned by Nolte, the American version vanished without a trace, given a perfunctory release by its studio and just barely crossing the million-dollar mark at the box office.

Michael Haneke

Original Film: *Funny Games* (1997)
Remake: *Funny Games* (2007)
Ten years after the Austrian version of his brutal home invasion film arrived in theaters and generated controversy and critical hosannas, Haneke came to the United States to make the exact same movie again, only this time in English and with acknowledged stateside stars like Naomi Watts. As with Gus Van Sant's *Psycho*, reaction to his shot-for-shot remake wasn't entirely kind, particularly from viewers who had seen the original. Those who hadn't, however, tended to be more impressed by the remake's sustained atmosphere of tension and dread as well as its formal playfulness—all things that were directly replicated from its predecessor.

Sam Raimi

Original Film: *The Evil Dead* (1981)
Remake: *Evil Dead 2: Dead by Dawn* (1987)
Don't let the "2" in the title throw you; some consider Raimi's second *Evil Dead* film, which returns viewers to a haunted cabin in the woods, to be as much a remake of the original film as it is a continuation. The first time around, Raimi worked guerrilla style, making do with a roughly $400,000 budget. For the follow-up, he was gifted with the astronomical (by compari-son) amount of $3.6 million to help with his bloodletting. That money

bought a lot more fake blood, a lot more dismembered body parts, and a lot more zany humor.

Takashi Shimizu

Original Film: *Ju-on: The Grudge* (2002)
Remake: *The Grudge* (2004)
One of the most popular Japanese horror franchises, Shimizu's *Ju-on* series started with two direct-to-video installments before making the leap to the big screen in 2002, the same year that *The Ring*—the Hollywood version of another hit J-horror feature, *Ringu*—took the domestic box office by storm. Eager to find the next *Ring*, the Columbia Pictures arm of Sony hired Shimizu to translate his particular sensibility to American audiences. The resulting film earned $110 million, making it the second-highest-grossing horror remake of all time after *The Ring*.

George Sluizer

Original Film: *Spoorloos* (1988)
Remake: *The Vanishing* (1993)
A worldwide sensation during its initial theatrical release, the Dutch thriller about a man's dogged quest to learn what happened to his vanished lover earned comparisons to none other than Albert Hitchcock. After enlisting Sluizer to make an American version that would be equally acclaimed, 20th Century Fox then forced him to change virtually everything that people loved about the original, most notably the dark but entirely appropriate ending. As a result of their interference, *Spoorloos* is still watched and recommended today, while the remake is a mere footnote.

FILM FIRST FILE #2: FIVE GREAT POST-*PSYCHO* HORROR REMAKES

Most of the horror movie remakes to come along post-*Psycho* have been middling to lousy—charges some have leveled at Gus Van Sant's film itself. The following five films, though, actually merit positive comparisons to their predecessors.

Dawn of the Dead (Zach Snyder, 2005)

Snyder's slick revise of George A. Romero's 1978 zombie classic lacks the potent satiric edge of the original, but functions quite nicely as a tense, exciting action movie. It's not particularly scary, but it is especially bloody.

The Hills Have Eyes (Alexandre Aja, 2006)

The sheer brutality depicted in Aja's update of Wes Craven's 1977 men vs. mutants survivalist tale is bracing stuff, leaving the film constantly teetering on the edge of being too much. But what routinely pulls it back from the brink is the skill with which it was made—a skill that often surpasses the roughly assembled original.

The Wicker Man (Neil LaBute, 2006)

Let's be clear—LaBute's update of the Robin Hardy cult classic completely violates the spirit of its source material by transforming Hardy's chilling story into something utterly absurd thanks to laughable dialogue, inept direction, and a Nicolas Cage performance that's over the top even for Nicolas Cage. But those absurdities are what make the remake such a kick to watch; believe it or not, one of the funniest comedies of the '00s happens to be a horror movie.

Let Me In (Matt Reeves, 2010)

The American remake of the 2008 Swedish vampire tale *Let the Right One In* ups the fear factor but, for once, not at the expense of the original's thoughtful thematic material or overall emotional power. *Let Me In* is a tenser sit than its slow-burning predecessor, while still hitting the same final haunting note.

Don't Be Afraid of the Dark (Troy Nixey, 2011)

Nixey's background as a comic book artist came in handy for his Guillermo del Toro–produced remake of a '70s made-for-TV haunted house tale. *Don't Be Afraid of the Dark* has a formal elegance and eye for detail that too many modern horror films—not to mention the original TV movie—lack.

Chapter 15

The Matrix (1999)

The Film: Lana and Andy Wachowski's breakthrough cyberspace adventure invited audiences to come for the cutting-edge action sequences and stay for its deep philosophical underpinnings.

There are several ways of answering the question that lies at the center of *The Matrix*,[1] namely: "What is the Matrix?" The first and most obvious response is that it's a thrilling science-fiction action film from the filmmaking duo then known as the Wachowski Brothers that set Hollywood on its ear when it hit theaters in 1999. The second is rooted in the movie's plot: the Matrix is a computer simulation of the real world built and maintained by artificial intelligence–enabled machines to keep humanity enslaved. And then there's the third answer, which is that the Matrix is a state of mind—a way of viewing the world and one's place in it that's based in a unique fusion of Eastern and Western philosophies and film genres. This latter explanation is likely the one that the directors themselves would endorse first and foremost. Strip away the movie's groundbreaking technical advances, game-changing action sequences, and crisply plotted narrative, and what you're left with is a philosophical tract in the guise of a next-gen blockbuster. To borrow a line from Laurence Fishburne's in-movie guru, Morpheus, *The Matrix* isn't just out to rock your world—it wants to free your mind.

The film accomplishes that goal through a mixture of high (theological texts, sociological and philosophical surveys) and—by some people's definition, anyway—low (kung-fu movies, Japanese animation or *anime* and video games) culture that reflects the disparate interests of its makers. Born almost three years apart into middle-class surroundings in Chicago, Larry and Andy Wachowski earned their geek cred early on, falling into comic books, sci-fi movies, and marathon *Dungeons & Dragons* sessions at a young age.[2]

(Today, Larry is Lana Wachowski, having officially come out as transgender in 2012.)[3] They retained their enthusiasm for those mediums even as they grew up and their horizons expanded to include weighty tomes like Jean Baudrillard's *Simulacra and Simulation*, which would later top the list of key influences on *The Matrix*. In fact, the film's star, Keanu Reeves, has said that *Simulacra* was one of three books the Wachowskis required him to read before they would cast him in the role of Neo,[4] the computer hacker who is awakened to the fact that the world he (or to be more precise, his avatar) is inhabiting is a digital invention created out of 1's and 0's. After an extensive amount of physical and, more importantly, mental training, he learns that he has the power to bend and shape that simulated environment instead of being a slave to it.

The Wachowski siblings eventually went from reading comics as kids to writing them as adults, penning a series for Marvel Comics in the early '90s. They branched out into screenplays as well, all while running a construction business as a day job. It was in the process of brainstorming pitches for a new comic book that they hit upon the idea that would blossom into *The Matrix* and decided to pursue it as a feature rather than a comic. By this time, one of their scripts was already in the process of being turned into a feature—the Warner Bros.–produced Sylvester Stallone star vehicle *Assassins*—and while the finished product bore only a passing resemblance to what they had originally written, it made people interested to see what other scripts they might have up their sleeves. So they sent an initial draft of *The Matrix* out into the world, where it was met with a resounding . . . silence.[5]

The one person who did seem to get the movie's mixture of chop-socky action and cyberpunk philosophy was veteran producer Joel Silver, who had also produced *Assassins*. It was Silver who encouraged the Wachowskis to flesh out their dense, complicated script with detailed storyboards (many of which were drawn by celebrated comics artist Geof Darrow)[6] that would better represent the kind of movie they told him they wanted to make: a live-action version of an *anime* feature.[7] Even with an illustrated guide to the film, though, nobody was willing to take a chance on a pair of untested directors, so the duo went off to write and direct another movie as a calling card—the low-budget but highly stylish thriller *Bound*. It was on the strength of that film that Warner Bros., which had eventually ponied up the money for the script, decided to give *The Matrix* the go-ahead, even though it remained an open question whether the Wachowskis could deliver on the ambitious spectacle they had described on the page.

The studio's doubts were understandable considering that the directors' artistic vision hinged on them successfully executing several technical processes that they had no direct experience with and, in some cases, hadn't even been invented yet. For starters, they wanted the actors—rather than their stunt doubles—to perform the extensive martial-arts sequences and specifically wanted them to be trained in the Hong Kong school of fight choreography under the tutelage of master choreographer Yuen Woo-ping, whose work on the 1994 Jet Li feature *Fist of Legend* shaped the way they wanted the hand-to-hand combat in *The Matrix* to look. Before a frame of film was even shot, Reeves and the rest of the core cast spent four months in intensive training sessions with Woo-ping and his fight crew, sessions that the Wachowskis were able to observe and learn from as well.[8] (Although directors like John Woo and Tsui Hark had brought Hong Kong style to Hollywood by the time *The Matrix* was in production, few American-born filmmakers had attempted to use Hong Kong–specific techniques such as wire work, where harnesses and rigs are employed to give the performer's moves extra oomph.) While the use of stunt doubles would have cut down on preproduction time, it would have resulted in a vastly different shooting style for the action sequences, with the directors being forced to cut around the performers to hide the fact that Keanu wasn't Keanu. Hearing Reeves utter the immortal line "I know kung fu" and then actually seeing him *do* it heightens the viewer's connection to his character. More importantly, it reinforces one of the movie's central ideas, which is that within the artificial environment of the Matrix, a person can become his or her idealized self given the right tools and state of mind.

In addition to learning the ins and outs of shooting Hong Kong fight choreography, making *The Matrix* demanded that the already tech-savvy Wachowskis receive a serious schooling in special effects. Lessons like shooting against a greenscreen and incorporating practical and digital F/X in the same scene proved challenging but teachable thanks to the experienced crew. However, accomplishing the film's most important (and defining) effect—bullet time—required the directors and the effects team to write an entirely new lesson plan. Essentially a stylized version of slow motion, bullet time was intended to be a means by which the directors could control the speed of a specific piece of action while also choreographing elaborate camera moves that wouldn't be possible in an ordinary physical space. The earliest bullet time tests were conducted in 1996—two years before the film started shooting—under the supervision of John Gaeta,[9] who would later win a Visual Effects Oscar for his work on the film.

Through trial and error, Gaeta eventually devised a system by which the performers were positioned in front of a greenscreen (upon which a digitally rendered environment would later be inserted) and surrounded by a series of still cameras, as well as two motion picture cameras all arranged in a specific order to mimic the effect of a single camera moving through space. The still cameras would photograph the action one frame at a time while the film cameras rolled at different speeds. At the end of the process, the directors are left with a scene in which they have the ability to manipulate the frame rate to speed up or slow down the action while the camera moves around it in a fluid, constant motion.[10] At the time and still today, bullet time is a remarkable effect, one that rarely fails to make the viewer's mouth drop no matter how many times he's seen it. It also doubles as an important thematic device; within the Matrix, bullet time functions as a way for Neo to demonstrate his ability to defy the rules of a physical reality that the computer simulation gives the illusion of replicating, but which can actually be reshaped and rewritten.

It's this intrinsic connection that the Wachowskis carefully established between the movie's themes and its technology-driven spectacle that continues to make *The Matrix* (as well as its two underrated sequels) a vital, relevant science-fiction tale. The action sequences are viscerally exciting, yes, but they also frequently serve as expressions of the film's deeper ideas instead of distractions from them. Using Baudrillard's notion that modern society has become a simulation of itself as a jumping-off point, the directors marry that idea to the story of an individual's intellectual awakening, as well as his more spiritual journey to enlightenment and beyond. (Indeed, as the series progresses, the familiar Christian myth involving saviors and rebirths that pervades the first movie gives way to a more multifaceted religious allegory, with healthy doses of Buddhism and Hinduism stirred into the mix.) The majority of the action sequences in *The Matrix* are specifically designed to be part of Neo's self-discovery, as his ever-evolving mind eventually allows him to become the master of his simulated environment. And while some of the technology within the movie has dated—the boxy computers used by the characters look ancient compared to the sleek machines sold at Apple stores today—its depiction of a pristine virtual reality that's impossible to tell apart from the "real thing" continues to resonate, particularly as so much of our daily life continues to migrate into digital spaces. "The Matrix has you," read several of the one-sheet movie posters that advertised the film prior to its release, a tagline that suggests that you're a slave to the status quo, be it in computer space or meatspace. But what the Wachowskis seek to teach you is that you have the power to challenge and even change it—first by thought, then by action.

The First: *The Matrix*'s blockbuster posttheatrical life on DVD helped transform that still-young technology into the dominant home entertainment system . . . for a few years at least.

One of the defining trends of the past four decades of movie history is the creation and ongoing evolution of home entertainment technology. Prior to the late 1980s, the only way a moviegoers could see a specific film was in theaters—either in a first- or second-run house for more recent releases, or a repertory theater if it were a significantly older title—or wait for it to potentially pop up on television on a local station's late-night lineup or a national network's designated "movie of the week" time slot. (By the late '70s, fledgling cable channels like HBO became another posttheatrical outlet for feature films, although they initially reached a very limited audience.) The notion of being able to own a movie—let alone an entire library of movies—to watch at home whenever you wished seemed like a privilege reserved for those with the funds to construct a private theater in their own residences, complete with a projector and healthy collection of film prints.

The inklings of an impending sea change were first felt in the early '70s thanks to the advances that were being made in the realm of video technology, particularly the advent of videocassettes—the video equivalent of audiocassette tapes, which eliminated the cumbersome reel-to-reel approach of early video playback machines.[11] One of the first videocassette recorders (or VCRs), Sony's U-Matic, arrived on the market in 1971,[12] and while that particular model didn't find its way into many living rooms (largely because of its high sticker price),[13] it did make technology companies see the potential in pursuing the idea of a videocassette machine specifically intended for the home market. Sony went on to develop the Betamax system, while its rival JVC unveiled the Video Home System or VHS; a full-scale format war ensued that ultimately ended in the '80s with VHS declaring victory, thanks to, among other reasons, its cheaper manufacturing costs and significantly longer recording length.[14]

Even while the format war was raging, the Hollywood studios saw the value in home video, as it provided them with another way to make money off their film catalogues that didn't require them to involve theaters, which took a healthy chunk of the profits. Selling movies to video rental stores and later directly to consumers seemed to promise—and, in fact, delivered—lucrative returns. In time, the emergence of a home entertainment market would fundamentally alter the industry business model; studios could potentially recoup costs on movies that bombed in theaters via their video afterlife, while other films could be greenlit specifically with the home audience in mind. Thanks to the arrival of the home video age, a theatrical release was no longer the beginning and the end of a movie's life—it was just the beginning.

The dominance of VHS was a triumph from a business perspective, but as a piece of technology, it was always problematic. The image and audio quality of a film-to-video transfer was a significant step down from what viewers could experience in theaters, and it only further degraded with time and multiple re-viewings.[15] (A serious film buff could also go on and on for hours about the eternal "pan and scan vs. letterboxing" debates that plagued the format, referring to the common practice of cropping films so they'd fit the exact dimensions of a TV screen.) In the early '90s, another home-viewing option arose in the form of laser discs, optical discs that resembled vinyl record–sized CDs. In addition to looking and sounding better than VHS tapes, laser discs had the capacity to offer dual audio tracks, one of which would play the movie's soundtrack while the other could be reserved for, say, a commentary track from the director or other key talent involved in the film.[16] On the downside, laser discs were cumbersome and their playback capacity much shorter than VHS tapes; viewers could count on having to flip the disc over from Side A to Side B halfway through the film, and longer movies were spread across multiple discs.

While laser discs failed to make a serious dent in the VHS market (it did become the preferred format among cinephiles, though), the benefits of the optical disc format were clearly apparent. The next evolution in that technology came with the mid-'90s debut of DVDs, which offered many of the same benefits of laser discs (superior picture and audio quality, greater capacity for bonus features accompanying the film) without its limitations (longer playback time, smaller size). Released on the American market in 1997, DVDs initially ran up against the challenges confronted by any emerging technology, among them lack of consumer awareness, higher costs, and limited catalogue offerings. A crossover hit was needed—a release that highlighted the unique qualities of the format and convinced skeptics that *this* was the machine worth replacing their VCRs for.

Enter *The Matrix*, which Warner Bros. released on DVD (and, as part of standard operating procedure, VHS) in September 1999, six months after its theatrical premiere. A year later in August 2000, the studio issued a press release trumpeting that it was the first disc to sell three million copies, making it, at the time, the best-selling DVD in the format's young history.[17] Although that number seemed paltry compared to some of the highest-grossing VHS tapes, it was a sign that DVDs were gaining a firmer foothold on the home entertainment market, with *The Matrix* in particular almost certainly helping to pull in new consumers. Indeed, the movie's status as a cultural and box-office phenom accounts in large part for its impressive sales figures, but the Wachowskis and Warner Bros. also put together a terrific disc filled with supplements that highlighted the format's unique benefits over VHS.

That list of supplements begins somewhat innocuously with a standard half-hour making-of documentary originally produced for HBO and a solid but not exceptional commentary track anchored by one of the movie's costars, Carrie-Anne Moss; its editor, Zach Sternberg; and its special effects guru (and inventor of bullet time), John Gaeta. (The Wachowskis themselves declined to add their own voices to the mix; to this day, they have only recorded one DVD commentary track, which appeared on the disc for their debut feature, *Bound*.) Things get progressively more interesting from there, starting with another separate audio track that allows viewers to watch the film with just the music playing, as well as the occasional comment from composer Don Davis. The images of two red pills—the pills that Neo pops to awaken his true self outside of the Matrix—are also hidden amongst the DVD menus and, when found and accessed, lead viewers to separate short documentaries. (These sorts of hidden extras are known as "Easter Eggs" in DVD parlance.)

By far the most innovative extra at the time was the "Follow the White Rabbit" feature, referring to one of the many allusions to *Alice in Wonderland* that recur throughout the film. When this feature was activated, the image of a white rabbit would pop up on-screen at nine specific points in the film. Clicking on the rabbit would take viewers to a short behind-the-scenes clip about the scene in question, and, when the clip was complete, they'd be returned to the exact point where the disc had branched off.[18] This kind of branching between the film proper and the supplemental material was a feature VHS couldn't replicate, and the technology has been further refined over time, now allowing for an entire "second screen" DVD experience where viewers can seamlessly move back and forth from the feature and bonus content with the push of a button.

Given the movie's digital setting, it's no surprise that the *Matrix* DVD also came with a host of bonus features that could only be accessed via a computer. When the disc was inserted inside a DVD-ROM drive, viewers had access to special trivia questions, storyboards, a series of essays covering topics that ranged from comic-book movies to martial-arts films, trailers for *The Matrix*, and announcements of special web-only events like online chats with members of the movie's crew. (The Wachowskis participated in one of these chat sessions in November 1999, answering fans' questions while watching a virtual screening of the film.)[19] The message to consumers was clear: if you wanted to have the full *Matrix* experience in the comfort of your own home, you had to upgrade to DVD.

In the years following *The Matrix*'s DVD release, those shiny silver discs did, in fact, come to supplant VHS tapes as the dominant home entertainment format. (The final studio production to be widely released on VHS was *A History of Violence* in 2006, and the format was phased out altogether in 2008.)[20] Along with DVD sales, the breadth of bonus features included on future releases continued to grow, and *The Matrix* remained on the cutting edge of that as well. In 2004, Warner Bros. issued the entire trilogy in an "Ultimate Collection" box set that was packed with hours and hours of supplemental material. But DVD didn't have long to rest on its laurels. By 2006, high-definition optical discs were hitting the market, resulting in another format war, this time between Sony's Blu-ray and Toshiba's HD-DVD. (Unlike the VHS vs. Betamax face-off, though, Sony eventually emerged victorious from this particular battle.) And by 2012, the rise in streaming video services such as Netflix, iTunes, and Video on Demand channels seemed poised to make the very idea of physical media irrelevant. Even as the DVD market shrinks, however, home entertainment itself is most certainly here to stay, as it's become too important a revenue stream for the studios to abandon entirely, not to mention too prevalent a way that contemporary audiences consume films. If anything, "going to the movies" these days more commonly means sitting down in front of your television and/or computer and logging onto Netflix rather than driving to your local multiplex. And considering the way technology is so rapidly evolving, one day in the not-too-distant future it might even be possible to watch a streaming copy of *The Matrix* inside a computer-simulated replica of the Matrix.

FILM FIRST FILE #1: FIVE CINEMATIC WORLDS WITHIN WORLDS

Beyond its superbly executed action sequences, perhaps the aspect of *The Matrix* that resonates most with viewers is the way it taps into the potent idea that the world around us isn't real—that we're instead part of an artificial construct beyond which the real "real world" lies. The following films similarly each take place in a reality that's nestled inside a larger reality, be it virtual or man-made.

Dark City (Alex Proyas, 1998)

Movie World: A sprawling city that seems forever shrouded in darkness and features architecture straight out of a German expressionist feature and fashions from a *noir*ish detective potboiler.

Real World: The city has actually been constructed by a dying alien race in deep space and serves as a plus-sized petri dish where they can conduct their experiments on humankind.

Open Your Eyes (Alejandro Amenábar, 1997)/*Vanilla Sky* (Cameron Crowe, 2001)

Movie World: Both the original Spanish-language film and its inferior Hollywood remake take place in a reality that appears on the surface to be exactly like our own . . . until a series of strange, otherworldly events befall the main character, a handsome playboy disfigured in a terrible car accident.

Real World: He's living inside his own head, while his body lies preserved inside a cyrogenic tube, possibly in the present or potentially the distant future.

World on a Wire (Rainer Werner Fassbinder, 1973)/*The Thirteenth Floor* (Josef Rusnak, 1999)

Movie World: The 1964 Daniel F. Galouye novel *Simulacron-3* served as the basis for a German TV miniseries and an American studio-backed feature, both of which revolve around a cutting-edge scientific corporation that has successfully constructed a virtually simulated world.

Real World: It turns out that the corporation itself exists inside of a virtual simulation, and there's still at least one more level of reality above it.

The Truman Show (Peter Weir, 1998)

Movie World: Ordinary guy Truman Burbank is a lifetime resident of the idyllic small town of Seahaven, a place filled with lovely homes, beautiful scenery, and the friendliest people you'd ever hope to meet.

Real World: Seahaven exists entirely within a dome-sized Los Angeles–based television soundstage where Truman's life is filmed (without his knowledge) by hundreds of cameras 24/7 for the amusement of audiences around the globe.

The Village (M. Night Shyamalan, 2004)

Movie World: In a nineteenth-century woodland village, the citizens work hard to uphold time-honored traditions and avoid the monsters lurking inside the surrounding forest.

Real World: That forest is actually part of a wildlife preserve, outside of which exists a twenty-first-century landscape, a time period that the village elders have shunned in favor of an older way of life.

FILM FIRST FILE #2: FIVE MUST-LISTEN DVD COMMENTARY TRACKS

Originally introduced during the brief heyday of laser discs, the commentary track—a separate audio track that could be played over a film featuring running commentary from the people involved with making it—became an especially popular bonus feature during the DVD era. The following discs boast some of the finest commentaries ever recorded for DVD editions of good (and bad) movies.

Citizen Kane: 70th Anniversary Collector's Edition (Warner Bros., 2011)

Want to know why Orson Welles's 1941 masterpiece is so widely considered one of the greatest films of all time? America's best-known film critic, Roger Ebert, makes the case in a dense, informative, and highly enjoyable commentary track. Having seen the movie over 100 times and analyzed it shot-by-shot in front of audiences, Ebert brings a wealth of knowledge about the movie's production history and Welles's specific techniques to his audio lecture. It's a commentary track that doubles as a film history class.

The Limey (Artisan, 2000)

Typically when directors and screenwriters sit down to chat about a film they've collaborated on, the result is a chummy, backslapping affair. That's decidedly not the case with Steven Soderbergh's crime drama, penned by

Lem Dobbs. Almost from the moment the commentary begins, a disgruntled Dobbs assails Soderbergh's choices in translating his script to the screen, while the director good-naturedly (if defensively) responds to his criticisms. It's a tense, fascinating conversation that reveals how extensively a film's screenplay can be written and rewritten during production and in the editing room.

The Matrix Reloaded/The Matrix Revolutions (The Ultimate Matrix Collection, Warner Bros. 2004)

While the first *Matrix* is almost universally adored, its two sequels are far more divisive. The Wachowskis embraced the debate by including two separate audio commentaries for Parts 2 and 3 (plus the original film) on the trilogy's deluxe box set release, one led by a pair of philosophers (Dr. Cornel West and Ken Wilber) and the other anchored by a trio of film critics (Todd McCarthy, John Powers, and David Thomson). Both groups are given the opportunity to air their respective hosannas and grievances about the sequels, allowing the viewers to decide which camp they belong to.

Mimic: The Director's Cut (Lionsgate, 2011)

Guillermo del Toro's first Hollywood creature feature was a trial by fire experience during which he repeatedly argued with the producers and had the film more or less taken away from him in the editing room. Given the opportunity to reconstruct his preferred version years after the fact, del Toro's fascinating commentary track walks viewers through his ordeal in calm, measured (but still ever-so-slightly annoyed) tones. His version of events is at once both a horror story and a source of inspiration as no matter how bad the situation on set got, the director never gave up on making the best movie his circumstances would allow.

Zardoz (20th Century Fox, 2001)

If you're left baffled and annoyed by John Boorman's 1974 futuristic parable, don't worry—the director is right there with you. Less a defense of a deeply flawed movie than an extended apology, Boorman alternately sounds befuddled and amused by the questionable creative choices his younger self made decades ago. Rarely has a filmmaker been this honest about his own failings.

Chapter 16

The Blair Witch Project (1999)

The Film: By faking it so real, the makers of *The Blair Witch Project* struck box-office pay dirt and launched the found-footage horror genre.

An awful lot of fiction went into making the ostensibly factual horror movie *The Blair Witch Project*,[1] a reality. Start with the premise, which is handily summarized in a title card preceding the film: in 1994, three film students armed with more cameras than common sense wandered into the Maryland woods to investigate the legend of the Blair Witch. They never returned, but a year later the footage of their doomed trip was unearthed and presented for the world to see. Let's debunk this scenario point by point. First, the footage seen in *The Blair Witch Project* was shot in 1997, not 1994. Secondly, the film students weren't actual film students, but actors who had auditioned to be part of this half-inspired, half-foolhardy production. Finally, the Blair Witch herself—along with all her accordant mythology—was an invention, dreamed up by the movie's directors, Daniel Myrick and Eduardo Sánchez, and later embellished beyond the film in a series of tie-in books by other writers.

About the only thing in *The Blair Witch Project* that is authentic are the scenes of the three "students," Heather (played by Heather Donahue), Josh (Joshua Leonard), and Mike (Michael Williams), hiking through the forests surrounding Burkittsville, Maryland. The trio really did spend several days in the wilderness, carrying their own supplies, making up their own dialogue (extrapolated from a detailed story outline typed up by the directors),[2] and filming their journey with a pair of cameras, a Hi-8 video recorder, and a 16mm camera shooting black-and-white film.[3] But even that nugget of truth is wrapped in fiction, as the actors were following a path prepared for them by the filmmakers, who plotted the course through Maryland's Seneca Creek State Park with GPS units.[4] And during the shoot, the directors regularly interacted with the performers off camera, requesting multiple takes of the same scene and passing along acting notes, story reminders. and things to react to, be they physical objects or suitably spooky noises. The cast and crew even had a special code word—"Taco"—that they used whenever they needed to escape the movie's reality into actual reality.[5] For a film that derives its drama and its scares from being immediate and in the moment, so much of it was carefully planned out in advance.

And yet the impressive thing about *The Blair Witch Project* is that, while you're watching it, you don't see the strings. Sure, there are cracks in the scenario if you laser in closely enough, especially during repeat viewings. But all that advance legwork that the filmmakers put in lends the film an internal consistency and a narrative drive that its descendants in what has become known as the "found-footage" genre often lack. A found-footage descendant like 2007's *Paranormal Activity*, for example, operates mainly on a scare-to-scare basis, using the found-footage aesthetic (commonly defined by a first-person point-of-view camera, jumpy editing, and mock-documentary interviews and/or confessionals, among other elements) to stage effective "Boo!" moments, but not necessarily putting a great deal of thought or effort into what comes between them. In contrast, *The Blair Witch Project* doesn't isolate its predesignated scary bits—the scenes the filmmakers have specifically designed ahead of time to elicit screams from the crowd—from the rest of the narrative; instead, the whole movie flows together, building naturally and inevitably toward the characters' horrific fates.

Although *The Blair Witch Project* is correctly regarded as having kickstarted the contemporary found-footage boom, which has since spread from horror into other genres, it isn't technically the first of its kind. The obscure 1980 Italian film *Cannibal Holocaust* employed the same "group of filmmakers go missing in the woods and here's their footage" premise, using—as the title suggests—cannibals rather than witches as its central boogeyman. And even before that, exploitative pseudo-documentaries like the infamous 1962 hit *Mondo Cane* sought to pass off faked footage of gruesome deaths and general mayhem as the real thing. Despite not being the first out of the gate, *Blair Witch* has had a more lasting impact than its predecessors, due to the deftness of its execution, the scale of its success, and, most importantly, the appropriateness of its timing. (Interestingly, the documentary approach was initially born out of financial rather that creative necessity. As Sánchez told *Entertainment Weekly* in a 1999 interview, "It was supposed to look like a documentary because we had no money.")[6] Released in 1999 on the cusp of the reality television boom—CBS's industry-changing reality TV competition *Survivor* was still a year away, but MTV's *The Real World* had already been through several cycles—the movie presaged a time when recording your life on a camera would be second nature, particularly amongst tech-savvy youngsters like the characters in the film. Heather, the director of the documentary within the faux-documentary, has a habit of letting the camera run, even when she's not collecting material for her student film. When asked early on why she feels required to "have every conversation on video," she pauses a moment before replying matter-of-factly, "I have a camera. Doesn't hurt." To her mind, the camera's mere presence justifies its use; it would actually be odder to *not* have it running all the time.

Obviously, the movie's central narrative device demands that Heather adopt this attitude, because if she wasn't constantly filming herself as well as Josh and Mike, there'd be no footage for us to "find." But there's another level to her compulsion to just keep shooting no matter how dire their situation becomes; as one of her companions remarks at one point, by treating her life as a movie Heather is able to distance herself from what's actually going on. Reality seems a little bit grander, a little bit more fun, and a little less horrific when viewed through a camera lens. At several points throughout *Blair Witch*, especially when their situation grows increasingly dire, her companions beg and even threaten her to stop filming, a request she can't bring herself to comply with, insisting that, "It's all I have left."

In Myrick and Sánchez's initial vision for *Blair Witch*, the plight of the student filmmakers was only going to be part of a bigger faux-documentary canvas.[7] After the Maryland shoot wrapped, production shifted back to the filmmakers' home base in Florida, where they started work on what they described as "Phase II" of *The Blair Witch Project*, which would incorporate additional elements, like fake interviews with occult experts and the parents of the missing students, who were actually played by actors.[8] While reviewing and editing the footage of Heather, Josh, and Mike, however, they began to feel that that material was strong enough to stand entirely on its own.[9]

Thus, the film's reality was reshaped once again in the editing room, as the directors constructed whole sequences out of different takes—much like in a conventional narrative feature—and omitted or cut around the cast improvisations that didn't fit what they wanted from the characters or the scene. For instance, Myrick and Sánchez found the tone of much of the early footage too angry, with the actors squabbling with each other before they even arrived in the woods. So they snipped those fights out while retaining the lighter, funnier moments—rendering the characters' relationships as more harmonious than they actually were.[10] In essence, the filmmakers were creating scripted moments out of unscripted raw material, in the same way that the majority of contemporary reality television programs do. In that industry, the task of manufacturing a dramatic reality out of actual reality falls to story editors, who employ many of the tactics that Myrick and Sánchez used in making *Blair Witch*, including recontextualizing footage, coaching the cast members on what to say in a particular scene, and dropping them into artificial circumstances that are guaranteed to generate conflict. In that way, one could make the case that a series like *Duck Dynasty* owes as much to *The Blair Witch Project* as more obvious descendants like *The Devil Inside* do.

The illusion of reality was *Blair Witch*'s main selling point and the thing that tempted moviegoers into the theater in droves. Thanks to films like *Scream*, the horror genre was drowning in heightened self-awareness by the late '90s, dominated by movies that knew they were movies and took pleasure in winking at the audience in between murders. Myrick and Sánchez's film stood as the antithesis to that in that it wanted the audience to believe that what was happening on-screen was authentic, rather than deliberately artificial. The movie's seriousness, along with its then-unfamiliar style, is undoubtedly what shocked and surprised the first wave of audiences who experienced it during its world premiere at the 1999 Sundance Film Festival. It was in Park City that *The Blair Witch Project* first acquired the reputation as being the scariest movie to come along in years, one guaranteed to terrify even the hardiest soul. The distributor that acquired the film—the now defunct Artisan Entertainment—continued to successfully bolster that impression in *Blair Witch*'s ad campaign, aided by the breathless Sundance coverage. By the time the movie opened in general release that summer, few people knew what the movie was about, but they did know that it was supposed to be—as the Peter Travers pull quote emblazoned on one of the film's posters promised—"Scary as Hell."

While the hyperbole surrounding *The Blair Witch Project* raised its profile, it also put a big target on its back. Viewers walked into the theater expecting to lose their minds with fear, and when that didn't happen, they walked out angry and confused—as well as maybe a little nauseous due to the movie's handheld camerawork. Although the movie was successful, it also proved wildly divisive, with a significant portion of the audience not caring for the brand of horror it was practicing, one that was more rooted in psychology than blatant, in-your-face scares. The fact is, the movie's real subject—as well as the source of its horror—isn't the titular witch at all, but the way seemingly ordinary, well-adjusted people can turn on each other (and themselves) when placed in extreme situations. At heart, *The Blair Witch Project* is a depiction of the breakdown of the social order played out in microcosm, as well as the destruction of an individual's sense of self. And as such, it's more unsettling than overtly terrifying, which is bound to disappoint anyone purely looking for a steady stream of shocks and jolts.

The mixed reaction that mainstream moviegoers had to *The Blair Witch Project* may be one of the reasons why most of the found-footage horror films that came after have employed the style to more conventional ends. For example, *Paranormal Activity* and its sequels are little more than straightforward haunted house stories complete with a ghost that goes bump in the night, while *The Last Exorcism* incorporates many of the same devil-based theatrics made famous by William Friedkin's 1973's smash horror hit

The Exorcist. In both cases, the faux-documentary style is primarily a gimmick to deliver familiar scares in a semifresh way. Intentionally or not, *Blair Witch* possesses higher aspirations; it's using documentary elements not necessarily to make the story authentic, but rather to make the *feelings* inspired by the story—fear, rage, and despair—authentic. The footage may be fictional, but the emotions are real.

The First: At the dawn of the Internet age, it took an independently financed horror movie with limited resources to show Hollywood how to harness the marketing power of the World Wide Web.

For perfectly preserved examples of what online movie marketing looked like in the early years of the Internet, point your browser in the direction of the still-functioning sites for the films *Space Jam* and *You've Got Mail*, released by Warner Bros. in 1996 and 1998 respectively. Both sites were built, launched, and maintained by the studio to function as an additional advertising arm for its Bugs Bunny/Michael Jordan basketball comedy and Tom Hanks/Meg Ryan romantic comedy and bear all the hallmarks of early webpage design—from limited graphics and lots of text to a small color palette and blocky frames. Beyond their retro design, what stands out about both sites when visited today is how perfunctory they feel. While each contains a fair amount of content (particularly the *Space Jam* site), neither does a particularly strong job selling visitors on the experience of seeing the movie. That makes sense as, at the time, television and print advertising was still the primary way that the studios marketed their wares to the general public; the Internet was still an addendum to the marketing campaign rather than the integral part it has become today.

Even as the Web's toolkit—to say nothing of its reach—grew during the '90s, the deep-pocketed major movie companies mainly stuck with the traditional (and pricey) advertising methods, leaving the exploration of the digital frontier up to outsiders like the makers of *The Blair Witch Project*. From the beginning, Myrick and Sánchez seemed well aware that getting their independently financed feature seen and released would, in many ways, pose an even greater challenge than getting it made in the first place. By the time the duo began shooting *Blair Witch* in 1997, the indie film industry had become a big business, and while that meant that the market for low-budget, convention-defying movies was larger than before, it was also that much easier for films to get lost in the shuffle, either on the festival circuit where they all vied for the attention of the same distributors or, if they made it that far, in theaters.

But Myrick and Sánchez were also fortunate in that their movie came with a salable hook—namely, was *Blair Witch* fact or fiction? Unlike today, where found footage has become a genre unto itself, in the late '90s, there was still the potential to persuade moviegoers that the film's manufactured reality might in fact be the real deal. (The illusion was further bolstered by *Blair Witch*'s deliberately amateurish camerawork as well as the fact that the three young stars were complete unknowns.) The directors made the question of the film's authenticity a selling point early on, when they were still making the fund-raising rounds to finance the feature in the summer of 1997. One person who saw potential in the idea was indie film producer/booking agent/gadfly John Pierson, who invited Sánchez and Myrick to air part of an early test reel they had done for the film—along with additional material that he would finance—as a segment for his television series *Split Screen*, which was wrapping up its first season on the cable channel, IFC. The show presented the footage as fact, and after the episode aired, the filmmakers were excited to learn that viewers seemed to believe it.[11] By October, the funding was in place, and the *Blair Witch* cast and crew walked into the woods for a roughly weeklong shoot.

The following April, footage from the now-completed *Blair Witch Project* was once again featured on *Split Screen* as part of the show's second-season premiere. But a more significant milestone occurred in February 1998, when the directors launched the first version of the film's website, blairwitch.com. Initially, the site featured very little in the way of information, offering up the wholly invented explanation that potential legal issues were preventing the filmmakers from going into more detail about the footage featured in the film.[12] (Although that might seem like a too-convenient-to-be-believable dodge, it wound up piquing the interest of more than a few visitors; in one of his journals, Sánchez describes being contacted by a detective wondering whether the site's description of three missing students was real. They eventually made the decision to let him on the secret.)[13] The traffic to both blairwitch.com and haxan.com (the official site for Haxan Films, Myrick and Sánchez's production company) experienced a major bump after the movie's second *Split Screen* airing, with posters speculating about its veracity, a debate that the filmmakers allowed to play out without tipping their hand.[14] Then in October 1998, a caller to the popular Los Angeles–based morning radio talk show *The Mark & Brian Show* spoke about the movie and its website on-air, a mention that brought the site 2,500 visitors in only two days.[15] The advance attention undoubtedly came in handy when *The Blair Witch Project* was admitted to Sundance, helping attract capacity crowds to the film's first festival screenings.

After Artisan acquired *Blair Witch* at Park City, they directed the filmmakers to continue developing the site, adding copious amounts of content that bolstered the movie's (false) claims to fact, including purported police photos, interviews with fictitious experts, and an invented mythology for the Blair Witch herself. As the film's midsummer release drew closer, blairwitch.com was attracting two million hits every day, and visitors professed to being alternately fascinated and frightened by the film's carefully crafted imitation of real life.[16] The website proved such a powerful marketing tool that Artisan made the decision to bypass paying for any thought-to-be requisite television commercials—although the film did receive some TV play in the form of an hour-long special made for the Sci-Fi Channel entitled *Curse of the Blair Witch*, which again presented the case of the missing students, as well as the unearthed footage of their hike, as being real.[17] All that online buzz paid off handsomely when *The Blair Witch Project* opened theatrically on July 16; initially released on 27 screens, the film earned $1.6 million in its first weekend, a number that swelled to $140 million by the end of its wide release run.

To this day, *Blair Witch* remains one of the most profitable independent films ever released, and much of that success can be attributed to the innovative way it used the Internet to attract the kind of attention for free that the bigger studios generally pay top dollar for. Blairwitch.com didn't just blandly sell the movie; it offered visitors a unique experience that existed separately from the film while still reinforcing the title and central concept in people's minds. In the wake of *The Blair Witch Project*, the Internet's role in movie marketing underwent a reassessment in Hollywood's boardrooms, with a greater emphasis placed on incorporating user-friendly original content ranging from games and exclusive behind-the-scenes videos to galleries of artwork and fan competitions. Today, virtually every blockbuster released by a big studio has a major Internet presence that encompasses a tricked-out website along with a Facebook page, a Twitter feed, and even a Tumblr account. If *Space Jam* or *You've Got Mail* were made in the present, it wouldn't be enough for them to simply have a website; they'd be expected to provide a full-fledged web *experience*.

FILM FIRST FILE #1: FIVE NON-HORROR USES OF FOUND FOOTAGE

The Blair Witch Project popularized the use of the found-footage aesthetic in the horror genre, paving the way for an extensive collection of first-person point-of-view frightfests, among them *Paranormal Activity*, *The Last Exorcism*, and *V/H/S*. The following five films took a found-footage approach to genres outside of the horror realm, and while none scaled the box-office heights of *Blair Witch*, they do highlight the adaptability of the format.

Chronicle (Josh Trank, 2012)

Genre: Superhero adventure

Synopsis: After exploring a hole in the woods that houses a strange artifact, three teenagers emerge with new powers, including increased strength, enhanced mental abilities, and, best of all, flight.

Who's Holding the Camera: Primarily moody outcast Andrew (Dane DeHaan), who winds up proving that absolute power can corrupt absolutely.

Cloverfield (Matt Reeves, 2008)

Genre: Monster movie/alien invasion
Synopsis: A giant creature from another world attacks New York, decimating the Big Apple like Godzilla decimated Tokyo.
Who's Holding the Camera: Boisterous, blustery Hud (T. J. Miller), part of a group of twentysomething pals who attempt to make their way from the Lower East Side to Central Park without becoming monster food.

End of Watch (David Ayer, 2012)

Genre: Cop drama
Synopsis: A pair of swaggering, supremely self-confident beat cops kick ass and take names on the mean streets of Los Angeles, which makes them stars within their department and the targets of a trigger-happy drug cartel.
Who's Holding the Camera: Officer Brian Taylor (Jake Gyllenhaal), who is recording his on-the-beat exploits for a film class he's taking as part of his after-hours college career.

Interview with the Assassin (Neil Burger, 2002)

Genre: Paranoid thriller
Synopsis: With his death rapidly approaching, an elderly, cancer-stricken man makes a remarkable on-camera confession: on a sunny November day in 1963, he fired the bullet that killed John F. Kennedy.
Who's Holding the Camera: The professed assassin's neighbor, Ron (Dylan Haggerty), who becomes obsessed with debunking the old man's claim ... an obsession that ends up implicating him in another assassination attempt.

Project X (Nima Nourizadeh, 2012)

Genre: Teen comedy
Synopsis: Three popularity-challenged high-schoolers stage the ultimate house party, which ends up exceeding their wildest expectations for drug-, alcohol-, and sex-fueled debauchery.
Who's Holding the Camera: AV geek Dax (Dax Flame), who manages to keep a firm grip on the camera despite the apocalyptic partying happening around him.

FILM FIRST FILE #2: FIVE OTHER INTERNET-SAVVY FILMS

The commercial success enjoyed by *The Blair Witch Project* showed the slow-to-adapt Hollywood that there was great potential in this whole "Internet" thing. These five movies exploited the digital frontier in new—and mostly lucrative—ways.

A.I. Artificial Intelligence (Steven Spielberg, 2001)

The Steven Spielberg by way of Stanley Kubrick futuristic drama was shrouded in secrecy from the moment it started shooting up until the film finally unspooled in theaters. To amp up the mystery, Microsoft was enlisted to design an elaborate online game called "The Beast" that began with a clue embedded in both the film's trailer and its poster. Over the course of three months, players followed a story line that embedded them in the world of the film through fake Internet sites, e-mails, and even phone messages, but avoided giving away any key details of the plot. Besides generating lots of prerelease hype for *A.I.*, "The Beast" also served as one of the flagship titles in an entirely new genre of gaming—alternative reality games, which require players to use real-life tools to participate in a fictional story line.

King Kong (Peter Jackson, 2005)

Peter Jackson got a crash course in the benefits of engaging Internet fandom while bringing J. R. R. Tolkien's *The Lord of the Rings* trilogy to the big screen. He made an effort to be as fan accessible on his follow-up film, a remake of the 1933 adventure *King Kong*. Throughout the movie's production, Jackson recorded regular video diaries that were posted on the website KongIsKing.net, run by the same team that operated one of the premiere *Lord of the Rings* fansites, TheOneRing.net. (Neither site was officially affiliated with the movies they were covering, but Jackson worked with them and fed them exclusive material.) The practice of posting regular behind-the-scenes production diaries online was quickly adopted by other blockbusters, including Bryan Singer's *Superman Returns* (which staged a crossover video diary stunt with *King Kong*) and Zack Snyder's *300*.

Snakes on a Plane (David R. Ellis, 2006)

Long before Tumblr, "I Can Has Cheezburger," and Grumpy Cat, there was *Snakes on a Plane*, the title of a Samuel L. Jackson movie that pitted the star against . . . well, snakes on a plane. The confluence of absurd premise and equally absurd title sparked the imaginations of thousands of bloggers with an Internet connection and too much time on their hands. All manner of memes and spoofs sprang up, including parodic posters, trailers, and even a tune or two. Initially surprised by the online outburst, the studio went on to actively court the Internet's attention, believing that hundreds of millions of page views would translate into hundreds of millions of dollars at the box office. It didn't quite work out that way—the film ended its theatrical run with only $34 million in the bank—but the *Snakes* experience effectively encapsulated both the power and limitations of Internet buzz.

The Dark Knight (Christopher Nolan, 2008)

Most comic-book movies release the first image of their hero and/or villain in full regalia on the Internet to great fanfare. Not Christopher Nolan's second Batman feature, which made people work to see the first shot of Heath Ledger as the Dark Knight's most iconic nemesis, the Joker. A full year before the movie's release, two tie-in sites hit the Web, one of which trumpeted the political ambitions of one of the movie's other major characters, Harvey Dent, while the other was more clearly the Joker's handiwork. A user who added his or her e-mail address to the latter page received a message that would allow him or her to swap out a pixel that was part of the current image. When all the pixels were replaced, the Clown Prince of Crime's visage stood clearly revealed. It was one of the first signs that *The Dark Knight* wasn't going to be your ordinary superhero picture.

Veronica Mars (Rob Thomas, 2014)

Ever since his *noir*ish TV series about a high school private eye ended its three-season run, writer/director Rob Thomas hoped to bring his eponymous heroine back in a feature film. Frustrated by the lack of studio interest, Thomas turned to the crowdsourced funding site Kickstarter.com to help finance his dream. If the project raised $2 million in 30 days, the movie would become a reality, and as extra incentive, Thomas offered various prize packages for big-ticket pledgers. (For example, $200 bought you a signed poster, a Blu-ray/DVD edition, a T-shirt, and a copy of the shooting script, while one lucky individual willing to pledge $10,000 would get a small role in the movie with actual dialogue.) The film cleared its $2 million goal in the first 24 hours, and immediately fans of other canceled-too-soon TV shows started speculating which series Kickstarter would revive next.

Chapter 17

Crouching Tiger, Hidden Dragon
(2000)

The Film: Ang Lee's initiation into the *wuxia* genre fuses Western storytelling techniques with Eastern action sequences.

Originating some 2,000 years ago, *wuxia*—which translates as "martial hero" in its native China—is one of the world's oldest storytelling genres, although it has gone by different names since its inception. But the content hasn't radically changed: *wuxia* stories are traditionally epic tales of action and adventure set in China's distant past pitting highly skilled martial-arts warriors against the forces of oppression wherever they might exist. Unlike medieval European stories of virtuous knights on virtuous quests, these soldiers generally don't fight for a ruler. Instead, they wander the vast countryside as solitary figures, offering their services to whoever might need them.[1] Over the centuries, oral *wuxia* tales gave way to written stories and novels and, eventually, such contemporary forms of media as comic books, TV shows, movies. and even video games. No matter the medium, it's a dominant genre in East Asia, if slightly less so in Western territories.

Growing up in Taiwan in the '50s and '60s, future film director Ang Lee was exposed to *wuxia* from an early age, and he had a particular affection for the genre's movies[2]: action-packed, if sometimes technically inelegant productions with titles like *Dragon Inn* and *The One-Armed Swordsman*. He dreamed of making his own *wuxia* epic one day, but when filmmaking became his career, he wound up pursuing more down-to-earth subjects and genres, with a particular interest in stories about families. The critical and commercial success of his first three Taiwanese-produced features (1992's *Pushing Hands*, 1993's *The Wedding Banquet*, and 1995's *Eat Drink Man Woman*) brought him to Hollywood's attention, and between 1995 and

1999, he made a trio of studio productions, one of which (1995's *Sense and Sensibility*) received a Best Picture nomination.

Following the disappointing reception of Lee's 1999 Civil War–era drama *Ride with the Devil*, the director decided to try his luck abroad again, accepting an offer from the producer of his early Taiwanese films, Li-Kong Hsu, to helm *Crouching Tiger, Hidden Dragon*,[3] a full-scale martial-arts production that would be shot on location in China—his first time making a movie in that country. The source material was the fourth entry in a series of *wuxia* novels by celebrated author Wang Dulu, who had passed away in 1977. Working with his frequent collaborator James Schamus, Lee adapted the story into a vehicle for two of Asia's biggest action stars, Chow Yun-Fat and Michelle Yeoh, who respectively play Li Mu Bai and Yu Shu Lien, warriors who are fearless in battle but don't have the courage to admit their unspoken love for each other. And in the pivotal role of Jen Yu—the young woman who causes a heap of trouble by stealing Bai's powerful sword, the Green Destiny—Lee cast newcomer Zhang Ziyi.

But the primary star of *Crouching Tiger* were the gravity-defying action set-pieces Lee had planned, hiring legendary Hong Kong action-movie choreographer Yuen Woo-ping (who had recently worked his magic on an Asian-influenced American blockbuster called *The Matrix*) to execute them on-screen. An action novice, Lee got a crash course in *wuxia* spectacle courtesy of Yuen, and the battles they designed—beginning with a chase over the rooftops of Peking and ending with a swordfight atop swaying bamboo trees—are thrilling to watch. (Although Lee's inexperience did create some offscreen drama early on, after the bond company hired to guarantee the film's completion got nervous when the shooting of the first action sequence dragged on longer than initially anticipated, necessitating some serious reassurances on the director's part.)[4]

While *Crouching Tiger, Hidden Dragon* displays many of *wuxia*'s hallmarks, Lee specifically crafted the film's narrative with an eye toward Western audiences. In adapting the original novel to the screen, he and Schamus structured and expanded the plot in ways that a more traditional example of the genre would not. For example, where most *wuxia* productions open with a big action sequence, *Crouching Tiger* allows 15 minutes to elapse before the first blows are struck, instead devoting that time to exposition—an approach that Lee and Schamus have since joked about. ("[This is] what you have to sit through to get to the good stuff," Schamus cheekily remarks on a commentary track recorded for the film's DVD release.)[5] Additionally, conventional *wuxia* warriors wouldn't engage in the kinds of meaning-fraught personal conversations shared by Bai and Lien. Schamus put those words in the characters' mouths because they fit traditional Hollywood models of storytelling, where characters are expected to vocalize those kinds of feelings so that the audience is crystal clear about their motives and goals. In classic *wuxia* narratives, though, the characters wouldn't have addressed their emotions so directly. Schamus compared the liberties he took in writing the film's screenplay to "[a] Chinese writer [writing] some kind of contemporary *Law & Order* courtroom drama in which the DA comes into the judge's chambers and bows like nine times before he speaks to him. I wrote, basically, Martians."[6]

While *Crouching Tiger*'s emotional embellishments might seem alien within the context of the typical *wuxia* narrative, they also achieve the filmmakers' desired effect of easing international audiences, particularly those in America, into a genre that may not be as familiar to them as it is to viewers from China or Lee's native Taiwan. Furthermore, they serve to position Bai and Lien as a classic Ang Lee couple: throughout his career, the director has frequently been drawn to stories about love denied or suppressed, so bringing that dynamic to this particular genre—as he later would in his 2005 western *Brokeback Mountain*—is a natural storytelling choice on his part. These scenes also give both of the movie's stars the opportunity to show that their dramatic range extends beyond holding their own in action sequences. Yeoh in particular delivers a rich, nuanced performance as a woman who has spent a lifetime mastering her craft at the expense of her personal feelings. That's part of the reason she and Jen are destined to find themselves at odds, as the younger woman operates primarily on emotion; whether it's stealing the Green Destiny in the first place or impetuously challenging Lien to a duel, Jen's actions are dictated by her feelings in the moment, whereas Lien is careful and cautious to a fault.

With *Crouching Tiger, Hidden Dragon*, Lee finally realized his childhood goal of making a *wuxia* film, doing so in a way that united his two cultural backgrounds—the Eastern genre aficionado and the Western filmmaker. To be sure, the cross-cultural fusion didn't resonate with everybody; in China and Hong Kong, for example, viewership was noticeably low, with some complaining about the film's slower pace and the Cantonese-speaking star's lack of facility with the Mandarin dialogue.[7] But the film's success in other regions, including America, proved that worldwide audiences will turn out for a production—no matter its country of origin—that speaks the common language of spectacle.

The First: The combination of savvy marketing campaign and action-hungry audiences helped *Crouching Tiger, Hidden Dragon* become the first foreign-language film in history to cross the $100 million threshold at the American box office.

It's an odd quirk of the international movie distribution system that while Hollywood blockbusters are exported to multiplexes all over the world, many of the foreign films that are imported onto American screens head straight for the art house. Every year, the list of foreign productions that manage to score an American release consists primarily of film festival favorites, new film from directors with proven followings in the United States (think Pedro Almodóvar or Michael Haneke), and highly targeted genre movies (particularly horror and action releases) that have similarly built-in audiences. Even when a significant international box-office hit makes its way to the United States, it rarely, if ever, sees the kind of wide release that Hollywood fare receives on a weekly basis.

The reason for this state of affairs begins with the fact that most of the larger American movie studios have international distribution arms—or deals in place with prominent international distributors—that possess the financial muscle necessary to give their products a high-profile release in almost every major movie market. (China remains a notable exception, with the government holding tight restrictions over the number of international productions that are allowed onto domestic screens every year.) In contrast, many overseas companies don't possess built-in channels into American theaters, instead having to reach stateside audiences by partnering with a U.S.-based distributor. And, by and large, the companies that specialize in bringing foreign films to U.S. audiences are specialty distributors like Fox Searchlight, IFC Films, and Sony Pictures Classics (the company that released *Crouching Tiger, Hidden Dragon* in America), which employ platform releases with the majority of their titles. Under this approach, the films open in a handful of markets and then expand outwards over the course of several weeks or months or don't, depending on how the box office in those initial markets goes. So where international audiences can see a big American film in almost any theater, U.S. moviegoers have fewer screens on which to see foreign releases. A market for foreign releases certainly exists, but it's generally been small . . . and getting smaller.

Beyond the business aspect of how foreign films are released in America, there's also the very real fact that the domestic audience for international movies is limited to begin with. Where Hollywood has big stars (Tom Cruise, Will Smith) and even bigger name-brand franchises (*Iron Man, Die Hard*) that are familiar to moviegoers around the world, the most high-profile actor in India's Bollywood industry or the most successful action movie franchise in Hong Kong would only be recognizable to a certain cross-section of the U.S. market. Even though both Chow Yun-Fat and Michelle Yeoh had appeared in several Hollywood films (he in *The Replacement Killers* and she in the James Bond adventure *Tomorrow Never Dies*) prior to the stateside release of *Crouching Tiger, Hidden Dragon*, they weren't immediately recognizable in America to the point where Sony Pictures Classics could tempt a sizable audience into the theater by simply placing their names above the title on a poster. Neither could they just hype the film's association with the *wuxia* tradition or connection to Wang Dulu's novels, both elements that would have been highly marketable in Asia but significantly less so across the Pacific. Finally, the language barrier was a significant hurdle to overcome; most American movies that are released overseas are usually dubbed into the local language, but it's rare that foreign films are given similar treatment before opening stateside. In fact, most domestic distributors and consumers of foreign-language features prefer subtitles to dubbing, a choice that may preserve the original intent of the filmmaker and performers, but also limits the audience appeal as reading subtitles is not a mainstream moviegoing habit. (Lee himself is no fan of dubbing and resisted releasing a dubbed version of *Crouching Tiger* for its U.S. run.)[8] Still, Sony Pictures Classics knew that they had a movie that would translate well to the American market provided they found the right way to sell it.

One guaranteed hook that the company could rely on was *Crouching Tiger*'s status as a film festival favorite. The movie premiered at Cannes in May 2000, and the first screening was met with cheers and extended applause. A flood of rave reviews followed and carried the film along to its second major platform at that year's Toronto International Film Festival. The ecstatic word of mouth from these screenings would be enough to galvanize the usual audience for foreign fare, but Sony—and Lee as well—hoped to extend the movie's reach to markets where moviegoers didn't typically think to seek out non-Hollywood productions. That's where those gravity-defying, crowd-pleasing martial-arts sequences came in handy. It didn't hurt that *Crouching Tiger* was released a year after *The Matrix* popularized some of the Hong Kong action techniques that Lee employed and the set pieces from that blockbuster were still fresh in moviegoers' minds. In the run-up to *Crouching Tiger*'s release, the tone of the coverage focused heavily on those combat sequences, giving spectacle-hungry audiences incentive to seek the film out.

That approach worked. *Crouching Tiger, Hidden Dragon* opened in December 2000, right in the middle of the crowded holiday moviegoing season. As usual, Sony Pictures Classics started small with the film, releasing it in just a few markets. The demand was there from the beginning; by the end of its second week of release, it had earned over $2 million playing on just 31 screens. Over the next few months, it traveled to more cities and encountered an equally enthusiastic response. A nomination and eventual victory in the Foreign Language category at that year's Oscars further elevated its profile. By its fourth month in theaters, the movie crossed the $100 million line at the box office, the first foreign film to hit a number virtually every Hollywood blockbuster is expected to reach or else be classified as a failure.

Unfortunately, *Crouching Tiger*'s box-office feat has yet to be repeated in the decade since its release. In fact, no other foreign-language feature released stateside since Lee's film has come within striking distance of $100 million, even movies that promise equally visceral and dynamic action sequences. Meanwhile, the titanic worldwide grosses that Hollywood spectacles regularly earn has made the American industry more dependent on overseas moviegoers than ever before. Much of the reason for this disparity can be chalked up to the difficult climate facing all specialty releases—a category that includes foreign films, independent films, and documentaries—in the contemporary American moviegoing marketplace. The rise of alternate viewing options, from DVD to video on demand, has meant that these films can still potentially find sizable audiences, but rarely in theaters. The result is that foreign films are increasingly marginalized on U.S. screens, receiving token and often very limited theatrical releases before arriving on DVD or streaming video services like Netflix where they'll do the bulk of their business.

There are exceptions, of course. In 2013, Lionsgate scored a theatrical hit with the Mexican comedy, *Instructions Not Included*, which the studio targeted directly at the Latino audience, But again, the film wasn't advertised as—and thus didn't become—a crossover success with non-Spanish speakers. Rather than try to appeal to a wide swath of audiences as Sony Pictures Classics did with *Crouching Tiger*, distributors of foreign releases are now more commonly selling their product to specific niches. In fact, had it been released after 2010, there's a very real chance that—even with the same combination of ecstatic reviews, compelling trailers, and action-movie hook— *Crouching Tiger, Hidden Dragon* wouldn't have achieved its singular success. At the time, its appeal transcended the usual challenges facing foreign films in America. In the current climate, it might get lost in translation.

FILM FIRST FILE #1: FOUR OTHER ASIAN ACTION MOVIES THAT LEFT THEIR MARK ON HOLLYWOOD

Crouching Tiger, Hidden Dragon may currently hold the title of America's highest-grossing Asian action film (not to mention its highest-grossing foreign-language film, period), but it's not the only one to have had a major impact on these shores. The following films also made a significant contribution to Hollywood's action movie assembly line.

Enter the Dragon (Robert Clouse, 1973)

Plot: Experienced fighter Lee (Bruce Lee) agrees to participate in a martial-arts tournament in order to spy on its organizer, a major league crime lord.

Background: After a largely unsatisfying stint in Hollywood, actor and martial artist Bruce Lee returned to Hong Kong and starred in a series of action movies that became enormous hits throughout Asia and attracted a significant American following as well. Lee's star burned so brightly, Warner Bros. agreed to finance this feature in partnership with one of Hong Kong's leading production companies, Golden Harvest—the first time a Hollywood studio ever funded a Hong Kong–made film.[9] The movie was an immediate critical and commercial hit in both Asia and America, but Lee himself was unable to enjoy its success, passing away suddenly six days before its release.

Lasting Legacy: In some ways, Lee's fame only increased after his untimely death. To this day, he continues to be recognized as one of the all-time great action stars the world over, and his movies—particularly *Enter the Dragon*—have inspired countless homages, rip-offs, and parodies. Additionally, Hollywood has only built upon the inroads it paved into Asian film production with *Dragon*; for example, such recent studio blockbusters as *The Karate Kid* remake and *Iron Man 3* have been joint American/Chinese productions.

The Killer (John Woo, 1989)

Plot: A hitman (Chow Yun-Fat) is forced to team up with a cop (Danny Lee) when he's double-crossed by his employers.

Background: John Woo had been a mainstay in the Hong Kong movie industry since the '70s, but it was this highly stylized, surprisingly emotional action drama that brought both him and his frequent leading man Chow Yun-Fat to the attention of international audiences. It was the first exposure many viewers outside Hong Kong had to the heightened approach to violence and gunplay that had become a distinct staple of the territory's cinema. The melodramatic flourishes in the storytelling also set it apart from the typical action fare being produced in America at the time.

Lasting Legacy: On the strength of *The Killer* and 1992's *Hard Boiled*, Woo made the jump to Hollywood with 1993's *Hard Target*, the first in a wave of Hong Kong directors who would be hired to helm American action movies during that decade, among them Ringo Lam and Tsui Hark. Woo's distinctive style also had a profound impact on American action films, influencing such directors as Quentin Tarantino and Andy and Lana Wachowski.

Rumble in the Bronx (Stanley Tong, 1995)

Plot: On a trip to New York, Keung (Jackie Chan) manages to accidentally run afoul of both a street gang *and* a local crime syndicate.

Background: A major movie star across Asia for well over a decade, Jackie Chan entered into *Rumble in the Bronx* specifically targeting the U.S. market (hence the New York setting . . . although the film was actually shot in Vancouver). *Bronx* was acquired by the Warner Bros.–owned New Line and released in February 1996—a full year after its Asian premiere. It topped the box-office charts in its opening weekend, the first Hong Kong film to accomplish that feat. (Even *Crouching Tiger* never reached the number-one spot.)

Lasting Legacy: Chan went on to star in such successful Hollywood films as the *Rush Hour* series and *The Karate Kid* and remains a major media personality in his native country and abroad. His success also inspired Hollywood to import other Asian action stars like Jet Li and Michelle Yeoh.

Hero (Zhang Yimou, 2002)

Plot: A swordsman (Jet Li) protects a powerful warlord from three assassins.

Background: Produced in the wake of *Crouching Tiger, Hidden Dragon*, Zhang Yimou's *Hero* was, at the time, the most expensive film ever made in China.[10] Like *Crouching Tiger*—a film in some ways it almost seems to be competing with—it's a visually lush take on the traditional *wuxia* genre, with a rich color scheme and beautifully choreographed set pieces. An international hit, the film did inspire some controversy regarding its seeming endorsement of China's centrally controlled Communist government.

Lasting Legacy: The film grossed over $50 million during its American theatrical release and became the second Asian martial-arts film (after *Crouching Tiger, Hidden Dragon*) to receive an Oscar nomination for Best Foreign Language Feature.

FILM FIRST FILE #2: THE TOP TEN FOREIGN LANGUAGE RELEASES IN THE UNITED STATES[11]

1. *Crouching Tiger, Hidden Dragon* (Ang Lee, 2000; Taiwan): $128 million
2. *Life Is Beautiful* (Robert Benigni, 1997; Italy): $57.5 million
3. *Hero* (Zhang Yimou, 2002; China): $53.7 million
4. *Instructions Not Included* (Eugenio Derbez, 2013; Mexico): $44.4
5. *Pan's Labyrinth* (Guillermo del Toro, 2006; Mexico): $37.6 million
6. *Amélie* (Jean-Pierre Jeunet, 2001; France): $33.2 million
7. *Jet Li's Fearless* (Ronny Yu, 2006; China): $24.6 million
8. *Il Postino* (Michael Radford, 1994; Italy): $21.8 million
9. *Like Water for Chocolate* (Alfonso Arau, 1992; Mexico): $21.6 million
10. *La Cage aux Folles* (Edouard Molinaro, 1978; France): $20.4 million

Chapter 18

The Lord of the Rings Trilogy (2001–2003)

The Film: Don't think of Peter Jackson's dazzling fantasy spectacle as three individual films—think of it as one movie told in three movements.

Although it was released theatrically in three separate installments spread out over three years, *The Lord of the Rings*,[1] Peter Jackson's sprawling adaptation of J. R. R. Tolkien's even more sprawling landmark work of fantasy fiction is designed to be consumed in one gulp. Whether that gulp takes the form of a single 9-to-11-hour marathon viewing session (the exact timing varies based on if you've elected to watch the original theatrical versions or the longer extended editions) or spread out over the course of three nights or even three weeks is up to the viewer. The point is to think of it as a single continuous narrative rather than a collection of distinct narratives that involve some of the same characters and story points, as is the case with most blockbuster trilogies from the *Indiana Jones* series to the *Iron Man* films. In that way—and in lots of others, of course—Jackson is very much honoring the source material; Tolkien himself had intended for *The Lord of the Rings* to be released as a one-volume text (with its companion book, *The Silmaril-lion*, published as a second volume), but his publisher divided it into three books—*The Fellowship of the Ring* (released in England in July 1954), *The Two Towers* (November 1954), and *The Return of the King* (October 1955) —in order to hold down the costs of publishing and selling the author's mammoth tome about the all-powerful One Ring and the fantastical menagerie of hobbits, human, dwarves, and elves whose lives it touches.[2]

Economics was also the primary reason behind the decision to split the long-in-the-works live-action movie version into three films, as neither Hollywood's existing production nor distribution structure could support the wide release of a single 10-hour film. Indeed, the industry had already proven barely capable of supporting previous and considerably shorter attempts at bringing Tolkien's medieval-inspired Middle-earth to the big screen. In the late 1960s, British director John Boorman distilled the three volumes into a single film that United Artists was poised to make but then was unable to afford.[3] Animator Ralph Bakshi got closer almost a decade later, releasing the first of two planned animated features—which spanned *Fellowship* and *The Two Towers*—but the studio (UA again) declined to make the second.[4]

When Jackson set his sights on *Rings* in the early '90s, he was prepared to settle for a shorter version as well. Having prevailed upon Harvey Weinstein, then-head of Miramax—which had handled the American release of his fourth feature, *Heavenly Creatures*—to help him secure the rights to the books from producer Saul Zaentz, the New Zealand-born and bred director agreed to make a pair of three-hour films. Those two movies almost became one when Weinstein experienced a case of price tag–inspired cold feet and demanded that Jackson scale back his vision, which the director had no intention of doing. The clash led Miramax to put the movie in turnaround, with Weinstein giving Jackson only three weeks to find another studio willing to foot the bill.[5] Enter New Line, which not only agreed that *The Lord of the Rings* should be two films—they wanted Jackson to expand it to three.[6]

With New Line's blessing—and, more importantly, its cash—Jackson shot *The Lord of the Rings* as one movie, with principal photography for the entire production taking place in one 15-month chunk on location in New Zealand. But the theatrical release of the saga was staggered, with one three-hour installment arriving in multiplexes each December between 2001 and 2003—a strategy dictated first and foremost by the realities of theatrical exhibition, where three hours is already past the norm for most wide mainstream releases. At the same time, it proved a financial boon for New Line in that it allowed the studio to profit from each individual release, thus upping their overall take. It was also a creative benefit for Jackson, who used the annual gap between movies to reshoot and reshape material as need be and, of course, complete the complex and extensive special effects. And from moviegoers' perspective, there was the pleasant buzz that accompanied the heightened anticipation of waiting 12 months to see the continuing adventures of hobbits Frodo (Elijah Wood) and Sam (Sean Astin), as well as king-in-training Aragorn (Viggo Mortensen), wizened wizard Gandalf (Ian McKellen), elf and dwarf odd couple Legolas (Orlando Bloom) and Gimli (Jonathan Rhys-Davies), and all the other major and minor inhabitants of Middle-earth.

More than a decade removed from its initial pass through movie theaters, *The Lord of the Rings* no longer needs to be viewed as three separate films. Individual theaters can and do program marathon screenings of the entire feature, while home viewers can take their DVD box sets down from the shelf and consume the adventures in a single weekend or a single day. And— despite the time commitment it demands—this is really the ideal way to watch Jackson's entire epic and best appreciate its structure, pacing, and immersive storytelling. The key to the movie's overall success is the way it builds its world from the inside out, starting off small and contained and gradually expanding its horizons and its borders, yet consistently staying in lockstep with its large cast of characters rather than rushing ahead of them. Following an expertly condensed prologue that distills thousands of years of dense history into roughly ten digestible minutes, *Fellowship of the Ring* sets viewers down in the idyllic community of Hobbiton and introduces us to our soon-to-be ringbearer, Frodo. It's subsequently through him that we meet the other major players in this narrative, who will go on to establish the titular fellowship before going their separate ways as the story shifts into its next act.

It's a sign of Jackson's confidence in the actors' characterizations and the way that he and his cowriters Fran Walsh and Philippa Boyens have adapted source material that he allows this initial three-hour stretch to be so intimate and small scale compared to what comes later. That's not to suggest that there isn't a grandeur to *Fellowship*; the spectacular New Zealand locations and lavish production design lend it an impressive sense of scale. But it's also carefully contained scale, as the journey that the fellowship of nine embark on as well as the obstacles they encounter along the way rarely dwarf the capabilities of their group. It's only after they split up that the threats grow larger, the enemies more powerful and more numerous, the challenges more insurmountable, and their need for new allies greater.

Keeping the first part of the story contained allows Jackson to build outward organically; if Frodo served as our primary guide in *Fellowship*, by *The Two Towers* the viewer knows the surviving members of the group well enough for each of them to be capable of introducing new story lines, locations, and characters. And by the time we reach *The Return of the King*— where the very fate of Middle-earth hangs in the balance—having those firmly entrenched multiple perspectives gives Jackson the freedom to cut from setting to setting as the War of the Ring rages on, allowing the viewer to take in the totality of what's at stake without losing track of individual characters. There's a very real sense that we've become participants rather than mere observers in this world, and that level of immersion speaks to how effectively Jackson has paced his saga, allowing the narrative to flow naturally from minute to minute and movie to movie.

Although the three installments are made to function in concert, if one were forced to pick a favorite, there are compelling arguments to be made for why any one part might stand out from the other two. Certainly, *Fellowship* benefits from the thrill that comes with being introduced to Middle-earth and embarking on what promises to be a grand adventure, before the traumatic reality of what lies ahead really sets in. (Savor every one of Frodo's smiles in *Fellowship*, because you won't be seeing them again until the final act of the entire saga.) But *The Two Towers* boasts the trilogy's single-best battle sequence (the extended siege at Helm's Deep) as well as its most fascinating character (the ring-obsessed madman Gollum, played to perfection by Andy Serkis) and a running thematic meditation on the nature of heroism that's summed up in a moving speech delivered by Sam in the closing moments. As for *The Return of the King*, it's the most purely emotional entry of the saga, filled with triumphs, failures, and teary farewells to favorite characters.

In the end, though, it's the cumulative power of the entire journey—rather than any single stage—that makes *The Lord of the Rings* resonate so deeply with audiences. That's what Tolkien understood and why Jackson sought to preserve the author's intended structure: one story that's only divided into three sections primarily for commercial, rather than strictly creative, reasons —reasons that, frankly, no longer need apply. Today you can sit down to read or watch the entirety of *The Lord of the Rings* and experience all of the adventure, joy, and heartbreak contained in its epic narrative at your own preferred pace.

The First: *The Return of the King*'s Best Picture victory at the Oscars was a first for a fantasy film, as well as a new kind of blockbuster trilogy.

Going into the 76th Annual Academy Awards—which were held on February 29, 2004, at Hollywood's Kodak Theater—the main question wasn't "Will *The Return of the King* win any Oscars?"; it was "How many Oscars will *The Return of the King* win?" Each of the previous installments had been nominated in multiple categories (including Best Picture) and won a number of statues, primarily in the technical categories like Best Visual Effects and Best Makeup. But the big prizes—Best Director, Best Screenplay, and Best Picture among them—had eluded the series thus far, and there was a palpable sense amongst the media and the industry at large that voters were simply waiting for the final installment in order to honor the trilogy as a collective achievement.

That supposition proved correct. *The Return of the King* received 11 nominations and won 11 Oscars, including Director and Picture. (The series was continually overlooked in the acting categories; of the large ensemble, only Ian McKellen ever received a nomination—as Supporting Actor for *Fellowship* at the 2001 awards—but lost to Jim Broadbent and was never singled out again.) That made the film only the second sequel after 1974's *The Godfather Part II* to be named Best Picture (the third if you choose to count 1991's *The Silence of the Lambs*, which is technically the second film to be made about Dr. Hannibal Lecter following 1986's *Manhunter*, but the two movies aren't directly linked) and the first-ever "Part 3" to win the top prize.

More significantly, it was the first fantasy film to be crowned Best Picture, a genre that—along with science fiction—had historically been overlooked by the Oscars, even when individual films found an audience beyond the typical collection of freaks and geeks that the industry assumed was the primary demographic for those movies. (Perhaps the most famous example of this was when George Lucas's mega-hit *Star Wars* received a Best Picture nomination in 1977, but Woody Allen's *Annie Hall* emerged victorious. On the other hand, while that may not have been the popular call, it was the correct one.) Indeed, if one wanted to place a demarcating line where so-called geek and nerd culture began to be taken seriously by Hollywood for its artistic, as well as its commercial, potential, *The Lord of the Rings* stands as a useful reference point. Viewers who didn't typically consider themselves the target audience for swords-and-sorcery tales were nevertheless swept away by Jackson's presentation of Tolkien's Middle-earth saga for reasons beyond its entertainment value.

There are a host of reasons why this particular fantasy managed to cross demographic borders other films of its type had failed to traverse. Certainly, one of the popular theories is that the series' presentation of a fractured, unsettled nation coming together to combat a growing threat resonated with moviegoers in the immediate aftermath of September 11, 2001.[7] (The first installment, *Fellowship of the Ring*, arrived in theaters almost exactly three months later on December 19.) There's also the fact that the books themselves had been a pop-culture touchstone for decades and enjoyed a readership that went far beyond fantasy devotees. And one shouldn't minimize the contribution of New Zealand, which provided the exotic backdrop necessary to transport audiences to Tolkien's vividly described realm. The natural beauty of that country, coupled with the exacting detail of the sets, costumes, makeup, and special effects created by Jackson and his team at Weta Workshop—the special-effects house founded in the late 1980s by the director's friend and collaborator Richard Taylor—lent the film's version of Middle-earth a rich, lived-in feel that distinguished it from more artificial-seeming cinematic fantasy worlds like those glimpsed in such movies as *The Beastmaster* or *Willow*. Fairly or not, the genre had a history of being dismissed by a wide audience as cheesy and silly, in part due to the challenge of creating an authentic environment that's filled with so many *inauthentic* things, be they elves and wizards or dragons and hobbits. *The Lord of the Rings* is a fantasy, yes, but the world it depicts feels all too real, and that's what moviegoers—and Oscar voters—responded to.

Still, *The Return of the King*'s Best Picture victory wasn't primarily a case of the Academy begrudgingly getting around to recognizing the artistry of the fantasy genre. It was more a case of voters' genuine admiration and respect for the mammoth undertaking of making three back-to-back blockbusters and the new technical ground that Jackson and his crew broke along the way. Although it's been a long-standing practice for a pair of movies to be shot at the same time (*Superman* and *Superman II* were filmed back-to-back, as were *Back to the Future Parts II* and *III*, *The Matrix Reloaded* and *The Matrix Revolutions*, and *Pirates of the Caribbean: Dead Man's Chest* and *At World's End*), *The Lord of the Rings* was the first instance where a spectacle-driven, hugely expensive Hollywood trilogy was shot in one go, to the tune of almost $300 million.[8] (Polish director Krzysztof Kieślowski's renowned *Three Colors* trilogy had been shot back-to-back in the mid-'90s, but the scale of that production was considerably smaller.) Due to the excessive amount of time and money required for making three films at once, it wasn't a feat that was repeated anytime soon . . . at least, not until Jackson himself returned to Middle-earth a decade later to make another trilogy of fantasy adventures based on the predecessor to *The Lord of the Rings*, Tolkien's 1937 novel *The Hobbit*. In both cases, Jackson's achievement was showing that it was possible to shoot three large-scale movies in one super-sized production. And as the major studios increasingly look for ways to maximize production schedules to fill up their release calendars, it's entirely possible to imagine a case where another three-film blockbuster franchise goes before cameras all at once.

Of course, pulling off that monumental task requires a cast and crew as famously dedicated as the *Rings* staff as well as a creative partner as resourceful and innovative as Weta Workshop, which almost overnight became a worldwide leader in visual effects based on its heralded work for these films. The company realized the various locations and races of Middle-earth through a mixture of practical and digital wizardry that included traditional standbys like miniatures, as well as then-cutting-edge technology like Massive, a piece of computer software specifically designed to manufacture large crowds of realistic-looking computer-generated characters.[9]

By far, Weta's most significant technical achievement for *The Lord of the Rings* films were the advancements it made in the realm of motion capture, a style of computer animation that involves a recording of a physical person or object that is then translated into the digital space and used as the basis for a computer-generated three-dimensional person or object. (These recording sessions typically take place on a soundstage with the live actor wearing a specialized suit covered with reflective balls that allow the camera to "capture" his or her movements, and that information can be passed along to the computer.)[10] Initially developed for use in video games, motion capture entered live-action cinematic territory with *Star Wars: Episode I—The Phantom Menace*, via one of the film's most polarizing characters, Jar Jar Binks. But the second installment of *The Lord of the Rings* series, *The Two Towers*, became the first film to feature a believable motion-capture character, who could persuasively share the frame with flesh-and-blood actors. Jackson turned to motion capture as a way to successfully realize the pivotal character of Gollum, once an ordinary hobbit physically and mentally corrupted by his long possession of the One Ring. Leery about rendering Gollum as the kind of computer-animated critter that might star in a Pixar movie, Jackson enlisted actor Andy Serkis to perform the role opposite the other actors while clad in a motion-capture suit and then handed that footage over to digital artists to animate.[11] The results wowed moviegoers and filmmakers (James Cameron, for one, has cited Gollum as being the catalyst for convincing him to make *Avatar* with motion-capture technology),[12] particularly in the film's standout scene—which was actually written and directed by Jackson's partner, Fran Walsh[13]—in which the two sides of Gollum's split personality carry on a spirited debate with each other. This sequence speaks to the creative possibilities of motion capture when there's a real (and really good) actor performing the role underneath layers of computer animation. It's also yet another sign of how effectively Jackson and Weta employ technology in creating their fantasy world. Though he's a fantastical creature, Gollum's motivations, personality, and even appearance feel grounded in the reality we see unfolding on-screen.

For now, at least, *The Return of the King* remains an Oscar anomaly as no subsequent fantasy feature has followed its path to a Best Picture victory or even a nomination. (That includes the first installment in Jackson's second Middle-earth trilogy, *The Hobbit: An Unexpected Journey.*) When viewed in the context of the Academy's history, though, the movie's win seems like less of an outlier. Going all the way back to the very first Best Picture winner, 1927's *Wings*, that particular statue has frequently—though not always, especially in recent years—gone to the film that exemplifies the classic Hollywood ideal of impressive spectacle (often achieved with new advancements in technology and filmmaking methods) balanced by a great story. And that's the tradition that *King*—and the entire *Lord of the Rings* cycle—fits neatly into. The movie's victory may have been a first for its particular brand of fantasy, but it still belongs to a long line of larger-than-life fantasies that remain a vital part of the Hollywood landscape.

FILM FIRST FILE #1: FIVE MEMORABLE CINEMATIC FANTASY WORLDS

The Lord of the Rings brought J. R. R. Tolkien's Middle-earth to spectacular life using New Zealand (and more than a few practical and computer-generated sets) as a backdrop. While the following five cinematic fantasy realms don't share the same majestic Oceanic landscape, they are each transporting in their own way.

Dinohattan

Film: *Super Mario Bros.* (Annabel Jankel and Rocky Morton, 1993)

Distinguishing Features: The only inhabitable city on a parallel, dino-human hybrid–populated version of Earth (the result of a meteoroid colliding with the Blue Planet), Dinohattan boasts the same collection of skyscrapers and dive bars that grace its parallel namesake, but far more crime, urban decay, and freaky-looking Goombas.

Heroes: The missing heir to the royal line; two wisecracking, color-coded Brooklyn plumbers and brothers.

Villains: King Koopa, the self-appointed dictator of the realm and his army of the aforementioned Goombas.

Fantasia

Film: *The NeverEnding Story* (Wolfgang Petersen, 1984)

Distinguishing Features: The dreary Swamps of Sadness; an expansive Sea of Possibilities; and a resplendent Ivory Tower where the land's ruler, the Childlike Empress, surveys her territory.

Heroes: The aforementioned Empress, the heroic Plains People, and a furry doglike dragon.

Villains: A faceless, formless devourer of worlds known only as The Nothing.

Florin

Film: *The Princess Bride* (Rob Reiner, 1987)

Distinguishing Features: Fire swamps, oceans filled with fleets of dread pirates, the towering Cliffs of Insanity, and torture pits hidden at the bottom of large trees.

Heroes: A stable boy masquerading as a pirate, a lovely princess-to-be, a swordsman with severe daddy issues, and a giant with a heart of gold.

Villains: A vainglorious prince, his six-fingered sidekick, a kidnapper with an inconceivable ego, and rodents of unusual sizes.

The Labyrinth

Film: *Labyrinth* (Jim Henson, 1986)

Distinguishing Features: Brain-teasing puzzles, the Bog of Eternal Stench, drugged peaches, and a castle with stairs that were apparently built by M. C. Escher.

Heroes: A brave teenage girl; a surly dwarf; a foxy, one-eyed knight; and a hulking beast who isn't as scary as he looks.

Villains: A Goblin King with killer fashion sense of fantastic hair.

Asgard

Film: *Thor* (Kenneth Branagh, 2011) and *Thor: The Dark World* (Alan Taylor, 2013)

Distinguishing Features: Ornate castles, throne rooms as golden as the sky, and a closely guarded rainbow bridge that link Asgard to the nine other realms that make up the Norse world.

Heroes: A brave, virtuous king and his hammer-wielding favorite son.

Villains: The king's *other* son, a duplicitous, power-hungry usurper.

FILM FIRST FILE #2: FIVE UNLIKELY CONTEMPORARY BEST PICTURE WINNERS

As strange as it was to see a fantasy film take home Oscar night's biggest award, *The Return of the King* was, in many ways, a more traditional Best Picture choice than the five following winners culled from the past four decades of Academy Awards history.

Rocky (Sylvester Stallone, 1976)

Fellow Nominees: *All the President's Men, Bound for Glory, Network, Taxi Driver*

Although the Italian Stallion probably should have been KO'd by heavy hitters like Alan J. Pakula's journalistic classic, Sidney Lumet's bold social satire, and Martin Scorsese's galvanizing portrait of alienation, when the final bell rang on Oscar night, the underdog *Rocky* was unexpectedly still standing. No boxing movie had won the Academy's version of the heavyweight belt before, and none would again until Clint Eastwood stepped into the ring almost 30 years later with *Million Dollar Baby*.

The Silence of the Lambs (Jonathan Demme, 1991)

Fellow Nominees: *Beauty and the Beast, Bugsy, JFK, The Prince of Tides*

Warren Beatty's star power would seem to have given his gangster drama *Bugsy* the edge, but in the end, Bugsy Malone proved no match for Hannibal the Cannibal. *The Silence of the Lambs* overcame an early February release date as well as gruesome subject matter to become one of the few thrillers— and, arguably, the first and only horror movie to date—to be named Best Picture.

Shakespeare in Love (John Madden, 1998)

Fellow Nominees: *Elizabeth, Life Is Beautiful, Saving Private Ryan, The Thin Red Line*

With rapturous reviews, enormous box office, and weighty subject matter, Steven Spielberg's World War II epic seemed unbeatable going into the 1998 awards season. In the end, voters proved more susceptible to the wit and wisdom of the Bard's words as filtered through *Shakespeare in Love* screenwriter Tom Stoppard's pen.

Slumdog Millionaire (Danny Boyle, 2008)

Fellow Nominees: *The Curious Case of Benjamin Button, Frost/Nixon, Milk, The Reader*

The hyperkinetic tale of an orphan from India's slums seemed like a longshot alongside such weightier fare as a biopic of slain gay civil rights pioneer Harvey Milk and a David Fincher–helmed adaptation of an F. Scott Fitzgerald story. But those movies never got voters dancing in the aisles the way that *Slumdog*'s uplifting narrative and propulsive Bollywood beat did.

The Artist (Michel Hazanavicius, 2011)

Fellow Nominees: *The Descendants, Extremely Loud and Incredibly Close, The Help, Hugo, Midnight in Paris, Moneyball, The Tree of Life, War Horse*

Back at the dawn of the Academy Awards in the late 1920s, a silent comedy would be a natural contender—not so much in the twenty-first century. Still, *The Artist*'s loving re-creation of that vanished past wound up trumping all the tears George Clooney shed in the film's closest competitor, the present-day-set *The Descendants*.

Chapter 19

Funny Ha Ha (2002)

The Film: Mumblecore's founding film is what a glossy Hollywood romantic comedy might look like if it took place in the real world.

Originally shot in 2001 and first screened in 2002, Andrew Bujalski's *Funny Ha Ha*[1] is a movie that straddles two eras. On the one hand, it heralded the arrival of a new generation of independent filmmakers eager to capture the rhythms and hang-ups of twenty-first-century life as they knew it. At the same time, stylistically the film possesses the scruffy, homemade quality of the indie cinema of the '80s and '90s—films like Jim Jarmusch's *Stranger Than Paradise*, Richard Linklater's *Slacker*, and Kevin Smith's *Clerks*—largely due to Bujalski's decision to shoot on 16mm film. By the time *Funny Ha Ha* scored a limited theatrical release in 2005 (a delay that was due more to the challenges of independent film distribution rather than to the specific quality of the movie), the digital revolution had taken hold, and the indie filmmakers that followed in Bujalski's wake were generally opting for high-def video over film stock, due to its lower cost and greater flexibility. (When asked about his choice to use that format, Bujalski replied, "I love 16mm. It also happens to be the format that I'm trained in. . . . And, truthfully, I'm just not very knowledgeable about video. . . . I think that *Funny Ha Ha* would have felt extremely different on video—the loose, improv-y aspects I think would be much more easily dismissed. 'Oh, this is just a bunch of kids screwing around.' Whereas the inherent painterly quality of film lends a credibility."[2] The gap between the movie's formal elements and its content makes watching it an instructive experience; while the millennial characters are firmly rooted in the then-present, the film looks as though it was made in an earlier decade and beamed into the future.

One element that does feel timeless is the story, which is the same basic scenario that's fueled dozens of studio-backed star vehicles over the decades—the unlucky-in-love single girl who has to choose between some very different boys. The girl in question here is Marnie (Kate Dollenmayer), a recent college graduate who isn't quite sure how to navigate life in the real world. Since leaving school, she's been unable to find either a steady job or a steady boyfriend that she's truly passionate about. There are three relationship candidates in her orbit, though, starting with Alex (Christian Rudder), the funny, charming guy she's had a crush on for some time. The only problem is that he's just getting out of a relationship and has a tendency to do odd things . . . like getting married on a whim. And then there's Dave (Myles Paige), the steady, sturdy boyfriend of one of her close pals that may carry a torch for her as well, seeing as how they once shared a kiss. Bringing up the rear is Mitchell (Bujalski himself), the gawky geek that she worked with briefly at a temp job and who practically fell over himself trying to ask her out. Over the course of the film, Marnie drifts from guy to guy, weighing their pros and cons as potential partners and being judged by them in return.

The broad outline of this story could be (and has been) used as fodder for Hollywood vehicles for glamorous leading ladies—think Julia Roberts, Reese Witherspoon, or Kate Hudson. (The setup also can't help but recall Spike Lee's debut feature *She's Gotta Have It*, although Marnie is a very different personality type than Nola Darling and *Funny Ha Ha* has a far less provocative attitude towards sex and sexuality.) Those movies would most likely also involve a series of comic misunderstandings, tearful confessions, and, of course, the requisite climax involving the heroine pursuing her chosen lover to a public place—probably the airport—for a grand declaration of love. *Funny Ha Ha* offers none of those heightened rom-com shenanigans. In fact, it doesn't even end with Marnie making a definitive choice among one of the three guys. Instead, the film moves at the pace of real life; there are no outside forces pushing the narrative forward or manufactured obstacles put in the characters' way.

The unhurried rhythm Bujalski seeks to establish is also reflected in the way conversations between the characters are allowed to drag on or taper off suddenly, without obvious start or end points. These conversations are what distinguish *Funny Ha Ha* from the snappy patter filled with clever rejoinders and cleanly (perhaps too cleanly) scripted insights that defined so much of '90s independent cinema. Here, the characters are often fumbling for the right words to express themselves. (Although Bujalski and his cast are working from a script as opposed to improvising, the director made time for what he described as "happy accidents," where something would happen in the process of shooting a scene that was better that anything he could have planned for.)[3] It's that kind of rambling, mumbling delivery that must have, in part at least, inspired the cheeky label that was affixed to *Funny Ha Ha* and the wave of no-budget indie talk-a-thons that came after it: mumblecore. And while later mumblecore movies would depart from the stylistic and narrative template that *Funny Ha Ha* employs—most notably in the use of digital cameras rather than 16mm film—they do all attempt to retain the same low-key realism and steady stream of halting, awkward, circuitous, and yet still insightful and revealing conversations that Bujalski pursues here. It would be hyperbole to suggest that he establishes himself as the voice of a generation (a claim that the filmmaker himself would likely resist whole-heartedly), but *Funny Ha Ha* does possess a distinctly different sound from the indies that preceded it. And that sound is what makes its otherwise famil-iar story feel fresh; we've seen this scenario play out before, but never with these very specific individuals acting and speaking in this very specific way.

At the same time, it's fair to ask whether the movie's voice is one that can possibly resonate with an audience beyond the ages of the characters depicted on-screen. Bujalski was only 24 when he made the film, and its concerns complement those viewers in the same demographic. It's easy to picture a viewer outside this demo watching about 10 minutes of *Funny Ha Ha* and getting fed up with the amount of self-pity on display. And yet the film's insularity isn't necessarily a bad thing. Certainly, a greater offense would have been to try and speak directly to this specific audience without a clear understanding of who they are or what they sound like. Bujalski knows exactly who he is communicating with and does so with conviction. If nothing else, *Funny Ha Ha* may come to serve as a snapshot of a particular place and time for the director and his viewership. Decades from now, when the postcollegiate haze has completely worn off, they can glimpse back at this stage in their lives through the prism of *Funny Ha Ha* and alternately shudder and laugh in knowing recognition.

The First: Though he didn't know it at the time, with *Funny Ha Ha*, Andrew Bujalski inadvertently launched the next big indie film movement.

Neither the mumblecore movement, nor the very word "mumblecore" itself, existed when *Funny Ha Ha* hit the film festival circuit in 2002. That description wouldn't appear on the pop- culture radar for another three years, by which time Bujalski was already touring festivals with his second film, *Mutual Appreciation*. One of its earliest appearances came during a 2005 interview with the director, in which he mentioned that his sophomore feature had just screened at that year's South by Southwest film festival in Austin, Texas, alongside a few other like-minded movies that were similarly built around twentysomethings wrestling with their problems though long, rambling conversations. "There was some talk there of a 'movement' just because there were a bunch of performance-based films by young quasi-idealists," Bujalski said at the time. "My sound mixer, Eric Masunaga, named the movement 'mumblecore,' which is pretty catchy."[4]

The name "mumblecore" did indeed catch on, with the tipping point arriving in August 2007 when both the *Village Voice*[5] and the *New York Times*[6] published mumblecore-centric articles within days of each other. Suddenly, that word and the movies it applied to entered the pop cultural lexicon, with previously little-known directors with names Duplass and Swanberg and their off-the-radar films like *The Puffy Chair* and *Hannah Takes the Stairs* being referenced in major media outlets. Without question, the concept of a mumblecore movement was a mutually beneficial arrangement for both the filmmakers involved and the public. Audiences and media types could feel the excitement of being present for the beginning of a new and potentially influential cinematic form in the still-young twenty-first century. Meanwhile, the filmmakers had a way to distinguish themselves and the films from the overcrowded indie marketplace, which swallows up so many small movies, even ones of remarkable quality that only lacked a salable hook. Simply being grouped under the mumblecore umbrella could bring a movie some attention. And in several cases, being part of the mumblecore generation even opened doors at the studio level. For example, mumblecore It Girl, actress Greta Gerwig, found her way into studio productions like 2011's *Arthur* and forged creative partnerships with higher-profile filmmakers such as Noah Baumbach. And in 2009, mumblecore moviemaking brothers Mark and Jay Duplass helmed *Cyrus*, which was financed by Fox Searchlight and starred such big-name actors as Jonah Hill, John C. Reilly, and Marisa Tomei. Despite the upgrade, the duo didn't change the working methods they had honed during their time in the mumblecore trenches, once again relying on simple camera setups and a relatively aimless plot that's driven entirely by dialogue. (Mark Duplass has also gone on to score frequent acting gigs in films like *Zero Dark Thirty* and on TV shows like *The League* and *The Mindy Project*.)

What's interesting about the way mumblecore made its presence felt in comparison to other cinematic movements is that the precise definition of what constituted a mumblecore film was always somewhat amorphous. *Funny Ha Ha* may have acquired the reputation as being the movement's Ur-text—largely due to the fact that it was Bujalski's first feature and he helped popularize the phrase—but the films that came after it have their own stylistic quirks. In movies like *The Puffy Chair* and *Baghead*—to say nothing of their two studio-backed productions, *Cyrus* and *Jeff, Who Lives at Home*—for example, the Duplass brothers demonstrate a more hectic, in-the-moment visual sensibility that's very much removed from Bujalski's static, stationary style. Likewise, Lynn Shelton's movies, including *My Effortless Brilliance* and *Humpday*, have their own distinct rhythm and milieu—the older and supposedly more mature characters in *Humpday*, for instance, are in a different place in their lives than Bujalski's fresh-out-of-college navel gazers.

Those differences between the movies that were being slapped with the mumblecore label led Bujalski to announce his trepidation about grouping all of these films and filmmakers into one category. "I think it's probably a little reductive and silly to actually group any of them together. And if it is a movement I'm sure I'll want to get out of it and do something else."[7] Shelton expressed similar concerns, saying in one interview: "I always had an issue with lumping everyone together. . . . I'm happy to be associated with them because they're my friends and I think they're awesome, but I feel we're all very different directors. At the same time it was very useful when we were all starting out, because the mumblecore label shone a light on films that wouldn't have had a lot of light shined on them as individual movies, just because they were so tiny."[8]

Although the mumblecore moniker may have initially been as much a marketing hook as it was a cinematic movement, it's worth noting that there are actually several commonalities that unite the disparate movies grouped under its banner. For one thing, they're all committed to capturing an unstudied, unrehearsed naturalism that's not always present in most studio productions and even certain kinds of indie films. They also speak to a sense of intense longing for something—be it romance, friendship or simply a fulfilling job—that's very much present in the culture right now, particularly amongst millennials. And, finally, they present their characters as they are, not as aspirational figures viewers should try to emulate. Unlike so many Hollywood romantic comedies, *Funny Ha Ha* doesn't try to impart lessons about how actual twentysomethings should conduct their lives. It simply chronicles Marnie's experiences and invites us to observe her decisions without passing overt judgment.

Beyond the quality of the films, the buzz surrounding mumblecore was also the result of good timing, as its arrival on the scene helped give the independent film world of the mid-'00s a much-needed jolt. As the auteurs that defined indie film in the previous decade—men and women like Quentin Tarantino, Allison Anders, and Robert Rodriguez—aged into elder statesmen roles there seemed to be an absence of fresh new voices that could excite both the press and moviegoers. Mumblecore represented a way to fill that void, offering an interesting set of aesthetics and personable group of filmmakers that helped the movies stand out. And even though no mumblecore production has broken out at the box office in the same way *Pulp Fiction* or *Clerks* did, belonging to that club has been a benefit in terms of allowing its directors to get their movies made, screened, and (eventually) sold. Bujalski himself has gone on to helm three more films after *Funny Ha Ha*, most recently *Computer Chess*, an '80s-set period piece that seems to be both a departure from his past work and entirely consistent with his interests. Though mumblecore may turn out to be a blip on the radar rather than the lasting movement some might have hoped, in the short term, at least, it's allowed for the introduction of some compelling new voices.

FILM FIRST FILE #1: GET TO KNOW YOUR MUMBLECORE AUTEURS

Andrew Bujalski may be considered the first mumblecore director, but the genre's ranks swelled in his wake. Here are some other mumblecore names to familiarize yourself with.

Katie Aselton

Who She Is: A former beauty pageant queen turned actress and director. Married to her frequent collaborator, Mark Duplass.

Breakout Mumblecore Feature: *The Freebie* (2010), about a married couple (Aselton and Dax Shepard) who decide to give each other a one-night hall pass from their relationship.

Other Credits: *Black Rock* (2012), a mumblecore-lite thriller with a tinge of horror.

Lena Dunham

Who She Is: The daughter of two renowned New York artists who frequently write, direct, and star in her projects.

Breakout Mumblecore Feature: *Tiny Furniture* (2010), about a college graduate struggling to decide what her next step in life should be.

Other Credits: The much buzzed-about HBO series *Girls* (2012), a depiction of four single girls living and working in New York City.

Mark and Jay Duplass

Who They Are: A pair of filmmaking brothers from New Orleans; Mark is also a prolific actor, appearing in both his own films and numerous others.

Breakout Mumblecore Feature: *The Puffy Chair* (2005), about a couple (Mark Duplass and Katie Aselton) who hit the road to retrieve an eBay purchase: the titular chair.

Other Credits: *Baghead* (2008), *Cyrus* (2010), and *Jeff, Who Lives at Home* (2012); the latter two were produced and distributed by Hollywood studios and featured some major stars, including Jonah Hill and Jason Segel.

Aaron Katz

Who He Is: An Oregon-based writer/director who has helmed some of mumblecore's most acclaimed titles.

Breakout Mumblecore Feature: *Cold Weather* (2010), a lightly *noir*ish amateur detective story about the search for a missing girl.

Other Credits: *Dance Party USA* (2006) and *Quiet City* (2007), a Brooklyn-set talkathon about a pair of strangers who become friends over one long day and night.

Barry Jenkins

Who He Is: One of mumblecore's few minority voices, Jenkins is an African American filmmaker who lives and works in San Francisco.

Breakout Mumblecore Feature: *Medicine for Melancholy* (2008), about two people (Wyatt Cenac and Tracey Heggins) who wake up from a one-night stand and decide to spend the day together.

Other Credits: Numerous shorts, including *Remigration* (2011) for the online *Futurestates* project.

Lynn Shelton

Who She Is: An editor turned filmmaker, Shelton writes and directs features in and around her home base of Seattle.

Breakout Mumblecore Feature: *Humpday* (2009), about two straight guy friends (Mark Duplass and Joshua Leonard) who decide to make a porn film together as an art project/dare.

Other Credits: *My Effortless Brilliance* (2008), *Your Sister's Sister* (2011), and *Touchy Feely* (2013), the latter of which stars Oscar nominee Ellen Page.

Joe Swanberg

Who He Is: The "bad boy" of mumblecore—and also one of its more prolific directors—whose work dwells heavily on sex.

Breakout Mumblecore Feature: *Hannah Takes the Stairs* (2007), about a girl (Greta Gerwig) bouncing between two guys.

Other Credits: *Nights and Weekends* (2008), *Uncle Kent* (2011), and *Drinking Buddies* (2013).

FILM FIRST FILE #2: OTHER INDEPENDENT FILM MOVEMENTS THAT HAVE COME AND GONE

Mumblecore isn't the only cinematic movement to sweep through the independent film world in the past few decades. Here are some of the other movements that have burned brightly and then faded away.

L.A. Rebellion

What It Was: A West Coast–based collective of African American filmmakers directing movies about the areas of Los Angeles that Hollywood rarely, if ever, depicted on film.

Defining Characteristics: Unconventional narratives, urban settings, politically and racially charged material, documentary-style film techniques.

When It Began: 1967
When It Ended: 1989

Examples: *Killer of Sheep* (Charles Burnett, 1977); *Ashes and Embers* (Haile Gerima, 1982); *Bless Their Little Hearts* (Billy Woodberry, 1984)

No Wave Cinema

What It Was: A fiercely independent school of cinema made for and by the starving artists that populated New York's Lower East Side in the '70s and '80s.
Defining Characteristics: Lower East Side locations, frequently shot on black-and-white 16mm film, nonprofessional actors, and appearances by then-popular musicians and artists.
When It Began: 1976
When It Ended: 1985
Examples: *The Blank Generation* (Ivan Král and Amos Poe, 1976); *Men in Orbit* (John Lurie, 1979); *Stranger Than Paradise* (Jim Jarmusch, 1984)

Cinema of Transgression

What It Was: A more extreme version of No Wave that ventured into dark, disturbing realms of emotion and rage.
Defining Characteristics: Graphic displays of sex and violence, extreme satire of societal conventions,
When It Began: 1985
When It Ended: 1990
Examples: *Kiss Me Goodbye* (Nick Zedd, 1986); *Fingered* (Richard Kern, 1986); *Salvation!: Have You Said Your Prayers Today?* (Beth B, 1987)

New Queer Cinema

What It Was: The label that film scholar B. Ruby Rich in a 1992 magazine article applied to a wave of formally daring, as well as politically and sexually conscious films that explored a variety of issues important to the LGBT community.
Defining Characteristics: Unconventional narrative structures and cinematic techniques, a strong sense of rebellion against the status quo, sexually explicit.
When It Began: 1990
When It Ended: 2000
Examples: *Poison* (Todd Haynes, 1991); *The Living End* (Gregg Araki, 1992); *Swoon* (Tom Kalin, 1992)

Dogme 95

What It Was: A response to the artificiality of studio filmmaking that required participants to agree to a "Vow of Chastity" foreswearing digital effects and other visual gimmicks.
Defining Characteristics: Natural lighting, real locations, handheld camerawork, heightened emotions.
When It Began: 1995

When It Ended: 2005

Best Known Works: *The Celebration* (Thomas Vinterberg, 1998); *The Idiots* (Lars von Trier, 1998); *Julien Donkey-Boy* (Harmony Korine, 1999)

Neo-Neo Realism

What It Was: Coined by *New York Times* critic A. O. Scott, this description referred to American independent movies that explore characters and settings frequently unseen in Hollywood movies.

Defining Characteristics: Small-town or rural locations, frequent use of nonprofessional actors, and characters from distinctly working-class backgrounds.

When It Began: 2008

When It Ended: 2012

Best Known Works: *Wendy and Lucy* (Kelly Reichardt, 2008); *Goodbye Solo* (Ramin Bahrani, 2008); *Ballast* (Lance Hammer, 2008)

Chapter 20

Bubble (2005)

The Film: Purposefully moving away from the trappings of Hollywood, *Bubble* finds Steven Soderbergh striving to replicate ordinary life and mostly succeeding.

It's often said (frequently by the director himself) that Steven Soderbergh approaches filmmaking as more of a problem-solving process than an artistic one.[1] With each film, the director presents himself with at least one—and frequently more—key challenge and then proceeds to find a way to crack it. While making what would become his Hollywood breakthrough *Out of Sight*, for example, Soderbergh opted to shake up standard crime picture machinations by scrambling the movie's chronology, a structural device he's employed many times since. And for his sprawling drug saga *Traffic*, Soderbergh gave each of the film's three main story lines its own distinct visual texture as a way to help the audience distinguish between the wide range of settings and characters. In fact, he puts so much thought into the formal elements of his movies that he's frequently described as a cerebral director, which isn't necessarily intended as a compliment. Oftentimes, that label is used to imply that a filmmaker is somehow "cold" and "detached" from his or her own material, the assumption being that too much thinking gets in the way of a film's emotional resonance. And while it's fair to say that, based on his films, Soderbergh isn't a sentimentalist, his best movies are filled with feeling. Indeed, tapping into those emotions in ways that feel honest and true seems to be among the problems he seems out to solve in every new film that he undertakes.

The pursuit of truth is another important element of Soderbergh's working methods; although he's made his fair share of fanciful escapist entertainments (most notably the *Ocean*'s trilogy), he's routinely fascinated by the

intersection between reality and fiction. His 2011 virus-themed thriller
Contagion, for example, depicted a potentially apocalyptic scenario in an
ultrarealistic fashion, as opposed to the manufactured science seen in past
films like *Outbreak*. Still, that movie carried a touch of Hollywood glamour
with its all-star lineup of famous faces, from Matt Damon to Kate Winslet.
For Soderbergh's most radical rejection of moviemaking magic in favor of
absolute realism, you have to go back to 2005's *Bubble*.[2]

The first of six planned films that Soderbergh agreed to make for the independent distributor Magnolia Pictures (which is co-owned by prominent
entrepreneur Mark Cuban),[3] *Bubble* was shot entirely on location in and
around the neighboring communities of Belpre, Ohio, and Parkersburg, West
Virginia, and stars exclusively nonactors who lived and worked in the area.
Soderbergh's casting director, Carmen Cuba, filled out the ensemble by
essentially recruiting people off the streets of Belpre and Parkersburg;
she would approach individuals that she felt might be right for the various
parts and then interview them on camera for up to 30 minutes, sending those
tapes back to Soderbergh for him to make his final selections. (For example,
Cuba found the movie's star, Debbie Doebereine, working at a local KFC.)[4]
Once they got on set, Soderbergh made a point of stripping away as much
artifice as possible in pursuit of pure authenticity, often setting up one
or two static cameras and allowing his cast to move about the frame without
necessarily giving them specific blocking. He also largely eliminated the
other intrusive elements of filmmaking, such as complicated lighting setups
and boom mics hanging over the cast's head. Instead, *Bubble* was filmed
almost completely with natural lighting, and the performers were fitted with
wireless microphones to record their impromptu conversations with each
other.[5]

And they really were impromptu conversations, given that *Bubble* deliberately lacked a conventional script. While Soderbergh and his collaborator,
novelist Coleman Hough, sketched a general outline for the movie, they
mostly avoided writing specific lines of dialogue. As the director explained
it: "The biggest thing to confront [with nonactors] is if there's a way not to
have them memorize lines, you're headed in the right direction. That's what
locks them up, having to speak someone else's words."[6] So rather than put
words in their mouths, before shooting a specific scene, Soderbergh would
give them a basic idea of what the scene would be about and what information they needed to convey; the exact manner in which they delivered those
details was up to them. The film's cast has said that Soderbergh's off-
camera direction primarily consisted of lots of simple, straightforward
instructions—sit at that table, use that machine, pick up that object. He also
gave them scene-specific details, rarely hinting at the film's overall story line.
(The cast did speak extensively with Hough about their lives and experiences,
and some of the details in those conversations were integrated into their characters' own histories.)[7]

Not that there's much of an overall story line to give away. The nominal plot of *Bubble* hinges on the friendship between middle-aged Martha (Doebereine) and young twentysomething Kyle (Dustin James Ashley) coworkers at a rubber doll manufacturing factory. Their tight bond is threatened by the arrival of single mom Rose (Misty Wilkins), who strikes sparks with Kyle—a development that doesn't sit well with his older friend. The night after her first date with Kyle, Rose turns up dead, and the ensuing investigation points to Martha as the culprit.

Soderbergh has referred to *Bubble* as a "whydunit"[8] as opposed to a whodunit, and that's because the identity of the murderer is never really in doubt. Although the audience never sees the killing occur (at least in the moment anyway—there's a flashback at the end that shows us the aftermath), it's fairly apparent that Martha is the guilty party; the movie, though, is more interested in exploring what brought her to that moment than in the specific act and its consequences. In fact, Soderbergh dropped a story line that might have explained her actions: an alternate version of the film references a CAT scan that suggests she has a brain tumor that could be affecting her behavior. Eliminating that plot point leaves Martha's motivations entirely up to the audience's interpretation. Was she driven by envy about Rose's relationship with Kyle? Fury at the younger woman's self-entitled behavior? Or maybe the explanation is that there is no explanation; it was an action she took in the moment that she'll never completely understand.

Although designed and executed with impressive formal rigor, *Bubble* is a film that's more interesting for how it was made than for what happens in it. Part of the problem stems from Soderbergh's decision to use nonactors, a choice that may enhance the reality of the world he's trying to depict, but often causes the internal drama of a scene to fall flat. Even without the burden of having to memorize lines, there's a certain stiffness and self-consciousness present in the performances that can be hard to ignore. One of the things trained actors are taught is how to listen to the partners they're sharing a scene with, so that their responses feel natural. Watching *Bubble*, one gets the sense that the performers are talking at each other, but not really hearing what the others are saying beyond the specific details Soderbergh has instructed them to impart. The lack of variation in their expressions and speaking voices lends the movie a monotonous feeling as well that's not relieved by the straightforward, almost predictable story. *Bubble* is an intriguing film to watch, but it's not necessarily a very engaging one.

Perhaps Soderbergh recognized some of the limitations of his approach to *Bubble*, because his second film for Magnolia, 2009's *The Girlfriend Experience*, makes a few key changes to its predecessor's aesthetic. Although the director once again filled the movie with mostly nonactors, he cast an experienced performer—albeit one whose past experience was primarily in porn movies—at its center and designed a fractured narrative that keeps the audience involved by requiring them to piece the exact sequence of events together. Funnily enough, those flourishes actually make *The Girlfriend Experience* a more conventional film than *Bubble*, which aims for a kind of unfiltered realism that seems to run contrary to the very idea of fiction film-making, where reality is frequently heightened rather than painstakingly recreated. In keeping with Soderbergh's general career path, *Bubble* gave the director the opportunity to solve one problem that had been nagging at him and then allowed him to move on to the next one.

The First: It used to be that new movies by major directors could initially only be seen at a theater near you. In the years after *Bubble*, it can be just as easy as turning on your TV.

Bubble represented a formal and narrative experiment for Steven Soderbergh, but it also served as the test case for a new business model he and Magnolia head Mark Cuban had hit upon when they initially launched their six-movie partnership. The duo were out to accomplish nothing less than upending the status quo of how movies were released, specifically in regard to what are commonly referred to as "release windows"—the amount of time during which a film is available via a specific platform. Most commonly the term is applied to the gap between a movie's theatrical run and its subsequent appearance on various home entertainment platforms, be that DVD, video on demand (VOD), or cable television. When release windows were first instituted during the '80s as emerging home entertainment technology changed the way audiences could consume movies, the amount of time between a movie's theatrical and video release was fairly extensive. In recent years, however, it's shrunk considerably; for most titles there's a window of about three to four months between a movie's theatrical and home entertainment release.[9] Nevertheless, it remains the industry's preferred way of ensuring that all the various revenue streams for a single title are exploited to their fullest extent for all interested parties; theatrical exhibitors would stand to lose millions if, for example, a movie like *The Avengers* was made available on DVD or Netflix only a month following its premiere in theaters.

But the situation is different in the independent film world, where movies rarely receive the wide releases and omnipresent marketing campaigns studio productions can afford. Since their theatrical prospects are often limited in terms of both distribution and overall gross, wider exposure from the get-go can be crucial in helping them bring in an audience and, potentially, a profit. With *Bubble*, Soderbergh and Cuban planned to junk the concept of release windows in favor of a "day-and-date" approach, meaning that the film would be available on the same day in theaters and via a cable movie service. (Of course, this scheme was aided immeasurably by the fact that Cuban owned both the theatrical chain and the specific cable network that *Bubble* would be released on: Landmark Theaters and HDNet Movies respectively.) A DVD would then follow several days later.[10] The idea was that if moviegoers read about *Bubble* and wanted to see it, they wouldn't have to wait the weeks and months it might take for it to come to their local art house: they'd be able to view it out on VOD or DVD right away. It was a test of whether small, low-budget movies could seize upon word of mouth to attract the widest possible audience right away, instead of having to pass through various release windows that could dilute their hype and thus their earning power.

Although a day-and-date concept seemed beneficial for certain films—particularly independent productions—there were a number of reasons why the model hadn't been widely embraced in the past. First and foremost, theater owners weren't wild about it, as it had the potential to eat into their profits and detract from the perceived specialness of the theatrical experience.[11] As much as the introduction of the home entertainment model revolutionized where and how films could be seen, the theatrical release remains the most celebrated and closely watched segment of a movie's life span. And filmmakers idealize movie theaters as much as theater owners do; as many directors are quick to mention, one of the main reasons they make movies in the first place is to see them projected on the big screen in front of a packed crowd. At the time of *Bubble*'s release, it was rare for filmmaker with Soderbergh's successful track record and stature in the industry to want one of his films to potentially be seen first on TV screens rather than a movie screen.

And yet, speaking about that prospect on *Bubble*'s DVD commentary track, Soderbergh sounds remarkably indifferent to the "magic" of the theatrical experience. "I have no problem with someone experiencing *Bubble* for the first time on DVD or HDNet," he says without a trace of regret, adding, "I don't think it's going to destroy the moviegoing experience any more than having the ability to get takeout has destroyed the restaurant-going experience."[12] Furthermore, he cites the widespread and illegal practice of film piracy bringing about an unofficial day-and-date release anyway, with bootlegged copies of films turning up for sale on the street the same day they premiere in theaters.[13] By making *Bubble* legally available on DVD at the same time as its theatrical release, he could at least ensure that most of the discs sold would line the movie's pocket rather than someone unaffiliated with the production.

In its trial run, Magnolia's business model seemed to pay off. The weekend after the movie opened, Magnolia announced that *Bubble* grossed roughly $72,000 from its 32-screen theatrical engagement, but earned roughly $5 million overall when taking into account DVD pre-orders and other revenues.[14] That number may seem small, but considering that the film was made and marketed for around $2 million, the profit margin was significant. Magnolia employed the same strategy on several of their subsequent releases, but by the time Soderbergh's follow-up, *The Girlfriend Experience*, arrived in 2009, the company tweaked the model, leading off with a VOD release on April 30, followed by a theatrical run starting May 22.[15] A DVD edition subsequently followed months—rather than days—later in September. In other words, this strategy was closer to the traditional release window concept, albeit with the theatrical release relegated to second position.

Since *Bubble*, Magnolia—along with one of the other best-known distributors of independent cinema, IFC Films—has continued down that path, making many of their releases available on Video on Demand either before or on the same day as their theatrical debut, with a DVD coming several months later, an approach motivated by the declining fortunes of the DVD format as well as the always challenging theatrical landscape for indie movies. VOD, on the other hand, is widely regarded as having a bright future for the independent industry (although financial information regarding VOD earnings isn't always easy to come by and there has been a demonstrated impact on a movie's potential theatrical earnings), and because Magnolia in particular has its own branded On Demand site in addition to operating its own chain of cinemas, it's able to pursue this strategy without necessarily having to worry about upsetting exhibitors who still believe in the primacy of the theatrical experience. That's a freedom the bigger studios often don't have; for example, Universals plans to make their 2011 heist comedy *Tower Heist* available on VOD in select markets only three weeks after it opened in theaters were scuttled after several major movie chains refused to book the film on those conditions.[16] Still, it's likely only a matter of time until a major studio figures out a way to employ a VOD/theatrical day-and-date strategy. Perhaps it'll even be a movie directed by the supposedly retired Steven Soderbergh, if and when he decides to return to feature filmmaking.

FILM FIRST FILE #1: OTHER NONACTORS EMPLOYED BY STEVEN SODERBERGH

Bubble represents director Steven Soderbergh's most ambitious and extensive use of nonactors, but he's made room for nonprofessionals in some of his past projects.

Schizopolis (1996)

Himself: Soderbergh cast himself (and his ex-wife, actress Betsy Brantley) as the lead in his experimental hall-of-mirrors tale of a bored corporate drone whose life take a turn for the bizarre.

Traffic (2000)

Senators Harry Reid, Barbara Boxer, Don Nickles, and Orrin Hatch: To add more authenticity to the Washington, D.C., sequences of his sprawling drug drama, Soderbergh had his fictional Director of National Drug Control

Policy (played by Michael Douglas) interact with actual federal employees from both sides of the aisle, including Democratic senators Reid and Boxer and Republicans Nickles and Hatch.

Full Frontal (2002)

David Fincher: The director of such films as *Se7en* and *Fight Club* made a brief appearance in Soderbergh's divisive Hollywood satire playing a movie director.

K Street (2003)

James Carville and Mary Matalin: Returning to the nation's capital for this HBO series that explored the too-close relationship between special-interests lobbyists, political strategists, and those in power, Soderbergh put together an ensemble that included veteran strategists (and Washington power couple) Carville and Matalin in major roles opposite professional actors like John Slattery and Mary McCormack.

The Girlfriend Experience (2009)

Glenn Kenny: To play the so-called "Erotic Connoisseur" who evaluates the skills of a high-priced Manhattan call girl (porn star Sasha Grey), Soderbergh tapped veteran film critic Kenny to deliver a blistering review of her talents (or lack thereof).

Haywire (2011)

Gina Carano: Soderbergh and screenwriter Lem Dobbs crafted this project specifically as a star vehicle for Carano, a mixed martial-arts fighter who had never carried her own feature.

FILM FIRST FILE #2: OTHER NOTABLE MOVIES THAT HAVE PREMIERED ON VOD

Since Steven Soderbergh's *Bubble* helped break the previously sacrosanct day-and-date barrier that kept a movie's theatrical window separate from all other forms of distribution, other higher-profile films and filmmakers have followed suit. Here are some examples of what Soderbergh's pioneering strategy for *Bubble* has wrought.

Trespass (Joel Schumacher, 2011)

In the '90s, a home-invasion thriller starring two Oscar winners (Nicolas Cage and Nicole Kidman) and directed by an experienced studio filmmaker (Joel Schumacher) would have been granted a prominent theatrical release, no questions asked. But in the current climate—where movie stars sometime matter less than franchise familiarity—the studio behind *Trespass* looked to maximize whatever profits it could from what was reportedly a pretty terrible movie by making it available on VOD platforms the same day it was released in theaters.

Margin Call (J. C. Chandor, 2011)

A hit at the 2011 Sundance Film Festival, this Wall Street–set ensemble drama with a cast that included Kevin Spacey and Zachary Quinto performed well in its limited theatrical run, grossing a little over $5 million. But it doubled that number with a VOD run that brought in another $4 million thanks to strong word of mouth.

Take This Waltz (Sarah Polley, 2011)

After debuting to strong reviews at the 2011 Toronto Film Festival, Sarah Polley's sophomore directing effort—about a couple (Michelle Williams and Seth Rogen) experiencing marital troubles—sought to capitalize on that buzz with a VOD release prior to its theatrical release date in the middle of the crowded 2012 summer movie season, where it predictably sank from sight fairly quickly.

Get the Gringo (Adrian Grunberg, 2012)

Once one of Hollywood's most bankable movie stars, Mel Gibson saw his most recent film, a south-of-the-border action picture, bypass theaters altogether in America for a VOD- and DVD-only release.

Piranha 3DD (John Gulager, 2012)

Perhaps sensing that the sequel to their surprise hit *Piranha 3D* was a creative dud, the Weinstein Brothers–owned horror label Dimension released the mutant-piranhas-attack-a-waterpark frightfest on VOD platforms the same day as its repeatedly delayed theatrical release, trusting that its target audience wouldn't bother to read reviews or want to pay full price to see it in theaters.

Chapter 21

The Hurt Locker (2008)

The Film: Kathryn Bigelow's Oscar-winning depiction of modern warfare presents combat as both grunt work and a thrill ride.

The 10-minute sequence that opens Kathryn Bigelow's Iraq War–set combat film, *The Hurt Locker*[1], is a masterful minimovie in its own right. It's the year 2004, and the viewer is embedded with a three-man U.S. Army bomb disposal unit in Baghdad (although the film was actually shot in Jordan, not Iraq) roughly a year after the American invasion that toppled Saddam Hussein from power. The trio, who happily engage in a vigorous round of trash talking as they work, has been tasked with defusing an explosive device that's been left by the side of a city road. After the remote-controlled robotic machine they've been using suffers a minor breakdown, one of the soldiers, Staff Sergeant Matt Thompson (played by Guy Pearce) volunteers to don the heavy-duty safety gear and carry the charges intended to destroy the device himself. As he enters the "kill zone"—the radius within which any detonation would take his life—and lays the charges on the bomb, his colleagues are scanning their surroundings, eyes peeled and guns at the ready for any signs of suspicious activity. Bigelow heightens the tension by cutting between various vantage points—Thompson's point of view, the positions of the other two soldiers and cameras stationed above street level, mimicking the gaze of a bystander observing these soldiers from the window or balcony of one of the adjacent apartment buildings.

As Thompson prepares to return to safety, one of his colleagues spots an Iraqi civilian standing in the door of a butcher shop holding a cell phone—a potential trigger device for a bomb. He immediately shouts at the man to drop the phone and charges over, gun pointed. Meanwhile, Thompson breaks into a run, trying to clear the kill zone before the explosion goes off. But it's already too late—the trigger is activated and the bomb detonates and we watch

Thompson fall to the ground, blood splattering against his mask. This sequence sets the tone for the rest of the movie in the way it depicts these three soldiers matter-of-factly troubleshooting the task at hand, despite the ever-present specter of death looming in the background. *The Hurt Locker* is, in many respects, just a film about working stiffs on the job; it just so happens that their profession is warfare.

This depiction of combat as punch-the-clock day labor makes *The Hurt Locker* somewhat unique among war movies. Most films in this genre take place on a larger scale, focusing their attention on big, chaotic battles and prolonged missions into enemy territory, with themes that dwell on the futility of war or man's inhumanity to other man. *The Hurt Locker*, on the other hand, adopts a micro view of the Iraq War; there's little to no discussion about the broader political situation in Baghdad in the wake of the invasion or what the higher-ups back at the Pentagon might be planning next. As conceived by Bigelow—who has said she was attracted to the film in part because she viewed these soldiers as having the most dangerous job in the world[2]—and screenwriter Mark Boal, the film is structured as a series of assignments that these highly skilled professionals must complete without killing others or themselves. It's a film that's interested in the *process* of modern warfare rather than the act or art of war. Indeed, the central conflict in the film boils down to a fundamental disagreement over working methods. After Thompson dies, his former colleagues, Sergeant J. T. Sanborn (Anthony Mackie) and Specialist Owen Eldridge (Brian Geraghty), welcome a new coworker to their unit—Sergeant First Class William James (Jeremy Renner). Where his predecessor was a team player, James takes enormous risks that often endanger himself and his coworkers. His approach to the job understandably creates tension between him and the more by-the-book Sanborn, tension that inevitably boils over into fights both in the field and back at the barracks.

In another reflection of the movie's process-minded aesthetic, *The Hurt Locker* doesn't concern itself with explaining how James acquired his reckless streak. In fact, the movie studiously avoids the familiar war-movie convention of a (usually doomed) soldier launching into a monologue that reveals what exactly he's fighting for, be it a wife and child back home, the respect of his fellow soldiers, or just honor and glory. Boal had spent time embedded with a real bomb disposal team in Iraq to write the magazine article on which his screenplay is based, and while he didn't model James after any one soldier, the character does reflect a pattern of behavior that the writer observed. Because of the sheer number of IEDs (improvised explosive devices) that were routinely planted and set off, it could be difficult for the field units to follow standard operating procedures in each individual situation. As a result, some of the soldiers in the bomb disposal units made up the rules as they went along, much as James does during the course of the film.[3]

Although the filmmakers mostly avoid expository character profiles, they do lay bare one aspect of James's psychology with a quote that opens the movie, taken from the 2002 book *War Is a Force That Gives Us Meaning* by the journalist Chris Hedges: "The rush of battle is a potent and often lethal addiction, for war is a drug." As the film progresses, it becomes all too clear that James is hooked on that "rush of battle." He's at his most alive when he's one impulsive decision away from instant death. Tellingly, Boal and Bigelow avoid offering a definitive answer as to whether this is an admirable trait or tragic flaw. Viewers are also invited to read what they like into the film's closing scenes, which find James struggling to adapt to civilian life in the home he shares with his wife and their young son followed by his speedy return to Iraq for another yearlong tour. Should we feel sorrow and regret over his inability to find pleasure in a normal, quiet existence? Or pride that he's so eager to serve, no matter the personal cost? The filmmakers don't tip their hands either way, instead closing the film with a shot of James reentering Baghdad that echoes the image of an assembly-line worker marching into the factory where he works every day.

Although this depiction of combat-as-a-job is fascinating, it also rather cannily keeps the filmmakers from having to take a position on war in general and the Iraq War in particular. While *The Hurt Locker* can't exactly be described as a pro-war film, it also doesn't argue one way or the other about America's presence in Iraq. The film's relatively apolitical nature almost certainly helped it avoid the usual charges from certain quarters that Hollywood is a bastion of antiwar liberals who don't sufficiently honor the troops. It also may have contributed in some small way to the film's eventual win for Best Picture at the 82nd Academy Awards. Although more overtly antiwar movies like *All Quiet on the Western Front* and *Platoon* had won in decades past, in recent years the Oscars have seemed to shy away from more controversial material, particularly when it comes time to hand out their highest honor. (Just look at the roll call of winners over the last 10 years—among them *A Beautiful Mind*, *The Departed*, and *The Artist*—and you'll notice that escapism trumps more politically minded movies. Even the 2012 winner, *Argo*, about the Iran hostage crisis of the late '70s, treated history as the jumping-off point for a caper movie.) While arguments about the Iraq War raged on within the government and national press, *The Hurt Locker* simply concerned itself with presenting the work a select, specialized group of American soldiers was doing on the ground. A broader worldview might have lent *The Hurt Locker* more complexity, but the film deserves credit for carrying out its intended mission with clarity and conviction.

The First: Kathryn Bigelow's Best Director win on Oscar night finally broke that particular glass ceiling for female filmmakers.

When Kathryn Bigelow's name was announced as one of the five nominees for the Best Director Oscar at the 82nd Annual Academy Awards, she was the fourth female filmmaker in Hollywood history to be nominated for that statue. First came Italian director Lina Wertmüller, nominated in 1976 with her film *Seven Beauties*, about a reluctant volunteer soldier in World War II who is sent to a German prison camp for the crime of desertion. (Needless to say, it's a comedy.) Seventeen years later, Jane Campion's acclaimed 1993 drama *The Piano* was honored with a number of nominations, including Best Director. And a decade after that in 2003, Sofia Coppola became the third woman (and second Coppola) to compete for that prize.

All three of those filmmakers ultimately lost that statue on Oscar night, though not for reasons that were specifically due to their gender. Mostly, they had the misfortune of going up against more high-profile and wildly successful movies. For example, Wertmüller ran headlong into the fists of people's champ *Rocky*, which was '76's big success story, while in '93 Campion had to contend with the juggernaut that was *Schindler's List*, directed by Hollywood icon Steven Spielberg, who had yet to win a Best Director statue at that point. And in '03, Coppola's low-key culture-clash character study was steamrolled—along with virtually every other nominated film— by the last chapter in Peter Jackson's *Lord of the Rings* saga, which swept every category in which it was nominated (including Director and Picture) for a total of 11 awards. Bigelow herself seemed to face a similar predicament when she was nominated opposite her former collaborator (and former husband) James Cameron, whose 3D spectacle *Avatar* was riding high at the box office and on the awards circuit. Compared to the otherworldly action and state-of-the-art effects on display in that movie, *The Hurt Locker*'s emphasis on small-scale heroics seemed almost retro.

But history didn't repeat itself this time. Instead, on Oscar night—March 7, 2010—Bigelow took the stage at the Kodak Theatre and accepted the statue from the award's presenter, singing/acting legend Barbra Streisand (who had enjoyed a directing career of her own, helming three movies between 1983 and 1996) while Cameron applauded from the audience. As she had done throughout the awards season, Bigelow downplayed the historic nature of her nomination and victory in her acceptance speech, instead lavishing praise on Boal, her cast and crew, and closing with a dedication to the "women and men in the military who risk their lives on a daily basis in Iraq and Afghanistan and around the world. May they come home safe."[4] In that moment, she wasn't a female filmmaker—she was just a filmmaker.

That sentiment describes her overall career; as far back as her breakout feature film, the 1987 vampire thriller *Near Dark*, Bigelow refused to let her gender define her as a director, making a point of pursuing such traditionally male genres as cop movies (*Point Break*), science-fiction tales of the near future (*Strange Days*), and star-powered period action pictures (*K-19: The Widowmaker*). With *The Hurt Locker*, she ventured even further into "guy" territory to make her first combat film. Based on the finished product, you'd never know that it was new ground for her. Furthermore, it's difficult to discern the gender of the director behind the camera at all. In that way,

The Hurt Locker is more the work of an artisan than an auteur; it's first and foremost an excellent piece of craftsmanship that's less concerned with bearing the imprint of its maker than telling its story in the most compelling way possible.

While there's a great deal of satisfaction to be gained from the knowledge that the first female Best Director Oscar recipient was someone who had proved time and time again that she could hang with—and even surpass—the boys, one has to wonder if the fact that *The Hurt Locker* plays as such a guy movie (a feeling that's not just owed to the scarcity of women on-screen, but also its general theme of brotherhood amongst soldiers) gave it extra oomph with the male-dominated votership at the Academy of Motion Picture Arts and Sciences. Put another way, would Bigelow have taken home the Best Director statue had it put female soldiers front and center? Certainly, the Academy has had and continues to have a spotty track record when it comes to recognizing films made by women about women. Take Lisa Cholodenko, whose 2010 film *The Kids Are All Right* about a married lesbian couple was showered with awards and accolades including a Best Picture nomination. Cholodenko herself, however, missed the cut for a Best Director nod. Likewise, Patty Jenkins was entirely overlooked in the hoopla surrounding her 2003 film *Monster*, as the Academy chose to focus solely on Charlize Theron's star turn. Indeed, of the four women that have been nominated for the award, only Campion made a movie in which a woman is unquestionably the main character. (Coppola's *Lost in Translation* comes close, but Bill Murray just edges out Scarlett Johansson as the center of that film.)

To be fair, the list of factors that goes into determining which films and filmmakers receive Oscar nominations is too long and varied to chalk this state of affairs solely up to a case of institutional bias. And the fact that Bigelow now has an Oscar in hand represents a significant breakthrough that hopefully indicates things are changing for the better within the Academy. At the same time, though, her victory with *The Hurt Locker* highlights the difficult choice that female directors in Hollywood still bump up against: Make movies about women, for women, and watch them fail to catch fire at the box office and on the awards circuit, or show that you can flex your muscles like a dude by helming an action movie or a guy-centric character study and potentially score a wider audience of moviegoers and awards voters.

Bigelow experienced this firsthand when her two female-focused movies prior to *The Hurt Locker*—1990's *Blue Steel*, which starred Jamie Lee Curtis as a tough but inexperienced cop and 2000's *The Weight of Water*, about a newspaper photographer (Catherine McCormack) investigating a century-old murder—failed to attract the same commercial attention as the machismo-slathered 1991 action picture *Point Break*. On the other hand, her immediate follow-up to *The Hurt Locker*, *Zero Dark Thirty*, did feature a female lead (played by Jessica Chastain), and it became Bigelow's highest-grossing film by a wide margin, picking up several Oscar nominations to boot, including Best Picture. There again, though, Bigelow wound up being omitted from the Directing category, resulting in yet another all-male lineup. That seems sadly typical of the current status of female directors in Hollywood—for every step forward, there's a step back.

FILM FIRST FILE #1: THE IRAQ WAR ON FILM: A TIMELINE

March 19, 2003: American troops cross the border into Iraq, beginning "Operation Iraqi Freedom."

April 9, 2003: American troops seize control of the Iraqi capital, Baghdad.

July 2003: Iraqi poet Sinan Antoon returns to Baghdad with a camera crew and captures life in his native country post–Saddam Hussein. The resulting documentary, *About Baghdad*, is the first feature-length film to be made about the war and premieres on the festival circuit in 2004.

November 9, 2003: The made-for-TV movie *Saving Jessica Lynch*, based on the story of Private Jessica Lynch, airs on NBC. The film's version of events differs in significant ways from the account provided by the real Private Lynch.

January 2004: Jehane Noujaim's documentary *Control Room* premieres at the Sundance Film Festival and offers a look at the way the Iraq War was presented on American news networks versus the coverage seen on the controversial Qatar-based network Al Jazeera. A hit with critics, the movie receives a limited theatrical release in May.

May 22, 2004: Michael Moore's documentary *Fahrenheit 9/11*, a blistering critique of the George W. Bush administration's response to September 11 and its rush to war with Iraq, wins the Palme d'Or at the Cannes Film Festival. The movie is released in America on June 25, 2004 and becomes the highest-grossing non-fiction feature of all time, but is notably absent from the Oscar nominations for Best Documentary.

March 4, 2005: The grunt's-eye-view documentary *Gunner Palace* opens in limited theatrical release. Director Michael Tucker, who was embedded with a combat team that had taken up residence in one of Hussein's palaces, successfully appealed the original R rating the MPAA awarded the film for its language, and it was released with a PG-13 rating.

October 14, 2005: Italian actor/director Roberto Benigni directs and stars in *The Tiger and the Snow*, a fanciful romantic comedy set in Baghdad against the backdrop of the Iraq War. Reviews are resoundingly negative, and the movie doesn't open in America until December 2006.

December 15, 2006: MGM releases Hollywood's first narrative feature about the Iraq War, *Home of the Brave*, an ensemble drama starring Samuel L. Jackson, Jessica Biel, and the rapper 50 Cent. Reviews are mixed, and the film's box office stalls out at a little under $52,000.

July 27, 2007: Charles Ferguson's highly praised documentary *No End in Sight*, which harshly criticizes America's presence in Iraq, opens in theaters. It will go on to be nominated for (but not win) Best Documentary Feature at that year's Oscars.

September 2007–March 2008: A series of American films with Iraq War themes arrive in theaters, including *The Kingdom*, *In the Valley of Elah*, *Redacted*, *Grace Is Gone*, and *Stop-Loss*. While some receive strong reviews, box office across the board is weak, leading many within the industry to conclude that moviegoers simply aren't interested in seeing movies about the conflict.

February 24, 2008: Alex Gibney's *Taxi to the Dark Side*, which explores whether torture was used by U.S. forces in waging the War on Terror, becomes the first Iraq War-themed documentary to win the Best Documentary Feature Oscar.

September 4, 2008: *The Hurt Locker* premieres at the Venice Film Festival and screens again four days later at the Toronto Film Festival, where it is acquired by the distributor Summit Entertainment.

June 26, 2009: *The Hurt Locker* opens in limited release in U.S. theaters almost a year after its festival debut. It will eventually earn $17 million at the domestic box office.

March 7, 2010: *The Hurt Locker* wins the Oscar for Best Picture.

March 12, 2010: The Paul Greengrass thriller *Green Zone*, starring Matt Damon as an American soldier serving in Iraq, opens in theaters. The movie only grosses $35 million in its theatrical run, and Hollywood pulls back on producing more Iraq War–themed features.

November 5, 2010: One of the last high-profile studio features that directly involves the Iraq War, *Fair Game*, starring Naomi Watts as former CIA agent Valerie Plame, comes and goes quickly from theaters.

December 15, 2011: The last American troops leave Iraq, officially ending major combat operations.

FILM FIRST FILE #2: FIVE OTHER CONTEMPORARY FEMALE ACTION DIRECTORS

While Kathryn Bigelow is certainly the most renowned female director of action movies, other women have worked within a genre that's sadly too often considered "boys only" territory. Their ranks include:

Lexi Alexander

An ex-kickboxing champion turned filmmaker, Alexander became the first (and still, so far, only) woman to direct a comic-book movie with 2008's *Punisher: War Zone*, starring the famous Marvel Comics vigilante.

Virginie Despentes and Coralie Trinh Thi

These French filmmakers collaborated on the controversial 1999 feature *Baise-Moi*, a kind of modern-day *Bonnie and Clyde* where two women—a prostitute and a sometimes porn actress—go on a killing spree for the sheer hell of it.

Karyn Kusama

After making her debut with the indie boxing drama *Girlfight*, Kusama went on to helm the big-budget sci-fi action movie *Aeon Flux*, starring Charlize Theron.

Mimi Leder

Perhaps the second-biggest female name in action behind Bigelow, Leder made her feature-film debut with the George Clooney/Nicole Kidman thriller *The Peacemaker* and moved on to helm the disaster movie *Deep Impact*, one of two "asteroid threatens to destroy Earth" films released in the summer of 1998 (the other being Michael Bay's *Armageddon*).

Betty Thomas

Primarily a director of comedies, the former actress added action to her resume with the 2002 big-screen version of the '60s TV series *I Spy*, which starred Owen Wilson and Eddie Murphy as a secret agent and an athlete that team up to pull off a top secret mission.

Chapter 22

Avatar (2009)

The Film: Using state-of-the-art technology, James Cameron crafted a futuristic epic that feels appropriately old-school.

For a filmmaker who is famous for his facility—and not-so-secret obsession—with cutting-edge cinematic technology, James Cameron's instincts as a storyteller are decidedly more old-fashioned. Whether you're talking *Titanic* or *Terminator* or *Avatar*,[1] there's a square-jawed simplicity to his approach to storytelling and characterization that would seem to be at odds with the visual razzle-dazzle provided by the movies' exotic settings and boundary-pushing special effects. And yet the earnestness (some would say cheesiness) that's frequently present in his films winds up complementing the high-tech trappings. Sure, there are individual lines of dialogue—penned by Cameron himself, who has written or cowritten every one of his films—that induce involuntary eye rolling, but even those clunkers carry a strong sense of honesty behind them. And that honesty, perhaps more than any other weapon in Cameron's aesthetic arsenal, might explain why the films connect so strongly to a mass audience. He believes in the story he's telling to his very core, and that often sets his blockbusters apart from other, more cynically calculated effects-heavy spectacles like *Transformers*.

By any measure, Cameron demonstrated that he had his finger on the moviegoers' pulses when *Titanic* became a global phenomenon in 1997, shattering box-office records, dominating awards shows, and sending millions upon millions of viewers back into the theater for multiple viewings. The success of that film was the prelude to a 10-year sabbatical from filmmaking, during which time Cameron pursued other interests—most notably a deep-sea-diving career—leaving many to wonder if he'd ever helm a narrative feature again. Turns out, he was waiting for technology to catch up to his

imagination, which had conjured up a distant planet called Pandora populated by a race of blue alien creatures named the Na'vi. It was after seeing
Peter Jackson's *Lord of the Rings* trilogy—paying specific attention to the
motion-capture technology that created Gollum—that Cameron started to
actively pursue making the movie that would become *Avatar*.

The fact that Cameron had spent so much time away from filmmaking,
coupled with reports of the special technology he had commissioned for his
top-secret new project, meant that once production commenced, *Avatar*
almost immediately took on mythical status. That impression was further
stoked by the testimonials of filmmakers like Steven Soderbergh, who
famously described the early footage he had seen as "the craziest shit ever."[2]
Those kinds of sky-high expectations were almost inevitably going to tumble
back down to Earth. and, indeed, as actual footage from the film began to
leak out into the world via trailers and extended clips shown at major media
events like San Diego's Comic-Con International, there was some disagreement about how "game-changing" the finished product would actually be.
(As one early eye-witness put it, "The footage was good, layered, incredibly
detailed and full of imagination and incredible imagery, but I wouldn't go
so far as to say it's the next quantum leap forward in filmmaking.")[3] Also
at issue were the similarities *Avatar*'s story line appeared to share with such
films as *Dances with Wolves* and *The New World* as well as a trio of animated, environmentally themed kiddie pictures, *FernGully: The Last Rainforest*, *Battle for Terra*, and *Delgo*. Like several of those films, *Avatar*'s
central narrative concerns itself with the appropriation and exploitation of
another, supposedly more primitive culture's land and resources by a people
with greater technology and weapons. Eventually, one of the more enlight-
ened invaders "goes native" and helps his adopted family defend their home
against his former tribe.

In *Avatar*, this scenario plays out with far-future paraplegic military grunt,
Jake Sully (Sam Worthington), arriving on Pandora, where a militarized corporation mines for a precious mineral known as unobtanium while maintaining a tense relationship with the Na'vi. Sully has volunteered to be part of a
cutting-edge scientific experiment whereby his consciousness is downloaded
into a genetically grown alien body. Once inside this other skin, he begins
to spend time with the actual Na'vi and forms a strong attachment to one
in particular—Neytiri (Zoe Saldana), the daughter of the tribe's leader. It
isn't long before he willingly abandons his human identity and joins the fight
to protect Pandora from its unwelcome visitors.

In contrast to the distinctly twenty-first-century technology that was used
to make the movie, *Avatar*'s story is vintage pulp fiction, going all the way
back to the granddaddy of most contemporary space adventures, Edgar Rice
Burroughs's *John Carter of Mars* series, which were first published in 1912.
And Cameron's irony-free reliance on certain genre clichés, as well as the
archetypal characterizations and admittedly undistinguished dialogue, made

Avatar an easy target for ridicule when it was finally released. There's also the thorny issue of the film's racial politics; certainly, it's hard to miss the visual and narrative resemblance the Na'vi bear to Native American or African tribespeople, and having them rally around a white hero—even one that's able to don their blue skin—inspires a host of questions that Cameron either didn't contemplate or had no intention of ever addressing. Some critics were put off enough by the movie's perceived dramatic shortcomings to predict that *Avatar* would be an epic flop,[4] a prediction that was also made about *Titanic* before it opened.[5] In both cases, though, the general public flipped for the movie, powering *Titanic* to a record $600 million domestic box-office gross that was only broken by *Avatar*'s $760 million final tally, making it the domestic box office's highest-grossing film (unadjusted for inflation). And while a movie's cumulative gross is by no means the sole arbiter of its quality, achieving that level of success requires it to resonate with a mass audience—or at the very least, keep them thoroughly entertained—to the point where they're eager to make repeat trips. And that's precisely what *Avatar* achieves; it's a simple, primal story told with a showman's brio and an artist's sincerity.

Also working in the film's favor, of course, are those state-of-the-art visual effects, which received more hype (and were more prominently featured in the various ad campaigns) than the flesh-and-blood actors. By selling *Avatar* as a technological breakthrough, the studio made it seem like that increasingly rare movie that *had* to be seen in theaters. And it's true that Cameron's grand command of spectacle plays best on a towering theatrical screen. The climactic battle alone—in which the Na'vi soar through Pandora's skies atop mighty winged beasts attacking human-piloted military helicopters—is impressive enough to make one forgive the extra cost of an IMAX ticket. That image also perfectly encapsulates the movie's origins, resembling the tattered cover of an issue of a vintage pulp magazine like *Amazing Stories* or *Galaxy*.

Even when watched in the comfort of your living room, *Avatar* is an immersive experience, simply because Cameron's affection for the world he's creating is so evident. If the initial glimpses we see of Pandora resemble Earth-bound backdrops (like an early scene in a tropical rainforest that looks familiar enough to have been filmed on location in South America, despite actually being created in a computer), that's entirely by design. By presenting us with more recognizable environments upfront, Cameron is able to ease us gradually into this far-off planet, so that when we do see the landmarks that set Pandora apart—like majestic floating mountains and giant trees that pulsate with energy—it doesn't feel quite so . . . well, *alien*. George Lucas accomplished a similar feat in the Tatooine sequences of the first *Star Wars* movie; that desert planet seems unremarkable, until the audience sees Luke Skywalker gazing out at the horizon as twin suns set in the sky. And in that moment, we're reminded that this really is taking place in a galaxy far, far away. The sense of familiarity that's built into both the setting and the story is part of what audiences responded to about *Avatar*. It's the story of a future world told in a timeless way.

The First: By finally fusing both the art and commerce of 3D, and becoming the highest-grossing feature film of all time as a result, *Avatar* ensured that the process was around to stay. Or is it?

The history of 3D dates almost back to the invention of cinema itself. Inventor William Friese-Greene is generally credited with having dreamed up the earliest concept of a stereoscopic film in the 1890s, patenting a process by which a movie would be projected on two screens standing side by side while viewers gazed at them through a headset that would give the images being projected on-screen a sense of depth. Two decades later, pioneering filmmaker Edwin S. Porter (who directed the groundbreaking early cinema classic *The Great Train Robbery*) did his own series of tests using the red-green anaglyph process that relies on contrasting color filters to produce a 3D effect.[6] Much like the cinematic medium, though, 3D was viewed as a novelty in those early years and remained that way even after film became widely accepted as a legitimate art form. Not that the industry itself did much to make 3D respectable; rather than embracing it as they did such technological breakthroughs as sound and color, the process went ignored for decades, limited to infrequent experimental runs in individual theaters. And when 3D was made available on a wide basis in the 1950s, it was as part of a series of gimmicks—among them CinemaScope and VistaVision—Hollywood had adopted to try and combat the rising popularity of television. "Artistic" is certainly the last word you'd apply to Hollywood's first 3D color feature, 1952's low-budget African adventure movie *Bwana Devil*, which lured moviegoers into the theater with a poster that promised the sensation of feeling "A lion in your lap!" and "A lover in your arms!"[7]

As with most novelty acts, 3D went through cycles of popularity after its '50s heyday, each of which had an extremely short shelf life. When it cycled back again in the 2000s, its reemergence was initially fueled by family-friendly movies like *The Polar Express* and *Hannah Montana & Miley Cyrus: Best of Both Worlds Concert*. Again, the artistic aspects of 3D weren't paramount to many of these titles (excluding, perhaps, *The Polar Express*, as that film's director, Robert Zemeckis, generally tries to make movies where the technology services the art); rather, the renewed industry interest had a lot to do with the extra dollars that could be brought in from 3D-enhanced ticket prices. In order to prolong the current cycle of 3D spectacles, the industry needed a film that positioned the format as an integral element of the movie and not just an add-on gimmick; a film where 3D wasn't an option—it was essential.

Avatar became that movie, converting even entrenched 3D skeptics like Roger Ebert, who wrote in his 4-star review: "Cameron's iteration is the best I've seen—and more importantly, one of the most carefully employed. The film never uses 3-D *simply because it has it...*"[8] Provoking that kind of reaction was the primary reason Cameron waited so long to make *Avatar*, until he could find (or manufacture) the right technology to do 3D right. The live-action material in the film was shot with a new 3D-enabled camera that allowed Cameron to craft the most immersive experience possible. Where the 3D movies of yesteryear deliberately called attention to the process, Cameron wanted viewers to forget they were in a theater and vanish completely into the world he was creating on-screen.[9]

The "*Avatar* Must Be Seen in 3D" mantra was certainly beneficial for the movie's bottom line. Reports pegged the film's budget at almost $460 million, including production and marketing costs. With that kind of money on the table, breaking even would be a challenge, even for a director with such a proven track record as Cameron. But the movie scaled the charts both at home and abroad, earning $2 billion internationally, goosed in part by the higher ticket prices for 3D showings. Hollywood took careful notice of the movie's 3D bump; in the wake of *Avatar*'s enormous success, Warner Bros. quickly decided to convert their 2010 fantasy epic *Clash of the Titans* into a 3D version to capitalize on the renewed public interest in the format. And despite a chorus of complaints about the shoddy conversion job,[10] *Titans* opened extremely well in America and overseas, reaching almost $500 million worldwide. In recent years, it's become de rigueur for almost every studio blockbuster to be released in 2D and 3D versions, as audiences seemed to have adjusted to the format as part of the contemporary moviegoing landscape.

You might think that Cameron would have been pleased to see 3D become of such paramount importance to the industry. But in recent years, the director became an outspoken critic of Hollywood's rush to capitalize on the process. His primary objection centered around the fact that most of the 3D features arriving in theaters were converted to the format in postproduction, and the quality was rarely on par with what he had tried to achieve with *Avatar*. At one industry event, he publicly cited *Clash of the Titans* as an example of a rushed 3D conversion that didn't represent what the format was truly capable of, remarking, "If you want to release a movie in 3D—make it in 3D."[11] On the other hand, Cameron did express his opinion that, given the proper amount of time and attention, older films could be successfully converted, an idea he set out to prove by rereleasing *Titanic* in 3D in April 2012.

By then, though, some of the bloom was already off the 3D rose. Although a hit like *The Avengers* had its already sizable box office pushed even higher by the 3D bump, the industry also weathered some high-profile disappointments, among them *Fright Night*, *Wrath of the Titans*, and Martin Scorsese's much-acclaimed *Hugo*, which tried to make the case for the artistry of 3D in the same way that *Avatar* did. Audiences also weren't turning out in droves for conversions of classic titles either; Cameron's much-ballyhooed *Titanic 3D*, as well as converted versions of *Star Wars: Episode 1—The Phantom Menace* and *Jurassic Park* performed decently, but were far from runaway hits. For now, at least, the film industry at large seems committed to keeping 3D a viable format. Certainly, multiplex chains have already sunk too much money into outfitting their theaters with the latest in 3D-enabled technology to abandon it so quickly. And for the studios, there's still a fair amount of money to be made from 3D versions of big-budget blockbusters, particularly in the international market. China, for example, has been adding 3D screens at a rapid rate. and, not coincidentally, both *Avatar* and *Titanic 3D* have been enormous hits in that country. But it's likely going to take another creative breakthrough on the level of *Avatar* to keep the format from once more sliding back into novelty territory.

FILM FIRST FILE #1: THE BEST POST-*AVATAR* 3D MOVIES

Avatar gave new life to 3D, but that didn't please the format's detractors, who have routinely labeled it, at best, a distraction and, at worst, an eyesore. Still, as Cameron demonstrated in *Avatar*, 3D can be a terrific filmmaking tool when employed properly. These are the films made in the wake of *Avatar*'s release that have best demonstrated the artistry and/or entertainment value of that extra dimension.

Jackass 3D (Jeff Tremaine, 2010)

If one of the goals of a 3D film is to dazzle you with images that leave you speechless with shock and/or wonder, the third *Jackass* feature accomplishes that feat. The closing "Poo Cocktail Supreme" stunt is particularly...uh, *memorable*.

Piranha 3D (Alexandre Aja, 2010)

This remake of an old Roger Corman picture is much more of a gonzo comedy than a horror movie. Director Aja uses 3D to goose the laughs, resulting in such amusing (if admittedly sophomoric) moments as the sight of a piranha devouring a severed penis that's floated into the audience's field of vision or a nude underwater ballet with two well-endowed models.

The Adventures of Tintin (Steven Spielberg, 2011)

Spielberg's motion-capture interpretation of Hergé's hand-drawn hero contains some of the best 3D-enhanced action sequences this side of *Avatar*.

The standout set piece has to be the climactic chase through the winding streets of a seaside Middle Eastern town that appears to take place in one fluid take.

Hugo (Martin Scorsese, 2011)

Besides rendering '30s-era Paris as a kind of pop-up kids' storybook come to cinematic life, Scorsese's striking use of 3D adds a crucial touch of magic to the early silent films that serve as the crux of the plot, making them as transporting to today's young audiences as they were to him as a child.

Gravity (Alfonso Cuarón, 2013)

Speaking of immersive experiences, Cuarón's outer space disaster movie is a white-knuckle thrill ride that convincingly strands you above Earth with only Sandra Bullock (and occasionally George Clooney) for company. The 3D is a key component of that total immersion, emphasizing the vastness of space and the improbability of any rescue.

FILM FIRST FILE #2: QUIZ: *AVATAR, BATTLE FOR TERRA, DELGO,* OR *FERNGULLY?*

As details about *Avatar*'s proenvironmental message and narrative pitting fantastical forest dwellers against profit-minded human interlopers leaked out in the run-up to its December 2009 release date, one thought lodged itself in the minds of discerning moviegoers: hasn't this film been made before? In fact, hasn't it been made ... three times? Certainly, *Avatar*'s superficial similarities to the 1992 hand-drawn animated film *FernGully: The Last Rainforest* and computer-animated adventures *Battle for Terra* and *Delgo* (released in 2007 and 2008 respectively) were too striking not to be remarked upon. Here's a short quiz designed to test how well you can tell the different movies apart. Pick one answer for each of the below questions.

1) **Desperately in need of resources, mankind has come to a new planet via a ship known as *The Ark.***

   A) *Avatar*
   B) *Battle for Terra*
   C) *Delgo*
   D) *FernGully*

2) **A human male working for the invading company aligns himself with the natural-world natives after being shrunk to microscopic size.**

   A) *Avatar*
   B) *Battle for Terra*

C) *Delgo*
D) *FernGully*

3) The movie's hero falls in love with an alien princess who has a strict father and a nifty set of wings.

A) *Avatar*
B) *Battle for Terra*
C) *Delgo*
D) *FernGully*

4) Driven by greed, the humans chop down a mystical tree that contains an evil spirit.

A) *Avatar*
B) *Battle for Terra*
C) *Delgo*
D) *FernGully*

5) The hero and the princess fall in love, much to the disapproval of her dad, and consummate their affection by indulging in a little hair-pulling.

A) *Avatar*
B) *Battle for Terra*
C) *Delgo*
D) *FernGully*

6) The princess's favorite mode of transport is soaring through the skies atop a reddish reptile.

A) *Avatar*
B) *Battle for Terra*
C) *Delgo*
D) *FernGully*

7) An ex-Hannibal Lecter plays the military leader eager to wipe out all trace of the planet's native race.

A) *Avatar*
B) *Battle for Terra*
C) *Delgo*
D) *FernGully*

8) Comic relief is provided by a former *Saturday Night Live* cast member.

   A) *Avatar*
   B) *Battle for Terra*
   C) *Delgo*
   D) *FernGully*

9) An experienced linguist was recruited to create the alien language that's heard in the film.

   A) *Avatar*
   B) *Battle for Terra*
   C) *Delgo*
   D) *FernGully*

10) The tie-in soundtrack album contains tunes like "Batty Rap" and Elton John's "Some Other World."

   A) *Avatar*
   B) *Battle for Terra*
   C) *Delgo*
   D) *Ferngully*

Answer Key: 1) B; 2) D; 3) C; 4) D; 5) A; 6) C; 7) B; 8) C; 9) A; 10) D

Chapter 23

Life in a Day (2011)

The Film: Kevin Macdonald's documentary strives to capture a day in the life of planet Earth, one YouTube clip at a time.

From the moment they dreamed up the idea of *Life in a Day*,[1] the makers of this global collage—a crew that includes director Kevin Macdonald and producers Ridley Scott and the late Tony Scott—presented themselves with a difficult, if not impossible, task: crafting a nonfiction feature film that would somehow capture the way we live now, not just in the United States but around the entire globe. While not necessarily intended to be the definitive depiction of contemporary life on Earth, their production would provide some kind of summation of the state of the planet, a decade into the twenty-first century. But how can anybody, even a group of talented artists like Macdonald and the Scott brothers, hope to create a 90-minute film that represents every country, every culture, every *facet* of the world that more than 7 billion individuals call home? And then the answer came to them: YouTube, the video-sharing site with a worldwide audience.

In its finished form, *Life in a Day* isn't the all-encompassing vision of Earth that its makers may have at one point imagined creating. At the same time, though, the film does cross more borders than you might expect, in terms of both the countries it visits and the types of people it chooses to present. Macdonald and the rest of his creative team possess an obvious (and obviously genuine) curiosity about the world that suits the film well. Rather than a definitive global portrait, the film is a collection of brief moments in time that, when placed alongside each other, gives viewers a taste of the world that exists beyond their front door.

Just as interesting, if not more so, than the movie's content is the way it was made, with the cooperation of YouTube. In 2010, the Scott brothers' production company, Scott Free, put out a call on the site for footage from its millions upon millions of visitors and users. Interested participants were required to film and submit scenes from a single day in their life—specifically, July 24, 2010. (That date was picked because it came after the 2010 World Cup. The filmmakers no doubt correctly assumed that the world would be too football mad prior to that point to have the time to take part in their little experiment.)[2] Those scenes would be uploaded to YouTube and then screened by a sizable team of viewers, researchers, and language experts (as the clips obviously wouldn't be submitted with subtitles) to find the diamonds amidst the rough. The creative team behind the film expected to receive a few thousand videos; when the submission deadline passed, they had some 80,000 clips, for a total of 4,500 hours of footage.[3]

Working on a compressed schedule, the research team waded through the 4,500 hours, rating each clip on a 1-5 star scale (1 being the lowest and 5 being the highest; there was also a 6 rating for clips that were just too good—or too weird—to not be viewed). Eventually, the footage was culled down to some 350 hours that Macdonald and his editor, Joe Walker, screened over a three-week period. The duo then had another seven weeks to produce a 90-minute feature in time for the 2011 Sundance Film Festival,[4] where the film would premiere both in Park City and around the world through a YouTube-enabled simulcast.[5] To further drive home the idea that *Life in a Day* was a communal project, Macdonald made a point of crediting every single person whose footage appeared in the final cut; indeed, some of those directors even traveled to Sundance to attend the premiere. In this way, *Life in a Day* billed itself not as the product of a single author or country, but rather a movie that emerged from—and belonged to—the world.

Initially, Macdonald and Walker were uncertain how to impose a structure on the thousands of YouTube clips they had at their disposal. Eventually, they settled on the simplest and also the most appropriate way—by embracing the title and following the sunrise-to-sundown sequence of a single 24-hour period.[6] The movie begins in the darkness of July 24's early morning hours and ends in darkness as the clock approaches midnight, ushering in July 25. In between, we observe humanity going about its day, alternating moments of the ordinary (eating, shaving, shopping, driving) and the extraordinary (skydiving, mountaineering). For the most part, Macdonald doesn't linger on any one place or person, instead swiftly moving along to make room for as many different scenes as possible.

That said, there are certain individuals who emerge as full-fledged characters. For example, in the middle of a montage depicting people's morning routines, we're welcomed into a cramped, messy apartment somewhere in Japan that's shared by a father and his young son. As the father films them preparing for the day ahead, we get the sense that something (or someone) important is absent from their lives. That suspicion is confirmed when the man turns the camera toward the picture of a smiling young woman with candles and an incense bowl in front of it and instructs the boy to "Say good morning to mummy." At first, the child resists participating in this ritual, but eventually he acquiesces and, once it's over, walks away saying "All done." This scene lasts only two minutes but tells a complete story about these two people and the circumstances of their life. Other individuals that make a lasting impression include a Korean cyclist in the midst of a mission to circumvent the globe on a bicycle—a feat he hopes will unite the two Koreas once and for all—and a poverty-stricken family somewhere in the Middle East, who allow their tiny home to be filmed, all the while insisting that, although they don't have much (including basic necessities like electricity and running water that Western viewers too often take for granted), they are, at least, "still alive."

Moments like these point to how *Life in a Day* both succeeds and fails in its ambitious endeavor. While the film does provide windows into the way people from all walks of life, from all over the world, live day to day, too many of those windows are open for too brief a time to provide much in the way of insight. It's no accident that, after a while, all the faces and places seen in the movie blend together in the viewer's mind. Individuality melts away in favor of a grand "we are the world" sentiment. And while it's true that the planet's human population shares many of the same basic needs, hopes, dreams, and desires, what makes us truly interesting to each other are our differences—differences that can't be properly catalogued and explored in a short YouTube video. In a way, the very notion of editing these clips into a larger collage cuts against what is perhaps the biggest reason for the site's popularity, that it provides a platform for individuals to express something specific about themselves, even if it's just a short scene of them dancing to their favorite song. People post videos of themselves to YouTube hoping to gain attention and stand out from the crowd. *Life in a Day*, in contrast, puts its participants all on the same continuum. While this approach achieves great breadth, it sacrifices uniqueness, personality, and storytelling—three things that we go to the movies (and to YouTube) looking for.

The First: YouTube users generated enough content to fill one theatrical feature—could they do it again?

The first-ever video uploaded to YouTube is a 19-second clip entitled "Me at the zoo," which was posted on the still-fledgling website in April 2005 by one of its creators, Jawed Karim. In the video, Karim stands in front of the elephant pen at the San Diego Zoo and lets the world in on the secret of why these creatures are so cool. "They have really, really, *really* long trunks," he says sagely, going on to add, "And that's pretty much all there is to say."[7] Based solely on the content and production value of this clip, at the time, few would probably have predicted that YouTube would go on to change the way media is consumed in this country and around the world—let alone play a key role in the production of a feature-length theatrical documentary—in only five short years after it went live.

But today, YouTube's omnipresence is a fact of life, and the diversity and sheer amount of video content on the site is staggering. In addition to the always-popular user-uploaded clips (many of which are just as random and insubstantial as "Me at the zoo"), YouTube also houses movie trailers, episodes of TV shows, and entire feature-length films—both of the Hollywood and independent variety—some which cost money to watch (prices range from $1 to $15, less than the cost of many sell-through DVDs), while others can be viewed absolutely free. And then there are short movies that aspiring filmmakers make on their own dime uploaded in the hopes that the video will go viral, thus bringing them attention and, better still, more work.

Indeed, the site does so well as its own purveyor of content, it's surprising that they felt compelled to involve themselves in a project that was intended for something as quaint and retro as a movie theater. Then again, there's still a level of prestige associated with theatrical releases that direct-to-YouTube premieres have yet to attain. Just ask Wayne Wang, an established director of such studio vehicles as *The Joy Luck Club* and *Maid in Manhattan*, whose 2008 feature *The Princess of Nebraska* debuted exclusively on YouTube's Screen room section. Although Wang's decision to premiere the film this way attracted a fair amount of press and eyeballs—153,000 views in roughly three days, which is probably more people than would have seen it in theaters opening weekend[8]—the lack of a standard theatrical release was still a stigma the movie had to overcome, certainly within Hollywood if not necessarily with viewers. Getting involved with a movie that had the potential to be shown in theaters (and, in fact, *Life in a Day* was snapped up quickly by National Geographic Films just before its Sundance premiere) must have seemed to the site's operators like an ideal way for YouTube to attain a certain measure of legitimacy that perhaps still eluded it within the media at large. It also gave them bragging rights for being the first video-sharing website to have its logo attached to the front of a theatrical feature.

Nevertheless, the fact remains that the makers of *Life in a Day* needed YouTube far more than YouTube needed *Life in a Day*. While a project like this would theoretically have been possible prior to YouTube's creation, the difficult logistics as well as the cost involved (cameras or cameramen would have to be dispatched to countries all over the world, and confirming that all the footage was shot on the same, specified day would have been a nightmare) would likely have made it prohibitive. By involving YouTube from the beginning, the filmmakers were able to speak directly to an enormous audience—the site claims that its user base numbers in the billions and that they upload 100 hours of video every minute[9]—who were eager and willing to do the legwork for them. And certainly, the enormous amount of content they received (hundreds of movies could have been made out of the 4,500 hours that were uploaded specifically for the film) only reconfirmed the tremendous reach of the YouTube brand.

At the same time, though, by aligning themselves so closely with YouTube, the *Life in a Day* team was willingly accepting the site's limitations as well as its strengths. For starters, while YouTube is unquestionably a global phenomenon, there are several countries where access to the site is limited if not restricted outright, most notably China. That meant the filmmakers were cut off from millions of potential participants, with no way to alert them to the project's existence. The resulting lack of footage from what is currently the most populous—and certainly one of the most powerful—nations on Earth is a major oversight in a film that sets out to take a snapshot of our modern world. Other countries that play a sizable role on the international stage and yet aren't represented in this film include Iran, Iraq, and Pakistan, and their absence is keenly felt.

To their credit, the filmmakers did have a plan for how to involve regions of the world where access YouTube wasn't the problem—reliable Internet connections were. In those cases, they sent high-definition video cameras (450 in total) to volunteers in those parts of the world, who spent July 24 gathering material that they then returned to the England-based production office the old-fashioned way: via snail mail. That footage compromises about 20 percent of the finished film—the rest came entirely from YouTube.[10] The downside to that approach is the small but perceptible difference between the footage shot by YouTube-recruited users versus the scenes filmed by the volunteers. The former clips have a compelling intimacy, because the people wielding the camera are also the subjects; they're filming their own lives and inviting us to watch. The latter, on the other hand, feel more studied in their compositions and choice of subjects, to the point where it's more like a movie and less like life.

Despite its failings, *Life in a Day* is an honest attempt to bridge the gap between the old model of filmmaking and distribution still being practiced by the film industry and the new one represented by outlets like YouTube. The site provided the mechanics for making the movie, while the production company provided the team that was able to mold it into a conventional feature and then find a theatrical distributor. But based on the middling box-office returns—the film only grossed a little over $250,000 during its limited theatrical release—it's hard not to wonder whether a movie made in large part by YouTube should have stayed on YouTube. *Life in a Day* can currently be viewed in its entirety for free on the site, and the number of viewers who watch it there will almost certainly come to dwarf the number that paid to see it in theaters. And with the distribution model for independently financed features moving more in the direction of TV and web-based video-on-demand services anyway, a theatrical release for a film of this type is increasingly coming to seem, at best, an afterthought and, at worst, an indulgence.

Going forward, YouTube seems more interested in producing and/or purchasing original content that premieres on the site first, not elsewhere. With hundreds of different channels showing all kinds of material, from video diary entries to music videos to short films to features, the site is its own multiplex already, one that's the destination of choice for the young viewers that Hollywood covets. Fact is, we may never see another theatrical feature preceded by the YouTube logo. It's more likely that we'll one day see the logo of a major motion picture studio preceding a film that's premiering exclusively on YouTube.

FILM FIRST FILE #1: THE MOST FAMOUS YOUTUBE CLIPS

When it launched in 2005, few people probably would have guessed that YouTube would become such a dominant pop-culture force in such a short amount of time. And while millions upon millions of visitors drop by each day to view a variety of content, from movie trailers to music videos to random scenes from old TV shows, the site's bread and butter remains the user-generated clips that are shared, forwarded, Tweeted, and otherwise circulated all over the Web. While some of these short videos burn bright and fade away, many more have a surprisingly strong shelf life, racking up an enormous number of views months and years after they were first posted. Here are some of the most popular YouTube clips in the site's relatively brief history.

"Evolution of Dance" (Uploaded 2006)

One of the most-watched videos in the site's history, this six-minute clip features comedian Judson Laipply cramming roughly five decades' worth of dance crazes into a single performance in front of a hugely appreciative audience.

"Sneezing Panda" (Uploaded 2006)

It's a scene of domestic tranquility: a mama Panda sits snacking in her pen, while her baby lies on the floor in front of her. But the calm is shattered when the young 'un lets out an enormous sneeze that almost topples his mom over with surprise.

"Charlie Bit My Finger" (Uploaded 2007)

Like the title of this minute-long clip says, baby Charlie bites his older brother's finger. To be fair to Charlie, his brother had it coming by sticking his finger in his mouth in the first place.

"Leave Britney Alone" (Uploaded 2007)

Fed up with the way the public was trashing his beloved Britney Spears, young Chris Cocker takes to the Web to defend the pop star's honor, recording a two-minute rant that remains a major pop-culture meme.

"Keyboard Cat" (Uploaded 2007)

What's funnier than a cat tickling the plastic ivories of an electronic keyboard? Absolutely nothing.

"Double Rainbow" (Uploaded 2010)

While hiking in Yosemite National Park, Paul Vasquez witnessed a rare double rainbow sighting and preserved the moment (and his hilarious reaction) on video forever for all of us to appreciate . . . and laugh at.

FILM FIRST #2: YOUTUBE: A TRAINING GROUND FOR NEW FILMMAKERS

YouTube and video-sharing sites like it aren't just home to random video clips. It's also a place where filmmakers working outside of the Hollywood system can display the fruits of their labor to the world for their approval or dismissal. Here are four online shorts that inspired lots of online chatter.

Troops (Kevin Rubio, 1997)

The granddaddy of all online fan films, *Troops* cleverly sends up Fox's long-running reality series *Cops* with a *Star Wars* twist. It's so funny, even George Lucas dug it—his company, Lucasfilm, gave Rubio a special award in 2002.

Batman: Dead End (Sandy Collora, 2003)

Originally shown at the San Diego Comic-Con, this gritty eight-minute Batman adventure, in which the Dark Knight battles the Joker as well as an Alien and a Predator, helped comics fans recover from the epic flop that was Joel Schumacher's *Batman & Robin*.

Sita Sings the Blues (Nina Paley, 2008)

Paley didn't initially intend for her semiautobiographical animated film to end up premiering online, but licensing issues with the blues recordings that are so central to the narrative made the Web the only distribution avenue available to her at first. And while the film has since been released on an extremely limited DVD edition, the easiest way to see it is still via the Internet.

Kony 2012 (Jason Russell, 2012)

Created to draw awareness to the activities of Ugandan guerrilla leader Joseph Kony, this 30-minute film detailing Kony's various abuses and war crimes (including the use of child soldiers) became an instant viral sensation when it premiered on the Web in early 2012. The endorsements of Twitter-friendly celebrities like Rihanna and Taylor Swift gave it added momentum, despite reports the filmmaker manipulated facts and offered an overly simpli-fied summary of a complex situation.

Chapter 24

Margaret (2011)

The Film: Kenneth Lonergan's sophomore feature transforms a teenage girl's life into an opera with all of Manhattan serving as her stage.

Perhaps it's only appropriate that playwright and filmmaker Kenneth Lonergan's *Margaret*[1]—a film that paints one of the most nakedly honest portraits of teenage angst ever captured on celluloid—experienced severe growing pains itself as it traveled the long, winding road to a theatrical release. Originally filmed on location in New York City in 2005, the movie unfolds from the perspective of 17-year-old high school senior Lisa (Anna Paquin), the eldest daughter of a respected stage actress (Lonergan's wife, J. Smith-Cameron) who enjoys many of the privileges that come with being a member of the Upper West Side's upper-middle class, including enrollment at a prestigious private school, a healthy amount of disposable income and very little parental supervision.

As the movie begins, Lisa's chief concerns are grades, boys, and finding a cowboy hat (in that order) for an upcoming dude ranch vacation with her father (Lonergan himself) and his new girlfriend. In a strange twist of fate, her search for that hat makes her a witness to—and inadvertent cause of—a horrific bus accident that claims a woman's life (Allison Janney, in a brief but resonant performance). After watching this stranger literally die in her arms, Lisa spends the rest of the film wrestling with the kind of moral and ethical questions that even adults would find difficult to answer. And in fact, that's a big part of the problem; none of the actual adults in her life—from her mother to her favorite teacher (Matt Damon)—are able to offer any guidance that can quiet the grief and anger that's roiling inside her. Trying to get a handle on those emotions leads her to alternately lash out at the world, try to escape from it through the usual teenage avenues (like toking up in Central Park), or attempt to right its wrongs, starting with getting the bus driver (Mark Ruffalo) fired, despite the incident having been ruled an accident. But none of these courses of action bring her the peace she craves; if anything, her various experiences leave her more uncertain about the grown-up world and her eventual place in it.

Enough time elapsed between the movie's production and release date—six years in all—that for a while, there was a great deal of uncertainty about whether the world would even get to see *Margaret* (which takes its title from the poem "Spring and Fall" by Gerard Manley Hopkins) in the first place. After shooting on the movie wrapped in 2005, the famously exacting Lonergan—already a celebrated playwright, who made his feature film-making debut with the acclaimed 2000 drama *You Can Count on Me*—disappeared into the editing room and assembled a three-hour cut for release. Unfortunately, his contract with the film's twin backers—Fox Searchlight and independent producer Gary Gilbert—stipulated that the theatrical cut could run no longer than 150 minutes if the director wanted to maintain complete creative control. Excising those 30 minutes took Lonergan three additional years, during which time another editor was hired to cut a two-hour version of the movie that satisfied Gilbert but not the director, who did finally come up with a shorter cut in the summer of 2008. At that point, however, the producer refused to pay out his part of the movie's budget, which meant a prolonged court battle that lasted another three years. By the fall of 2011, three alternate versions of *Margaret* had been created: Lonergan's contract-stipulated 150-minute cut, Gilbert's approved 120-minute cut overseen, and what was supposed to have been a 160-minute compromise cut supervised by none other than Martin Scorsese, for whom Lonergan had done script rewrites on his period epic *Gangs of New York*. Even though Gilbert and Fox Searchlight had by now wiped the slate clean of lawsuits, the producer declined to approve the Scorsese-overseen version, so the studio wound up releasing Lonergan's 150-minute version of *Margaret*, which he had turned in three years earlier.[2]

At last the movie was in theaters, but the prolonged and public behind-the-scenes battle had taken its toll, and the scars are visible in the movie itself. The first half of *Margaret*'s theatrical version (the movie was subsequently released on DVD with an alternate three-hour cut that was closer to Lonergan's original vision) is exceptionally well paced, introducing the viewer to Lisa's world and then showing how the bottom drops out of it in the wake of the accident. (That 10-minute scene may be the movie's single best sequence; it's no wonder that it continues to haunt Lisa throughout the rest of the rest of the film.) Although it's not powered by a conventional plot structure, *Margaret*'s first hour does have a clear narrative arc with the disparate, seemingly random situations that Lisa subsequently involves her-self in—losing her virginity to a sarcastic slacker type, propositioning her teacher in his apartment, picking fights with her mother—tying back into the larger theme of a young woman trying to deal with the aftermath of a tragic situation by acting older than her years. (As more than one critic noted at the time of its release, *Margaret* is also rife with explicit and implicit allu-sions to the 9/11 tragedy; in that reading, Lisa's profound grief in a sense comes to mirror her city's collective mourning following the cataclysmic events of that day.)

It's in the movie's second hour where things get wonky. Scenes feel rushed and abbreviated, characters enter and exit the frame almost at random, and at least one seemingly important subplot is dropped entirely, referenced only once in such a way that the viewer can't quite tell whether it actually hap-pened or is just a figment of Lisa's overheated imagination. (This story line, which involves Lisa discovering that she's pregnant and then opting to get an abortion, is fully restored in Lonergan's extended cut.) At the same time, though, the back half of the movie does serve to snap Lonergan's end game into focus. As Lisa's heightened emotional state reaches a fever pitch—man-ifesting itself in prolonged outbursts shouted at occasionally eardrum-piercing volumes—and the first tragedy she's involved in is compounded by others, *Margaret* can clearly be seen pursuing the kind of grand melodrama and seismic release of feeling offered by opera. Lonergan drives this home in the final scene, which finds Lisa and her estranged mother attending a per-formance at Lincoln Center and both being moved to the point of tears and, finally, reconciliation by the sheer power of the experience. (The connection is made even more explicit in the alternate cut, where opera permeates the soundtrack.)

For all the trials and tribulations that Lonergan experienced making *Margaret*, the finished product is something worthy of admiration, both in its theatrical and alternate DVD versions. This is one of those instances where seeing both cuts is essential to the overall experience, as both follow the same general narrative trajectory but display some significantly different aesthetic choices. (For example, in the extended cut, Lonergan devotes more screen time to New York itself, making it clear that Lisa's story is one of many upon this bustling city stage.) In both cuts, it's striking to see this period of adolescence depicted with such sensitivity and nuance; even moments that aren't quite fully realized are balanced by scenes of extraordi-nary insight into the overburdened mind of its teenage protagonist. While it's doubtful that anyone, even Lonergan, would insist that Lisa is representative of all 17-year-olds, the larger questions and decisions she's confronted with do travel far beyond the Upper West Side of Manhattan. Like its heroine, *Margaret* endured a troubled coming of age, but emerges all the stronger for it.

The First: The brouhaha kicked up online over *Margaret*'s troubled release suggested a new function for twenty-first-century social media: cinematic activism.

Calling Fox Searchlight's belated theatrical release of *Margaret* half-hearted would be generous—after scheduling only a handful of press screenings for critics, the studio opened the movie on September 30, 2011, in a single theater in New York and another in Los Angeles, spending next to nothing on promotional materials advertising its long-awaited arrival. The mixed reaction from the press that had been able to see the movie didn't exactly help its box-office prospects (although those critics who did like it argued passionately in its favor); during that brief initial run, the movie earned a little under $50,000.[3] With little apparent interest from the studio in increasing the movie's profile, *Margaret* seemed destined to vanish back into the ether, most likely not to be seen or heard of again until an equally under-the-radar DVD release.

Fortunately, things didn't exactly work out that way, thanks to a wave of online activism that renewed interest in Lonergan's neglected film. *Margaret*'s second life began when Jaime Christley, a film reviewer for the online magazine *Slant*, posted a petition on the website Change.org that asked Fox Searchlight to expand the movie to more theaters, this time giving critics more opportunities to see it in consideration for their annual best-of-the-year lists, as well as any awards they might participate in. In his petition, Christley wrote:

> After a protracted post-production phase, news of which seemed to spell disaster, Kenneth Lonergan's MARGARET opened quietly in New York City and Los Angeles a few months ago, after which it seemed to disappear. (In fact, many major cities in the US didn't get the opportunity to see it at all.) In that time, the film became known as a miracle—a major work of cinematic art, against the odds—to almost all of the critics and cinephiles who were able to catch it during its brief appearance. It has all the earmarks of a grassroots-supported movie phenomenon. We, the undersigned respectfully request that film critics and other pertinent voting bodies be given the opportunity to view MARGARET prior to voting in applicable awards, or compiling applicable year-end "best of" lists.[4]

While it's not unheard of for reviewers to bemoan a movie's shoddy treatment by its distributor, typically those kinds of disappointed reactions appear in general think pieces or end-of-the-year wrap-up stories tallying up the best and worst in film. This was something different—a critic directly appealing to a studio to reconsider its practices in a form (not to mention a forum) more commonly associated with individuals championing various social and political causes. And what's more, other reviews signed their names to it as well. Christley's petition eventually collected 685 signatures, including such prominent respondents as *New York* magazine's Bilge Ebiri and *Time Out Chicago*'s Ben Kenigsberg, who wrote: "*Margaret* is a masterpiece ... the kind of layered, actor-driven family drama that awards bodies would probably go nuts for. Kenneth Lonergan's much-loved *You Can Count on Me* wouldn't have garnered Oscar nods without a push, and it certainly seems like *Margaret* has enough fans (and would-be viewers) to generate interest along those lines."[5]

But the Change.org petition was only the first step in the movie's web-based revival; the popular microblogging site Twitter came to play an even more prominent role. *Margaret*'s fans were able to win the film significant attention by utilizing one of Twitter's best-known features: the hashtag, which allows users to come up with a pithy tag at the end of their post that others can also join in their feed. In the case of *Margaret*, the hashtag was #TeamMargaret[6] and many of the critics who signed the online petition also made their allegiance to #TeamMargaret known on Twitter, as did civilian viewers who sought the film out and enjoyed it. The #TeamMargaret movement became prominent enough in film enthusiast circles that it was written about in various prominent news outlets, including *Time* magazine and the *Village Voice*. Even Lonergan—who isn't on Twitter himself[7]—was touched by the outpouring of online support. In one interview, the filmmaker remarked, "I despise the Internet, and as a matter of principle, I'm not supposed to like critics .... And yet I'm so grateful to the critical community for rescuing the film. I was just swept away by that, I must say. ... To see it become something of a cause célèbre was humbling. It makes you believe in critics."[8]

So what effect did all of this online chatter ultimately have on *Margaret*'s fortunes? In terms of box office, not much, as the film was mostly out of theaters by the time the online campaigning started. However, the petition and the media attention it attracted did convince Fox Searchlight to hold additional screenings for critics in cities where the movie didn't play theatrically[9] and send out screeners of the film—albeit at the last minute—to Oscar voters.[10] (The film ultimately didn't receive any nominations.) But perhaps the development that vindicated the efforts of #TeamMargaret the most was the studio's eventual announcement that the film's DVD release would include both the theatrical version *and* a three-hour alternate cut closer to Lonergan's original vision, which had taken on a mythical status thanks to all the conversations about the movie's editing-room woes. This was something that Christley hadn't asked for in his original petition and took even some of the movie's strongest advocates by surprise. Where Fox Searchlight's other actions—booking more critics' screenings and sending out awards screeners—were in direct response to the online activism, here was a case of a movie studio seizing the initiative to win the protestors back to their side (and, of course, sell more

DVD units in the process). Prior to the release of the DVD, Searchlight even held two special theatrical screenings of the longer version, both of which featured the director and several of his cast members in attendance. Suddenly, a movie that Fox Searchlight had essentially disowned was belatedly being celebrated, largely because a group of film lovers made their voices heard and campaigned hard for a movie they were genuinely passionate about.

Whether *Margaret*'s experience is replicable with other films certainly remains to be seen. Working in this movie's favor was the identity of its distributor—despite the poor way they handled *Margaret*'s initial release, Fox Searchlight is generally known to be a studio that's quite attentive to the movie press corps—as well as the always-compelling hook of the lone artist fighting to preserve his voice and vision in the face of industry indifference. Certainly the behind-the-scenes travails surrounding the movie helped make Lonergan a more sympathetic figure both to #TeamMargaret and the media at large that picked up on the story; just like in any sports movie, people want to root for the underdog athlete, not the people holding the purse strings. And then there's the fact that, despite its indie movie budget, *Margaret* is filled with well-known actors, which instantly elevates its profile. (It's safe to say that a campaign to save a movie *without* Matt Damon and Anna Paquin would have a harder time gaining traction, no matter how good the film itself is.) Regardless, the fact that a targeted social media campaign was able to rescue a movie from studio-imposed oblivion is a promising development for movie culture and an example of the power film critics—a group whose influence is often called into question—can wield in the right circumstances. As the case of *Margaret* indicates, the Internet offers new ways for overlooked and neglected films to be brought to the public's attention. It's another tool with which film lovers can rally behind the movies they believe in so that they don't languish forever in the dark.

FILM FIRST FILE #1: FIVE FAMOUSLY UNRELEASED FILMS

Margaret took six years to reach theaters, but some movies have spent an even longer time in limbo. These are a few of the titles that will probably never play at a theater near you.

The Day The Clown Cried (Jerry Lewis, 1972)

What It Is: Perhaps the most famous movie that no one (besides humorist Harry Shearer) has seen, this World War II drama about a German clown (director and star Lewis) who winds up in a POW camp for ridiculing Hitler. At one point the performer starts doing his act to entertain young Jewish prisoners and subsequently joins a group of children on a train to Auschwitz, where he leads them into the gas chambers.

Will It Ever Be Released? Signs point to no, as the movie only exists in a rough-cut form and lingering contractual issues would make a general release difficult even if Lewis showed any interest in completing it.

Cocksucker Blues (Robert Frank, 1972)

What It Is: In the tradition of D. A. Pennebaker's groundbreaking 1967 Bob Dylan-centric documentary *Don't Look Back*, *Cocksucker Blues* follows the Rolling Stones on their 1972 tour of North America, with Frank filming the band and their hangers-on engaging in all manner of bad behavior, from drug use to compromising sexual situations. The Stones went to the courts to block its release, and the resulting ruling gave the director permission to screen the movie five times a year only in specific venues (like museums) with himself in attendance.[11]

Will It Ever Be Released? Unless Frank tries to get that order overturned (which seems unlikely) or the Rolling Stones change their minds (which seems even more unlikely), the movie will never go into general release. But bootleg copies are floating around out there, including on YouTube.

Dark Blood (George Sluizer, 1993)

What It Is: River Phoenix was 11 days away from wrapping production on this drama about a young hermit living by a nuclear testing site when he died of a drug overdose at the age of 23. Following his passing, production shut down, but Sluizer held onto the footage, hoping to eventually find a way to finish it without his star.

Will It Ever Be Released? In 2012, Sluizer finally announced that he had managed to secure the funds to complete a reedited version of the movie and has since screened it at several film festivals.

The Fantastic Four (Oley Sassone, 1994)

What It Is: Back before Marvel Comics got smarter about licensing the movie rights to their characters, the German production company Neue Constantin Films held the option to produce a big-screen vehicle starring Marvel's blue-spandex-clad superhero family. With those rights set to expire in 1992, Constantin rushed a *Fantastic Four* movie into production on an ultra-low budget with the aid of B-movie guru Roger Corman. But the finished product went unreleased and Neue Constantin held onto the rights,[12] producing two big-budget movies based on the comic in 2005 and 2007, both of which *were* released in theaters.

Will It Ever Be Released? No, but bootleg copies are readily available online and at any comic book convention.

Nailed (David O. Russell, 2008)

What It Is: The director of *Three Kings* and *Silver Linings Playbook* teamed up with Al Gore's daughter Kristen to write this political satire about a receptionist (Jessica Biel) who becomes an activist for those suffering from bizarre injuries after she's shot in the head with a nail gun. Production repeatedly shut down due to various behind-the-scenes problems and eventually halted altogether before the movie could be completed. Russell made several attempts to finish it before walking away for good in 2010.[13]

Will It Ever Be Released? A year after Russell left the movie, the owner of the company that bankrolled it, Ron Tutor, made noises about ensuring its completion, screening it to a test audience and hiring a composer. But there's been no additional word on the movie's fate since then.

FILM FIRST FILE #2: SECOND TIME AROUND

The unwavering support of *Margaret*'s passionate fan base eventually helped it score critical reappraisal and a promising posttheatrical afterlife. The following films—all of which were written off as failures during their initial release—also benefitted from the enthusiastic championing of a small but devoted band of followers who eventually helped lead them to greater recognition through their own brand of advocacy.

The Rocky Horror Picture Show (Jim Sharman, 1975)

General audiences shrugged, but the midnight movie crowd ate up this film version of the offbeat British rock musical from the beginning. The key to its revival and subsequent longevity was transforming screenings of the film from passive to interactive experiences where audiences came in costume and participated in the show going on in front of the movie, from talking back to the screening to dancing along to key musical numbers. By making the film almost secondary to the experience, the *Rocky Horror* fans turned it into a party that every hip moviegoer felt they had to experience at least once.

The Thing (John Carpenter, 1982)

Granted, it faced some stiff competition during 1982's packed summer movie season, but Carpenter's horror-tinged survival story about a group of Antarctic researchers who confront a shape-shifting alien menace still deserved a better box-office fate than it received at the time. The good news is that the people who did see it then—or during its subsequent runs on TV—never forgot it. As many of them went on to enter the film world professionally as directors, writers, special-effects people, and critics, they frequently pointed to that film as a genre touchstone. Thanks to this generational shift, by the time a prequel/remake was made in 2011, Carpenter's *Thing* was revered as a classic.

The Boondock Saints (Troy Duffy, 1999)

Troy Duffy came practically out of nowhere when he wrote and directed this Boston-set crime thriller, and he was set to vanish back to nowhere following the movie's scathing reviews and dismal box office. But then Blockbuster Video flooded their stores with it, promoting it as a Blockbuster Exclusive, and *The Boondock Saints* picked up a sizable following, particularly amongst younger audiences who kept circulating the various DVD releases around to their friends in a pre-Internet form of viral marketing.

Donnie Darko (Richard Kelly, 2001)

DVD also proved pivotal to resurrecting Richard Kelly's trippy teen drama following its disappointing theatrical release. While the movie's demographic didn't turn up for its theatrical run, they did rent it regularly on disc to puzzle out its mysteries. The strong DVD sales allowed Kelly to release his director's cut of the film, which, funnily enough, most fans find inferior to the theatrical version.

Scott Pilgrim vs. the World (Edgar Wright, 2010)

Following the rapturous word of mouth that greeted this video-game-infused romantic comedy at special screenings held at San Diego's Comic-Con International, the studio was primed for the movie to cause a major youth quake when it opened in general release. But things didn't quite work out that way, as the movie only lasted one week in the Top Ten. As would happen with *Margaret* a year later, though, the film's Internet-savvy supporters refused to let it disappear from the pop-culture consciousness. A huge outpouring of online support instantly kicked in after the movie's disappointing opening weekend, and its cult status was solidified by sold-out midnight screenings—complete with *Rocky Horror*-like fan costumes—at revival theaters like Los Angeles' New Beverly Cinema.

Chapter 25

Red State (2011)

The Film: Seventeen years and nine feature films into his directorial career, Kevin Smith finally felt ready to step outside of his comfort zone and the result is perhaps his most ambitious—if flawed—movie.

Like Quentin Tarantino, Kevin Smith is often described as an "indie film-maker," but as the Jersey-born writer/director is fond of saying, he's only made two genuine independent features during the course of his career. The first was 1994's no-budget black-and-white comedy *Clerks* about two minimum-wage drones, which Smith paid for by maxing out his credit cards. A breakout hit at that year's Sundance Film Festival, the movie enjoyed an equally successful theatrical run that rocketed him out of the Red Bank, New Jersey, convenience store where he manned the register (and shot the movie) and onto a national stage. The second was 2011's *Red State*,[1] which Smith wrote, directed, and raised money for. In the 17 years separating his two true indie films, Smith wrote and directed eight other features, all of which were made for major and minor studios, ranging from Universal (*Mallrats*) to Miramax (*Chasing Amy*) to Warner Bros. (*Cop Out*).

So why after all that time within the studio world did Smith willingly return to the more unpredictable indie film market? Well, for one thing, his recent studio vehicles were only moderate commercial successes and mostly washed out with critics. More importantly, though, he couldn't find anyone—even his longtime friends and professional colleagues Harvey and Bob Weinstein, who essentially made his career when they acquired *Clerks* at Sundance—willing to finance the script. To be sure, *Red State* was a risky project to underwrite as it promised to be a wild departure from anything Smith had made before. Instead of yet another raunchy broad comedy, the filmmaker had penned a dark, genre-straddling story about a fundamentalist preacher (modeled after the controversial leader of the Westboro Baptist Church, Fred Phelps)[2] who, rather than simply preach about the sins of the modern world (with a particular emphasis on homosexuality), had decided to take an active role in meting out God's justice upon the heathens in his midst.

Red State begins like a more traditional Smith vehicle, with three horny small-town teens (Michael Angarano, Nicholas Braun, and Kyle Gallner) trolling the Internet for sex and eventually booking a session with a local prostitute (Melissa Leo). Too late do they discover, however, that she's actually a member of the Five Points Trinity Church, run by bloody-minded preacher Abin Cooper (Michael Parks). Brought to the Five Points headquarters inside a walled compound, the trio are intended to provide the congregation with sacrificial lambs, but two manage to escape, setting off a series of events that eventually results in a standoff between the Church and an army of federal agents who have gathered outside the front gate and granted the authority to storm the property and kill or capture (preferably kill) everyone inside.

Apart from the obvious potential for controversy, the bigger movie studios had to be concerned about whether Smith was the right guy to tackle this kind of material given that he was still best known for scripting debates about the merits of *The Lord of the Rings* movies vs. the *Star Wars* franchise and copious gags about blowjobs and/or cunnilingus. The fact that it is such a departure for him, though, makes *Red State* one of Smith's most interesting efforts as filmmaker. That's not to say that it's his best film, of course, as the finished product is rife with problems. But it is also quite clearly the work of a director that's actively engaged in the story he's telling as opposed to just going through the motions and hoping for the best, which is what appeared to happen in the film Smith made right before *Red State*, the listless buddy cop comedy *Cop Out*. The amount of effort that Smith is investing in *Red State* is felt throughout, and even when the film falls short of what he hopes to achieve, that attempt is still welcome.

Beyond meeting the challenge presented by the material, perhaps the element in *Red State* that prodded Smith into upping his behind-the-camera game is the movie's cast. *Cop Out* didn't gel for a variety of reasons, but chief among them was the tense relationship the director claims to have had with the movie's star, Bruce Willis, during shooting,[3] a tension that carries over into the film itself. And as the hired gun on a studio-backed star vehicle, Smith's influence on casting—particularly regarding the movie's leading roles—was limited. Returning to the independent world to make *Red State*, however, freed him up to cast the actors he liked, as opposed to who the studio wanted. That's largely how he was able to hand the movie's centerpiece role over to a veteran character actor like Michael Parks. And Parks proves to be absolutely inspired casting, as he projects an aura of charismatic menace that's essential to maintaining the movie's atmosphere of tension. The rest of the ensemble is populated by reliable performers as well, including John Goodman as a morally compromised ATF agent and acclaimed stage actress Kerry Bishé in a small but impressive turn as one of Cooper's granddaughters. Their committed performances go a long way toward smoothing over some of the rougher patches in Smith's screenplay.

Red State's low budget also demanded a higher level of engagement from the director than a studio production like *Cop Out*, where money is more readily available to throw at production problems. In discussing his experience of going from a budget of roughly $40 million to in the vicinity of $4 million, Smith often recounts a story in which he requested that *Red State*'s effects crew construct a ram's head that could be lowered over a human head for a key scene. Informed that the effect would cost $5,000, Smith initially agreed to the price without hesitation. He was then told that $5,000 was the entire effects budget for the film. That limitation forced Smith to rethink the scene, and he hit upon a solution that wound up pleasing him more than what he had originally written.[4]

Similarly, the accelerated production schedule brought about by the low budget clearly had an impact on the way Smith chose to shoot *Red State*. In the past, Smith's critics (and the director himself) have poked fun at his limited visual palette, which is generally defined by lots of static, stationary shots with the character or characters located dead center in the frame. From its first scenes, *Red State* establishes an entirely different visual language, one dominated by handheld camerawork, with shots that seem conceived on the fly rather than composed ahead of time. It's not a natural style for Smith, and, at times, one gets the sense that he's not always sure just what he wants the camera to capture. Again, though, there's an immediacy to the direction that suggests a level of involvement from the filmmaker that had been missing in some of his previous features. There's a feeling throughout that Smith is allowing himself to take chances that he used to avoid, preferring in those cases to settle for the easiest solution possible.

Smith's obvious enthusiasm for the film he's making does lead you to wish that *Red State* were a better movie overall. But the finished product is marred by choppy storytelling and some chaotic choreography in the final action sequence, as well as a certain amount of didacticism in the larger themes that Smith seems out to tackle. After setting up Cooper and his clan as the heavies, Smith tries to flip the script in the movie's second half, suggesting that the federal agents are just as hateful and morally compromised as the churchgoers they're about to execute on the orders of their soulless bureaucratic superiors. It's an equation that never quite makes sense, though, and neither does the film's ending, which feels cribbed from a key scene in the Coen Brothers' celebrated adaptation of the Cormac McCarthy novel *No Country for Old Men* in the way it presents the character who supposedly represents law and order (Goodman in this case) expressing uncertainty about his place in a crueler, more violent time.

Some directors would be reinvigorated by radically reinventing their well-worn style. As far as Smith was concerned, though, *Red State* marked the beginning of his final act as a feature filmmaker. While promoting the film, he frequently spoke of retiring after one more movie, the period hockey comedy *Hit Somebody*. Since then, his plans have changed; *Hit Somebody* is now set to be a television miniseries, while Smith has at least two more directorial efforts in the pipeline, *Clerks III* and an original screenplay entitled *Tusk*, which went before cameras in 2013.[5] (Smith was able to secure financing for that low budget film from an established production company, making it less of a "true indie" than *Red State*.) At the time of *Red State*'s original release, though, his insistence that he was willing to step away from filmmaking so readily was disappointing, given what the film suggested he might accomplish were he to continue displaying the same level of ambition (and a lot more discipline) in future projects. While there are a number of criticisms one can level at *Red State*, it's hard to accuse it of being a predictable career capper.

The First: Welcome to Indie Film 2.0, where filmmakers distribute their own movies in theaters and on VOD and publicize them solely via Twitter.

When Kevin Smith chose to premiere *Red State* at the 2011 Sundance Film Festival, it represented a homecoming of sorts. It had been 14 years since he had last appeared in Park City and 17 years since he had come to town with a movie to sell. But now he had returned to present his latest feature and join the ranks of filmmakers hunting for a decent distribution deal ... or so everyone assumed. Smith burnished that impression by announcing that an auction for the film's distribution rights would be held immediately following the premiere. And, indeed, following the screening, he did invite his producer, Jon Gordon, onto the stage to accept bids from the crowd. The first bid? $20 from the film's director, whom Gordon promptly declared the evening's winner.[6]

Turns out that handing *Red State* over to somebody else was never part of Smith's game plan; instead, he intended to use the stage offered by Sundance to announce a different release strategy for the film. Rather than sell the movie to an established distributor who would mount a standard theatrical release along with a multimillion-dollar ad campaign, the director planned a multitiered release, starting with a road-show tour complete with post-screening Q&A sessions with the cast and crew followed by a national theatrical rollout nine months later where he'd work directly with exhibitors to book the movie in their theaters. And best of all, he wouldn't spend a dime on marketing, relying on word of mouth—via the World Wide Web—to get people into the theater. "Welcome to Indie Film 2.0," he told the Sundance audience, as if ushering them into a brave new cinematic world.[7]

Of course, Smith was overstating things a bit, as several of the central tenets of "Indie Film 2.0" weren't exactly revolutionary concepts. By booking his film directly into theaters himself, Smith was following in the four-walling footsteps of Tom Laughlin, whose success at self-distributing his 1971 film *Billy Jack* played a key role in bringing about the wide-release strategy employed by every contemporary Hollywood blockbuster since *Jaws*. Meanwhile, the notion of a special road-show presentation hearkens all the way back to the Golden Age of Hollywood, when the major studios took some of their biggest titles (*Gone With the Wind* was an example Smith cited in his Sundance rant)[8] on tour. Still, Smith's plans did make him the first high-profile contemporary director to announce his independence from the distribution model most filmmakers at his level abided by. And what was new about his specific plan was the "no advertising" gimmick. The filmmaker devoted a healthy chunk of his Sundance speech to criticizing the current model, which, as he explained it, required that low-budget movies be sold off to companies that promptly sunk exorbitant costs into marketing them. And while more marketing potentially means more eyeballs, it also means that your average indie film is now further away from turning a profit, despite its low cost. A film like *Red State*, for example, was made for only $4 million, but Smith claimed a distributor would potentially spend anywhere from $10 to $20 million and above on ad dollars for a theatrical release, another $10 to $20 million that the film then has to earn back before it achieves profitability.[9]

Of course, most films require those kinds of advertising-related expenditures in order to create a brand awareness with moviegoers, thus luring them into the theater. Smith was in a more rarefied place in that *he* is already his own brand, one that comes with a built-in audience. A personable guy by nature, the filmmaker has worked hard to establish a rapport—both in person and, particularly, online, originally through Internet message boards and later via Twitter and other social media platforms—with his fans since the release of *Clerks* in 1994. As a result, Smith's flock readily turns out for all of his features while also following him beyond movies into his other pop-culture properties, including comic books, podcasts, and ancillary merchandise. Knowing that he possessed a sizable audience and, furthermore, had a direct, inexpensive avenue with which to communicate with them is what convinced Smith that he could forego traditional advertising methods when bringing *Red State* out into the world. After all, while a $30 million final gross—the number his films generally hit—might not have been enough to make *Cop Out* a success, it would more than pay off the $4 million that *Red State* cost to make.

Smith wasted little time putting his Indie Film 2.0 plans into action. Not long after the film's Sundance premiere, the official itinerary for the Red State U.S.A. Tour went live on *Red State*'s official website, CoopersDell.com (named for the small town in the movie where the action goes down). Smith also regularly hyped the movie and the tour through his fledgling podcast empire, which included an entire podcast devoted to *Red State* entitled "Red State of the Union," a series of Q&A's the director conducted with his cast and crew. The steady web-based drumbeat paid off; on March 5, 2011, the Red State U.S.A. Tour kicked off at New York's Radio City Music Hall in front of an audience of 3,800 people—a more than decent turnout considering that the venue could seat almost 6,000. In that one evening, *Red State* grossed $160,000, which made it the tenth-best per-theater average of all time. (Of course, it helped that cost of tickets for that screening ranged from $60 to $120.)[10]

The rest of the tour proved equally successful, with *Red State* playing to large crowds at every stop on his 15-city jaunt. And again, Smith reached those viewers almost exclusively through his online soapbox. In a blog post published on yet another one of his sites, TheRedStatements.com, Smith stated that 85 to 90 percent of the audience said that they heard about the tour from one of Smith's podcasts. In the same post, he claimed that between the money they grossed on the tour, an additional $1.5 million they acquired from selling the movie to foreign markets, and another $3 million they were likely to receive from selling off the rights for all North American distribution channels besides theatrical (i.e., video on demand, home video, cable television, and the like), *Red State* was well on its way to profitability without having to compensate at all for advertising dollars.[11]

While Smith's handling of *Red State* proved that it was possible to turn a profit on a low-budget film without spending exorbitant amounts of cash on advertising, it's worth noting that he didn't accomplish every one of his stated goals for Indie Film 2.0. First and foremost, *Red State* never received the traditional theatrical release he said it would at Sundance; the closest it came to that was a weeklong engagement at L.A.'s New Beverly Cinema in order to qualify for Academy Awards consideration[12] (it received no nominations) and a one-night only special screening in various theaters nationwide that included a live postscreening Q&A via Twitter and satellite.[13] In interviews, Smith confirmed that he abandoned the idea of a wide theatrical release when it became clear that theater exhibitors wanted him to spend more money on advertising the movie outside of the Web.[14] Instead of opening in theaters, *Red State* premiered on video on demand in September 2011, followed by a DVD release in October. (Smith repeated the roadshow model for the 2013 animated film, *Jay & Silent Bob's Super Groovy Cartoon Movie*, which played special engagements around the country, but never went into general release.)

The other question mark surrounding Smith's vision of Indie Film 2.0 is whether it would a replicable model for a director *not* named Kevin Smith. Certainly, Smith's second career as an Internet impresario, to say nothing of his built-in brand name, proved invaluable in allowing him to pursue the path he had chosen for *Red State*. It would be much harder for a director just starting out to attract the same kind of attention, even if he followed Smith's methods to the letter. (One example of someone who did succeed where Smith fell short is Shane Carruth, who self-distributed his 2013 film *Upstream Color* in theaters and on VOD and DVD with minimal—though not zero—advertising.) Perhaps recognizing that, in his Sundance speech Smith signaled his intentions to act as a distributor and spokesman for other indie films that he believed in, self-distributing them under his SModcast Pictures label.

On the one-year anniversary of *Red State*'s Park City premiere, the director moved forward with those plans in a characteristically tweaked fashion, announcing that SModcast Pictures had partnered with the distributor Phase 4 Films to release at least 12 films a year under the banner "SModcast Pictures Presents" (later changed to "The Kevin Smith Movie Club") four of which would play road-show style in addition to a VOD release, with each movie doing a minitour of a handful of cities featuring Q&A's with Smith and the filmmaking team.[15] (To date, "The Kevin Smith Movie Club" has released such low-budget films as *Miss December*, *Weekender*, and *The Dirties*.) Technically, striking a partnership with a distributor (even a smaller one like Phase 4) went against the tenets of Indie Film 2.0 that Smith had laid out in his Sundance speech. But even in its compromised form, Smith's plans for SModcast Pictures were forward-thinking: an established director actively extending his own brand name and sizeable media imprint to help other indie filmmakers get their start. That's a version of Indie Film 2.0 that may just have a future.

FILM FIRST FILE #1: KEVIN SMITH—KING OF ALL MEDIA?

Some filmmakers limit their careers to the silver screen. Not Kevin Smith, whose pop culture imprint extends far beyond movies. He are some of the other industries and mediums in which the writer/director has a strong foothold.

The Internet

Smith was an early adopter of the World Wide Web, launching his official website, ViewAskew.com in 1995, where he was a regular presence, often responding to reader-posed questions on the message boards and announcing information about upcoming appearances and projects. He launched a second site in 2001 as a tie-in to his fifth feature *Jay and Silent Bob Strike Back* entitled MoviePoopShoot.com. Originally intended as a parody site, it started to produce regular editorial content the following year and later changed its name to Quick Stop Entertainment. (In 2010, Smith turned the site over to another party and it has since been rebranded as Fred

Entertainment.) Smith also maintains a popular Twitter feed with over 2 million followers and then there's his Internet radio network, SIR (SModcast Internet Radio), which launched in 2011 and offers dozens of podcasts that can be streamed or downloaded. Many of these shows are anchored by Smith and also feature several of his regular collaborators, from former producer Scott Mosier, to former co-star Jason Mewes to his own wife, Jennifer Schwalbach.

Publishing

Smith has published four books, beginning with the 2005 collection *Silent Bob Speaks*. He has also enjoyed lengthy runs on several ongoing comic books (*Daredevil* and *Green Arrow* among them) and penned a number of limited series as well. Within the comic book realm, he also owns and operates the comic book and novelty store Jay and Silent Bob's Secret Stash, located in his hometown of Red Bank, New Jersey and is a regular fixture at San Diego's annual Comic-Con International.

TV

Jay and Silent Bob's Secret Stash served as the setting for the reality series *Comic Book Men* that Smith produced and appeared in. It premiered on the cable network AMC in February 2012.

Public Speaking

Smith maintains a lucrative side career as a kind of stand-up performer, touring the country (and even the globe) to live appearances where crowds of fans turn out to ask him questions. He responds to their queries with lengthy anecdotes that can last as long as an hour. His longest ever public engagement lasted seven hours, running from 8pm to 3am the next morning.

FILM FIRST FILE #2: OTHER WRITER/DIRECTORS WITH A SIGNIFICANT ONLINE PRESENCE

John August

The screenwriter behind *Big Fish* and *Charlie and the Chocolate Factory* regales readers with stories of his own Hollywood misadventures and helpful advice via his personal blog, **johnaugust.com**.

Joe Carnahan

The director of *The Grey* and *Smokin' Aces* maintains a lively Twitter feed under the handle **@carnojoe**.

Peter Jackson

The New Zealand filmmaker pioneered the use of web-based production diaries to build anticipation for films like his *Lord of the Rings* trilogy, *King Kong*, and the three *Hobbit* movies, available to view on **thehobbitblog.com**.

Rian Johnson

The mind behind such cult favorites as *Brick*, *The Brothers Bloom*, and *Looper* maintains his own site, **rcjohnso.com**, featuring behind-the-scenes snapshots and postings about his current films. He also has a Tumblr page at rcjohnso.tumblr.com/ and tweets frequently using his handle **@rianjohnson**.

Michael Moore

When he's not off making movies designed to annoy the country's right wing, the controversial documentary filmmaker and political gadfly blogs his opinions on his site, **michaelmoore.com**.

Edgar Wright

The *Scott Pilgrim vs. the World* director is a serial Tweeter and has some 250,000 followers on his **@edgarwright** feed.

Conclusion

Five Film Firsts to Come

This particular history of contemporary American cinema may end in 2011, but the pace of change within the country's film industry hasn't slowed down since then. If anything, the tempo has quickened, with both Hollywood and the independent film world preparing for a profound paradigm shift—one driven by new technology, new distribution strategies, and new financial avenues—that will have significant implications for both the art and commerce of filmmaking. While predicting what the overall landscape of the industry will look like a decade from now is difficult, based on recent developments, it's highly likely that we'll see several of the following film firsts happen before 2021.

THE FIRST INTERNATIONALLY FINANCED AMERICAN BLOCKBUSTER

It's already common for Hollywood's bigger movie studios and production companies to team up with foreign producers and coproduce globally minded blockbusters. One notable example is the comic-book movie powerhouse Marvel Studios, which partnered with one of China's biggest media companies, DMG Entertainment, for its 2013 sequel, *Iron Man 3*, ensuring the film's release in one of the world's biggest—and most tightly controlled—movie markets. But a more interesting test case for the role international money may play going forward is *Cloud Atlas*, the ambitious 2012 genre mélange written and directed by Andy and Lana Wachowski and Tom Tykwer. The filmmakers cobbled together the movie's $100 million budget from investors in such countries as South Korea, Singapore, and Germany, where the bulk of the film was shot. And while the cast included big-name Hollywood stars like Tom Hanks and Halle Berry, no American studio put a significant sum toward its production, with Warner Bros. attaching itself only as the movie's U.S. distributor.[1] Although *Cloud Atlas* ultimately proved to be a box-office failure stateside, the directing team's success at finding funding for their big-budget spectacle overseas provides a road map for others to follow. One day in the not-too-distant future, the next hugely successful American blockbuster won't actually have been made with American currency.

THE FIRST DAY AND DATE MAJOR STUDIO RELEASE

Steven Soderbergh and Magnolia got the ball rolling with *Bubble*—premiering the movie via video-on-demand platforms and in theaters on the same day rather than months apart as so often dictated by release windows—and other independent distributors have followed suit, to the point where a sizable number of smaller films now frequently premiere on VOD *before* turning up in cinemas. For now, the larger studios have been slow to commit to this practice, most likely still smarting from the *Tower Heist* fiasco, where Universal Pictures upset exhibitors by floating the idea of releasing that 2011 Eddie Murphy/Ben Stiller comedy on VOD in select markets after it had been in theaters for three weeks.[2] But it's only a matter of time before somebody—maybe even Universal, which is owned by the cable giant Comcast—tries again, especially if attendance for nonblockbusters continues to diminish, weakening exhibitors' bargaining power, and the studios continue to assert their control in the still-expanding marketplace for streaming entertainment. One studio is going to be the first to release a high-profile mainstream movie in theaters and at home on the same day, and once that dam bursts, the others will immediately follow.

THE FIRST MOVIE TO BYPASS DVD

The writing is on the wall for physical media across all spectrums from books to music to movies. Thanks to streaming services like Netflix, and Amazon Watch Instantly, sales of DVDs and the format's successor Blu-rays have largely stagnated. Much like the final days of VHS, the physical discs will continue to be manufactured—most likely in smaller and smaller quantities—for a few years yet, as enough homes still have players to warrant making them available. But it's clear that some of the major studios are already treating DVDs as afterthoughts; for example, a month before releasing its family-friendly animated hit *Wreck-It Ralph* on DVD and Blu-ray, the Walt Disney Company made the film available for digital download via outlets like iTunes.[3] So if your kids wanted to see *Wreck-It Ralph* immediately, you only had to download it with the click of a button. Otherwise, you'd have to wait another three or four weeks to hold that shiny disc in your hands. As more and more viewers get hooked on one-click viewing, it won't be long before studios opt to skip the DVD stage altogether in favor of a streaming-only option.

THE FIRST CROWDSOURCED MAINSTREAM HIT

One of the best-known names in the crowdsourcing field, the website Kickstarter started off as a way for creative-minded individuals to raise money from ordinary people for passion projects, ranging from demo albums to fashion lines to short films. But the site reached a whole new level of exposure in 2013 when television writer Rob Thomas used it as a way to fund his dream: a movie based on his defunct TV series *Veronica Mars*. The project met its original $2 million goal and eventually received almost $6 million in donations. In the wake of *Veronica Mars*, another TV star—Zach Braff, formerly of the medical sitcom *Scrubs*—posted his own film project on Kickstarter and raised a little over $3 million. Braff was followed by none other than Spike Lee, who raised $1.4 million for a new project with the aid of the site.[4] Still, raising money is one thing—earning it back is something else. All three of these movies have a built-in audience eager to see them, but it's unclear how mainstream their appeal might be. Nevertheless, as more filmmakers turn to Kickstarter, one (or more) of them might have a project with wide commercial appeal written all over it.

THE FIRST MOTION-CAPTURE OSCAR-NOMINATED PERFORMANCE

The drumbeat to secure Andy Serkis—commonly regarded as the most highly skilled motion-capture actor around—an Oscar nomination has been pounding since his breakthrough performance as Gollum in *The Lord of the Rings* proved what the technology is capable of. His equally celebrated turns as a giant monkey in *King Kong* and a super-smart monkey in *Rise of the Planet of the Apes* similarly attracted awards talk (his flesh-and-blood *Apes* co-star James Franco even penned an open letter to the Academy making the case for Serkis's nominability),[5] but ran up against the Academy's uncertainty about whether mo-cap acting qualifies as "acting." As technology that aids and abets performance becomes increasingly woven into the fabric of movies, however, it seems likely that a place will eventually be made for actors who rely on processes like motion capture to create memorable screen characters. And when that day comes, expect Serkis to be the first beneficiary.

Notes

CHAPTER 1: JAWS (1975)

1. *Jaws*, Blu-ray, directed by Steven Spielberg (1975; Universal City, CA: Universal Studios Home Entertainment, 2012).

2. Erik Hollander, "The Shark Is Still Working: The Impact & Legacy of *Jaws*," Blu-ray disc, *Jaws*, Blu-ray + DVD edition, directed by Steven Spielberg (Universal City, CA; Universal Studios Home Entertainment, 2012).

3. Peter Biskind, *Easy Riders, Raging Bulls: How the Sex-Drugs-and-Rock 'N' Roll Generation Saved Hollywood* (New York: Simon & Schuster, 1998), 266–67.

4. Ibid., 266.

5. Ibid., 263.

6. Laurent Bouzereau, "The Making of Jaws," Blu-ray, *Jaws*, Blu-ray + DVD edition, directed by Steven Spielberg (Universal City, CA; Universal Studios Home Entertainment, 2012).

7. Ibid., 263

8. Ibid., 259–60.

9. Bouzereau, "The Making of Jaws."

10. Ibid.

11. Hollander, "The Shark Is Still Working."

12. Ibid.

13. Bouzereau, "The Making of Jaws."

14. Biskind, *Easy Riders, Raging Bulls*, 276–77.

15. Bouzereau, "The Making of Jaws."

16. Dade Hayes and Jonathan Bing, *Open Wide: How Hollywood Box Office Became a National Obsession* (New York: Miramax Books, 2004), 160.

17. Biskind, *Easy Riders, Raging Bulls*, 277.

18. Hayes and Bing, *Open Wide*, 274–77.

19. Biskind, *Easy Riders, Raging Bulls*, 263.

20. Bouzereau, "The Making of Jaws."

21. Hayes and Bing, *Open Wide*, 157.

22. Ibid., 159–60.

23. Biskind, *Easy Riders, Raging Bulls*, 277.

24. Hayes and Bing, *Open Wide*, 158.

25. "Toys: Jaws Collectibles," LostEntertainment.org, June 27, 2012, http://www.lostentertainment.org/2012/06/toys-jaws-collectables.html.

26. Hayes and Bing, *Open Wide*, 158.

27. Ibid., 160.

28. Biskind, *Easy Riders, Raging Bulls*, 278.

29. *Hearts of Darkness: A Filmmaker's Apocalypse*, DVD, directed by Fax Bahr, George Hickenlooper, and Eleanor Coppola (1991; Hollywood, CA: Paramount Home Media, 2007).

30. *Burden of Dreams*, DVD, directed by Les Blank (1982; New York: The Criterion Collection, 2005).

31. Janet Maslin, "'Tootsie': A Woman Who Is Dustin Hoffman," *New York Times*, July 13, 1982, http://www.nytimes.com/1982/07/13/movies/tootsie-a-woman-who-is-dustin-hoffman.html.

32. Paul Miller, "Kate Winslet: James Cameron Justified in Losing Temper on Titanic Set," *Digital Spy*, March 30, 2012, http://www.digitalspy.com/movies/news/a374093/kate-winslet-james-cameron-justified-in-losing-temper-on-titanic-set.html.

33. Jess Cagle, "Craze the 'Titanic,'" *Entertainment Weekly*, September 13, 1996, http://www.ew.com/ew/article/0,,294065,00.html.

34. Borys Kit, "Disney's 'Lone Ranger' Shoot Nears an End," *The Hollywood Reporter*, September 26, 2012, http://www.hollywoodreporter.com/news/disney-the-lone-ranger-johnny-depp-shoot-end-374198.

35. BoxOfficeMojo.com.

36. Ibid.

CHAPTER 2: STAR WARS (1977)

1. *Star Wars*, DVD, directed by George Lucas (1977; Beverly Hills, CA: 20th Century Fox Home Entertainment, 2006).

2. Peter Biskind, *Easy Riders, Raging Bulls: How the Sex-Drugs-and-Rock 'N' Roll Generation Saved Hollywood* (New York: Simon & Schuster, 1998), 324.

3. Michael Kaminski, "In Tribute to Marcia Lucas." *The Secret History of Star Wars*, http://secrethistoryofstarwars.com/marcialucas.html.

4. "About George Lucas," the website of *American Masters*, PBS.org, January 13, 2004, http://www.pbs.org/wnet/americanmasters/episodes/george-lucas/about-george-lucas/649/.

5. "Good and Evil Rival for Top Spots in AFI's 100 Years ... 100 Heroes & Villains." AFI.com, June 4, 2003, http://www.afi.com/100Years/handv.aspx.

6. Carol Pinchefsky, "What Would Star Wars Cost in 2012 Dollars?" *Forbes*, January 17, 2012, http://www.forbes.com/sites/carolpinchefsky/2012/01/17/what-would-star-wars-cost-in-2012-dollars.

7. Marla Matza, "By George, He Can Thank His Lucky 'Stars.'" *Los Angeles Times*, February 6, 1997, http://articles.latimes.com/1997-02-06/business/fi-25849_1_star-wars.

8. Ibid.

9. Ryan Britt, "Weird Differences between the First *Star Wars* Movie and Its Preceding Novelization," Tor.com, January 24, 2013, http://www.tor.com/blogs/2013/01/weird-differences-between-the-first-star-wars-movie-and-its-preceding-novelization.

10. Emily Asher-Perrin, "The Star Wars Sequel That Never (Quite) Was: *Splinter of the Mind's Eye*," Tor.com, February 7, 2013, http://www.tor.com/blogs/2013/02/the-star-wars-sequel-that-never-quite-was-splinter-of-the-minds-eye.

11. "George Lucas' Galactic Empire," *Time*, March 6, 1978, http://www.time.com/time/magazine/article/0,9171,915986,00.html.

12. Matza, "By George," http://articles.latimes.com/1997-02-06/business/fi-25849_1_star-wars.

13. Jay West, " 'Star Wars' Flashback: Christmas '77 Left Fans with Empty Feeling," *Hero Complex* (blog), *Los Angeles Times*, January 10, 2012, http://herocomplex.latimes.com/movies/star-wars-flashback-christmas-77-left-fans-with-empty-feeling/.

14. Andy Greenberg, "Star Wars' Galactic Dollars," *Forbes*, May 24, 2007, http://www.forbes.com/2007/05/24/star-wars-revenues-tech-cx_ag_0524money.html.

15. Bruce Kirkland, "Merch Industry Bigger Than Movies," *Toronto Sun*, July 12, 2012, http://www.torontosun.com/2012/07/12/movie-swag-bigger-than-movies.

16. Dawn C. Chmielewski and Rebecca Keegan, "Merchandise Sales Drive Pixar's 'Cars' Franchise," *Los Angeles Times*, June 21, 2011, http://articles.latimes.com/2011/jun/21/business/la-fi-ct-cars2-20110621.

17. Claude Brodesser-Akner, "Spider-Man and the Half-Life of the Movie Reboot," *Vulture*, April 23, 2012, http://www.vulture.com/2012/04/spider-man-and-the-half-life-of-the-movie-reboot.html.

18. David Lieberman, "Harry Potter Inc." *Deadline*, July 13, 2011, http://www.deadline.com/2011/07/harry-potter-inc-warner-bros-21b-empire/.

19. Chmielewski and Keegan, "Merchandise Sales Drive Pixar's 'Cars' Franchise."

CHAPTER 3: SUPERMAN: THE MOVIE (1978)

1. "You Will Believe: The Cinematic Saga of Superman," Disc 13, *Superman: Ultimate Collector's Edition*, produced by Constantine Nasr (Burbank, CA: Warner Home Video, 2007),.

2. Ibid.

3. Jordan Riefe, "'Superman' Director Richard Donner Grilled on Choosing Christopher Reeve, Smashing Phones," *The Wrap*, http://www.thewrap.com/movies/article/superman-director-richard-donner-grilled-smashing-phones-choosing-reeve-28037?page=0,0.

4. "You Will Believe."

5. Jeremy Arnold, "Superman: The Movie," TCM.com, http://www.tcm.com/this-month/article/66930l0/Superman-The-Movie.html.

6. "You Will Believe."

7. Ibid.

8. Ibid.

9. Ibid.

10. Ibid.

11. Ibid.

12. *Superman: The Movie*. DVD. Directed by Richard Donner (1978; Burbank, CA: Warner Home Video, 2007).

13. "You Will Believe."

14. Ibid.

15. Jeff Jensen, "'Super' 5," *Entertainment Weekly*, June 17, 2005, http://www.ew.com/ew/article/0,,1073416,00.html.

16. Ryan Mac, "Investing in Batman: 30 Years Later an Executive's Gamble on The Dark Knight Pays Off," *Forbes.com*, July 14, 2012, http://www.forbes.com/sites/ryanmac/2012/07/14/investing-in-batman-30-years-later-an-executives-gamble-on-the-dark-knight-pays-off/.

17. James Van Hise, "Batman: A Retrospective of Tom Mankiewicz's Unfilmed Script," ComicBookMovie.com, August 3, 2010, http://www.comicbookmovie.com/fansites/mediageek/news/?a=21031.

18. Kara Warner, "Anne Hathaway's Catwoman Isn't First Controversial Costume," MTV.com, September 28, 2011, http://www.mtv.com/news/articles/1671706/dark-knight-rises-anne-hathaway-controversial-catwoman-costume.jhtml.

19. Scott Foundas, "Cinematic Faith," *Film Comment*, Winter 2012/2013, http://filmcomment.com/article/cinematic-faith-christopher-nolan-scott-foundas.

20. Devin Gordon, "Bat Trick," *Newsweek*, July 11, 2008, http://www.thedailybeast.com/newsweek/2008/07/11/bat-trick.html.

21. BoxOfficeMojo.com.

CHAPTER 4: STAR TREK: THE MOTION PICTURE (1979)

1. *Star Trek: The Motion Picture*, DVD, directed by Robert Wise (1979; Hollywood, CA: Paramount Home Entertainment, 2009).

2. Tim King, executive producer, "The Longest Trek: Writing the Motion Picture," *Star Trek: The Motion Picture*, DVD, directed by Robert Wise (Hollywood, CA: Paramount Home Entertainment, 2009).

3. Ibid.

4. Ibid.

5. "Star Trek," Roddenberry.com, http://www.roddenberry.com/entertainment-star-trek.

6. "A Bold New Enterprise," Disc 2, *Star Trek: The Motion Picture—The Director's Edition* DVD, directed by Robert Wise (Hollywood, CA: Paramount Home Video, 2001).

7. Ibid.

8. Chris Vespoli, "Dead Air: A Timeline of Failed Broadcast TV Networks," Gawker.com, April 7, 2010, http://gawker.com/5506656/dead-air-a-timeline-of-failed-broadcast-tv-networks.

9. Anthony Pascale, "Star Trek Loves Lucy," TrekMovie.com, August 6, 2011, http://trekmovie.com/2011/08/06/star-trek-loves-lucy/.

10. "Bjo Trimble: The Woman Who Saved Star Trek," StarTrek.com, August 31, 2011, http://www.startrek.com/article/bjo-trimble-the-woman-who-saved-star-trek-part-1.

11. "Phase II: The Lost Enterprise," Disc 2, *Star Trek: The Motion Picture—The Director's Edition* DVD, directed by Robert Wise (Hollywood, CA: Paramount Home Video, 2001).

12. Michael Okuda, "Text Commentary," Disc 1, *Star Trek: The Motion Picture—The Director's Edition* DVD, directed by Robert Wise (Hollywood, CA: Paramount Home Video, 2001).

13. "Phase II: The Lost Enterprise." Disc 2. *Star Trek: The Motion Picture—The Director's Edition* DVD.

CHAPTER 5: TRON (1982)

1. *Tron*, DVD, directed by Steven Lisberger. (1982; Burbank, CA: Buena Vista Home Entertainment, 2002).

2. Mark Millan and Marcus Chan, "'Pong Turns 40, but It's Not the Oldest Video Game," Bloomberg.com, November 15, 2012, http://www.bloomberg.com/slideshow/2012-11-16/-pong-turns-40-but-it-s-not-the-oldest-video-game.html.

3. Harold Goldberg, "The Origins of the First Arcade Video Game: Atari's *Pong*," *Vanity Fair*, March 28, 2011, http://www.vanityfair.com/culture/features/2011/03/pong-excerpt-201103. Excerpted from: *All Your Base Are Belong to Us: How Fifty Years of Videogames Conquered Pop Culture* (New York: Three Rivers Press, 2011).

4. "The Making of *Tron*," Disc 2, *Tron, 20th Anniversary Collector's Edition* DVD, directed by Steven Lisberger (Burbank, CA: Buena Vista Home Entertainment, 2002).

5. Ibid.

6. Ibid.

7. Tom Hormby, "The Pixar Story: Dick Shoup, Alex Schure, George Lucas, Steve Jobs, and Disney," *Tom Hormby's Orchard* (blog), revised January 22, 2007, http://www.lowendmac.com/orchard/06/pixar-story-lucas-disney.html.

8. "Our Story," Pixar.com, http://www.pixar.com/about/Our-Story.

9. "The Making of *Tron*."

10. Steven Lisberger, Donald Kushner, Harrison Ellenshaw, and Richard Taylor. "Audio Commentary," Disc 1, *Tron, 20th Anniversary Collector's Edition* DVD, directed by Steven Lisberger (Burbank, CA: Buena Vista Home Entertainment, 2002).

11. "The Making of *Tron*."

12. "Beyond Tron," Disc 2, *Tron, 20th Anniversary Collector's Edition* DVD, directed by Steven Lisberger (Burbank, CA: Buena Vista Home Entertainment, 2002).

13. "The Making of *Tron*."

14. Lisberger, "Audio Commentary."

15. Ibid.

16. "The Making of *Tron*."

17. "The Last Starfighter," AtariProtos.com, http://www.atariprotos.com/2600/software/tlsf/tlsf.htm.

18. Skyler Miller, review of *The Last Starfighter*, Mindscape Inc., All Game Guide, http://www.allgame.com/game.php?id=22206&tab=review.

19. "Cloak & Dagger," AtariProtos.com, http://www.atariprotos.com/8bit/software/cloakdagger/cloakdagger.htm.

CHAPTER 6: PARTING GLANCES (1986)

1. *Parting Glances*, DVD, directed by Bill Sherwood (1986; New York: First Run Features, 2000).

2. Clarke Taylor, "In Films, Gays Come Out in a Different Light," *Los Angeles Times*, March 2, 1986, http://articles.latimes.com/1986-03-02/entertainment/ca-1279_1_gay-film.

3. "Parting Glances Restored Premiere Kathy Kinney Bill Sherwood," YouTube video, 0:59, from a panel discussion following an October 29, 2007, screening of a restored version of *Parting Glances*, posted by Matthew Rettenmund on November 1, 2007, http://www.youtube.com/watch?v=w7bpjJdNxGo.

4. "Production Notes & Cast Photos," *Parting Glances*, DVD, directed by Bill Sherwood (New York: First Run Features, 2000).

5. Taylor, "Gays Come Out in a Different Light."

6. John Pierson, *Spike, Mike, Slackers & Dykes: A Guided Tour across a Decade of American Independent Cinema* (New York: Hyperion, 1995), 39–40.

7. "Production Notes."

8. Pierson, *Spike, Mike*, 41.

9. Ibid., 43.

10. Taylor, "Gays Come Out in a Different Light."

11. Pierson, *Spike, Mike*, 42.

CHAPTER 7: SHE'S GOTTA HAVE IT (1986)

1. *She's Gotta Have It*, DVD, directed by Spike Lee (1986; Beverly Hills, CA: 20th Century Fox Home Entertainment, 2008).

2. Spike Lee, *Spike Lee's Gotta Have It: Inside Guerrilla Filmmaking* (New York: Simon & Schuster, 1987), 66.

3. Ibid.

4. John Pierson, *Spike, Mike, Slackers & Dykes: A Guided Tour across a Decade of American Independent Cinema* (New York: Hyperion, 1995), 52.

5. Ibid., 70.

6. Stella Papamichael, "Getting Direct with Directors: No. 21 Spike Lee," BBC.co.uk, last updated November 2004, http://www.bbc.co.uk/films/calling theshots/spike_lee.shtml.

7. Pierson, *Spike, Mike*, 47.

8. Lee, *Spike Lee's Gotta Have It*, 253.

9. Ibid., 25.

10. Ibid., 81.

11. "About the Film," KillerofSheep.com, http://killerofsheep.com/about.html.

12. Pierson, *Spike, Mike*, 48–49.

13. Ibid., 58.

14. Ibid., 68–70.

15. Ibid., 75.

16. Diane Brady, "Spike Lee on Self-Financing *Red Hook Summer*," *Business-week*, June 28, 2012, http://www.businessweek.com/articles/2012-06-28/spike-lee-on-self-financing-red-hook-summer.

17. Michael Arceneaux, "Spike Lee Says No 'Inside Man 2,' " BET.com, July 5, 2011, http://www.bet.com/news/celebrities/2011/07/05/spike-lee-says-no-inside-man-2-.html.

18. Lee, *Spike Lee's Gotta Have It*, 38-39.

19. ABC News, "No Deposit, No Return on Rent Movie," ABC News.com, August 24, 2001 http://abcnews.go.com/Entertainment/story?id=102760&page=1.

20. Anne Thompson, "Spike Lee's Game," *New York*, http://nymag.com/nymetro/movies/columns/hollywood/n_8161/.

21. Tatiana Siegel, "The Most Famous Dodger Hits the Screen," *Hollywood Reporter*, August 8. 2012, http://www.hollywoodreporter.com/news/los-angeles-dodgers-jackie-robinson-42-359167.

CHAPTER 8: THE THIN BLUE LINE (1988)

1. *The Thin Blue Line*, Netflix Instant, directed by Errol Morris (1988; Los Gatos, CA: Netflix).

2. John Pierson, *Spike, Mike, Slackers & Dykes: A Guided Tour across a Decade of American Independent Cinema* (New York: Hyperion, 1995), 105.

3. "Making of The Thin Blue Line 1/2," YouTube video, 13:03, from a television documentary, posted by WOODDDDDDDYAMOVIES3, December 30, 2011, http://www.youtube.com/watch?v=2xa2CiiPJt8.

4. Pierson, *Spike, Mike*, 104.

5. Michael L. Radelet, "Randall Dale Adams," Northwestern Law, Bluhm Legal Clinic Center on Wrongful Convictions. http://www.law.northwestern.edu/legalclinic/wrongfulconvictions/exonerations/tx/randall-dale-adams.html.

6. "Making of The Thin Blue Line 1/2."

7. "Making of The Thin Blue Line 2/2," YouTube video, 9:05, from a televised documentary, posted by posted by WOODDDDDDDYAMOVIES3, December 30, 2011, http://www.youtube.com/watch?v=topEFBr3HFY.

8. Associated Press, "'Thin Blue Line' Prisoner Executed in Texas," NBCNews.com, June 30, 2004, http://www.nbcnews.com/id/5336585/ns/us_news-crime_and_courts/t/thin-blue-line-prisoner-executed-texas/#.UbO0dOvlUUs.

9. "Making of The Thin Blue Line 2/2."

10. Ibid.

11. "The Fog of War: 13 Questions and Answers on the Filmmaking of Errol Morris," *FLM*, Winter 2004, http://www.errolmorris.com/content/eyecontact/interrotron.html.

12. "Making of The Thin Blue Line 2/2."

13. Radelet, "Randall Dale Adams."

14. Pierson, *Spike, Mike*, 106-8.

15. Ibid., 111.

16. Radelet, "Randall Dale Adams."

17. Associated Press, "Freed Inmate Settles Suit with Producer Over Rights to Story," *New York Times*, August 6, 1989, http://www.nytimes.com/1989/08/06/us/freed-inmate-settles-suit-with-producer-over-rights-to-story.html?n=Top%2fReference%2fTimes%20Topics%2fPeople%2fM%2fMorris%2c%20Errol.

18. Linda Stewart Ball/Associated Press, "Texas Exoneree Featured in *The Thin Red Line* Dies," KHOU.com, June 24, 2011, http://www.khou.com/news/texas-news/Texas-exoneree-featured-in-Thin-Blue-Line-dies—124529789.html.

19. Pierson, *Spike, Mike*, 113.

20. Karen S. Schneider, "Blood Secrets," *People*, November 2, 1992, http://www.people.com/people/archive/article/0,,20109000,00.html.

21. Peter Kneght, "Decade: Andrew Jarecki on 'Capturing the Friedmans.' " *Indiewire*, December 14, 2009, http://www.indiewire.com/article/decade_andrew_jarecki_on_capturing_the_freidmans.

22. Tricia Romano, "Roman Polanski," *Crime Library* (blog), TruTV.com, http://www.trutv.com/library/crime/criminal_mind/sexual_assault/roman_polanski/1.html .

23. Kristal Hawkins, "Joyce McKinney and the Manacled Mormon," Crime Library (blog), TruTV.com, http://www.trutv.com/library/crime/criminal_mind/sexual_assault/joyce-mckinney/joy-to-the-world.html.

24. "Top 10 Imposters," *Time.com*, http://www.time.com/time/specials/packages/article/0,28804,1900621_1900618_1900789,00.html.

25. Madison Gray, " 'West Memphis Three' Freed After Plea Deal," Time.com, August 19, 2011, http://newsfeed.time.com/2011/08/19/west-memphis-3-to-go-free-after-plea-deal/.

26. Associated Press, "McDonald's Phasing Out Supersize Fries, Drinks," Mar 3, 2004, http://www.nbcnews.com/id/4433307/ns/business-us_business/t/mcdonalds-phasing-out-supersize-fries-drinks/#.Ud92xFPlXX8.

27. The official website of *Dear Zachary*, accessed June 8, 2013, http://www.dearzachary.com/.

CHAPTER 9: SEX, LIES, AND VIDEOTAPE (1989)

1. *sex, lies, and videotape*, Blu-ray, directed by Steven Soderbergh (1989; Culver City, CA; Sony Pictures Home Entertainment, 2009).

2. "Steven Soderbergh on *sex, lies, and videotape*," Blu-ray, directed by Steven Soderbergh (1989; Culver City, CA; Sony Pictures Home Entertainment, 2009).

3. Steven Soderbergh and Neil LaBute. "Commentary," *sex, lies, and videotape*, Blu-ray.

4. Ibid.

5. Ibid.

6. Steven Soderbergh, *sex, lies, and videotape* (New York: Harper & Row, 1990), 221–22.

7. Peter Biskind, *Down and Dirty Pictures: Miramax, Sundance, and the Rise of Independent Film* (New York: Simon & Schuster, 2004), 28–29.

8. Ibid., 29.

9. Biskind, *Down and Dirty Pictures*, 29.

10. Ibid., 29–32.

11. Benjamin Craig, "History of the Sundance Film Festival," Sundance Guide.net, http://www.sundanceguide.net/basics/history/.

12. Soderbergh, *sex, lies, and videotape*, 221.

13. Ibid., 222–25.

14. Ibid, 224.

15. Biskind, *Down and Dirty Pictures*, 30–31.

16. Soderbergh, *sex, lies, and videotape*, 230.

17. Biskind, *Down and Dirty Pictures*, 59

18. Ibid., 79.

19. Ibid., 80–81.

20. Soderbergh, *sex, lies, and videotape*, 244.

21. Biskind, *Down and Dirty Pictures*, 81–82.

CHAPTER 10: BLADE RUNNER: THE DIRECTOR'S CUT (1992)

1. *Blade Runner: The Director's Cut*, Blu-ray, directed by Ridley Scott (1992; Burbank, CA: Warner Home Video, 2012).

2. Charles de Lauzirika, "Dangerous Days: Making Blade Runner," Disc 3, *Blade Runner: 30th Anniversary Collector's Edition*, directed by Ridley Scott (Burbank, CA: Warner Home Video, 2012).

3. Kenneth Turan, "Blade Runner 2," *Los Angeles Times*, September 13, 1992, http://articles.latimes.com/1992-09-13/magazine/tm-1537_1_blade-runner-ridley-scott-orson-welles-othello.

4. Lauzirika, "Dangerous Days."

5. CBS Worldwide, "Ridley Scott," CBSNews.com, February 11, 2009 http://www.cbsnews.com/2100-500164_162-267597.html.

6. Ridley Scott, "Commentary," Disc 1, *Blade Runner: 30th Anniversary Collector's Edition*, directed by Ridley Scott (Burbank, CA: Warner Home Video, 2012).

7. Ibid.

8. Lauzirika, "Dangerous Days."

9. Ibid.

10. Ibid.

11. Ibid.

12. Ibid.

13. Ibid.

14. Ann Hornaday, "Now Starring on Video: The Director's Cut," *New York Times*, May 16, 1993, http://www.nytimes.com/1993/05/16/arts/film-now-starring -on-video-the-director-s-cut.html?pagewanted=all&src=pm.

15. Stuart Thornton, "Z Channel Created an Outlet for Marginalized Films to Blossom," *Monterey County Weekly*, July 28, 2005, http://www.montereycountyweekly .com/news/local_news/article_d86cc6de-4c5d-5b7d-94e3-136571de5df6.html.

16. Hornaday, "Now Starring."

17. Glenn Collins, "'Lawrence of Arabia' Returns After Restoration," *Chicago Tribune*, December 22, 1988, http://articles.chicagotribune.com/1988-12-22/ features/8802260689_1_sir-david-lean-restoration-arabia.

18. William M. Kolb, "Reconstructing the Director's Cut," in *Retrofitting Blade Runner*, edited by Judith B. Kerman (Madison: University of Wisconsin Press, 1997), 294–96.

19. Ibid., 295–97.

20. Ibid., 296–97.

21. Ibid,. 297–98.

22. Ibid., 299.

23. Owen Gleiberman, review of *Blade Runner*, Warner Bros., *Entertainment Weekly*, October 2, 1992, http://www.ew.com/ew/article/0,,311946,00.html.

24. Roger Ebert, review of *Blade Runner: Director's Cut*, Warner Bros., *Chicago Sun-Times*, September 11, 1992, http://www.rogerebert.com/reviews/blade-runner -directors-cut-1992.

25. Brent Hartinger, "Review: The Original '54' Really Deserves to be Seen." TheBacklot.com, April 15, 2010, http://www.thebacklot.com/review-the-original -54-really-deserves-to-be-seen/04/2010/.

26. Guillermo del Toro, "Commentary," *Mimic: The Director's Cut*, directed by Guillermo del Toro (Santa Monica, CA: Lionsgate, 2011).

CHAPTER 11: PULP FICTION (1994)

1. *Pulp Fiction*, Blu-ray, directed by Quentin Tarantino (1994; Los Angeles: Lionsgate and Miramax, 2011).

2. Peter Biskind, *Down and Dirty Pictures: Miramax, Sundance, and the Rise of Independent Film* (New York: Simon & Schuster, 2004), 195.

3. Oliver Lyttelton, "5 Things You Might Not Know About 'Reservoir Dogs' on Its 20th Anniversary," *The Playlist*, October 23, 2012, http://blogs.indiewire.com/theplaylist/5-things-you-might-not-know-about-reservoir-dogs-on-its-20th-anniversary-20121023.

4. Mark Seal, "Cinema Tarantino: The Making of *Pulp Fiction*," *Vanity Fair*, March 2013, 374–76.

5. Ibid., 376.

6. Ibid., 376–77.

7. Ibid., 376.

8. Ibid., 376-77

9. Lyttelton, "5 Things."

10. Biskind, *Down and Dirty Pictures*, 134–35.

11. Ibid., 135.

12. Ibid.,136.

13. Seal, "Cinema Tarantino," 377–79.

14. Ibid., 379.

15. Biskind, *Down and Dirty Pictures*, 170.

16. Seal, "Cinema Tarantino," 379.

17. Ibid., 379.

18. Biskind, *Down and Dirty Pictures*, 189.

19. John Pierson, *Spike, Mike, Slackers & Dykes: A Guided Tour across a Decade of American Independent Cinema* (New York: Hyperion, 1995), 332–33.

20. Biskind, *Down and Dirty Pictures*, 193.

CHAPTER 12: SHOWGIRLS (1995)

1. *Showgirls*. Blu-ray, directed by Paul Verhoeven (1995; Beverly Hills, CA: 20th Century Fox Home Entertainment, 2011).

2. Mark Caro. "The Heat Is On: Will NC-17 Go Legit?" *Chicago Tribune*, September 10, 1995, http://articles.chicagotribune.com/1995-09-10/news/9509100250_1_nc-17-showgirls-rival-movie-studios.

3. Ibid.

4. Roger Ebert, review of *Showgirls*, MGM, *Chicago Sun-Times*, September 22, 1995, http://www.rogerebert.com/reviews/showgirls-1995.

5. Kevin S. Sandler, *The Naked Truth: Why Hollywood Doesn't Make X-Rated Movies* (New Brunswick, NJ: Rutgers University Press, 2007), 175.

6. Jonathan Rosenbaum, review of *Romance*, Trimark, *Chicago Reader*, November 12, 1999, http://www.jonathanrosenbaum.com/?p=6439.

7. Sandler, *The Naked Truth*, 42.

8. Ibid., 45.

9. Anthony Breznican, "PG-13 at 20: How 'Gremlins' and 'Indiana Jones' Remade Hollywood," *Topeka Capital-Journal*, August 24, 2004, http://cjonline .com/stories/082404/ent_gremlins.shtml.

10. Sandler, *The Naked Truth*, 48.

11. Ibid., 63.

12. Ibid.

13. Ibid., 73.

14. Ibid., 85.

15. Ibid., 112–16.

16. Caro, "The Heat Is On."

17. Ibid.

18. Sandler, *The Naked Truth*, 179.

19. John Horn, "Showgirls: MGM Releases First NC-17 Film in Five Years," Associated Press News Archive, September 7, 1995, http://www.apnewsarchive .com/1995/-Showgirls-MGM-Releases-First-NC-17-Film-in-Five-Years/id-b3bd3e48f1 337b038526debcdb8e57ba.

20. Sandler, *The Naked Truth*, 174–75.

21. Ibid., 179.

22. Roger Ebert, review of *Showgirls*

23. BoxOfficeMojo.com.

24. Originally released unrated; rerated NC-17 after the creation of the rating.

CHAPTER 13: TOY STORY (1995)

1. *Toy Story*, DVD, directed by John Lasseter (1995; Burbank, CA: Buena Vista Home Entertainment, 2000).

2. "Toy Story: The Inside Buzz," *Entertainment Weekly*, December 1995, http:// www.ew.com/ew/article/0,,299897,00.html.

3. Walt Disney Home Video, "The Story behind Toy Story," Disc 1, *Toy Story, Collector's Edition* DVD. Burbank, CA: Buena Vista Home Entertainment, 2000.

4. "Treatment 3/91," Disc 3. *Toy Story, Collector's Edition* DVD.

5. "Treatment 9/91," Disc 3, *Toy Story, Collector's Edition*, DVD.

6. Walt Disney Home Entertainment, "The Story behind Toy Story."

7. "Toy Story: The Inside Buzz."

8. Ibid.

9. Ibid.

10. Ibid.

11. Brent Schlender, "Pixar's Magic Man," CNNMoney.com, May 17, 2006, http://money.cnn.com/2006/05/15/magazines/fortune/pixar_futureof_fortune _052906/.

12. Ibid.

13. Ibid.

14. Walt Disney Home Entertainment, "The Story behind Toy Story."

15. John Young, "Steve Jobs: 9 Ways He Changed the Movie Biz," *Entertainment Weekly*, October 11, 2011, http://www.ew.com/ew/gallery/0,,20535153_21064998,00.html.

16. "Toy Story: The Inside Buzz."

17. Roger Ebert, review of *Toy Story*, Disney/Pixar, *Chicago Sun-Times*, November 22, 1995, http://www.rogerebert.com/reviews/toy-story-1995.

18. Stacy Cowley, "How Shrek Saved DreamWorks," CNNMoney.com, November 14, 2011, http://money.cnn.com/2011/11/14/technology/katzenberg_techonomy/index.htm.

19. Laura M. Holson, "Disney Moves Away from Hand-Drawn Animation," *New York Times*, September 18, 2005, http://www.nytimes.com/2005/09/18/business/media/18disney.html?pagewanted=print&_r=0.

20. Ethan Smith, "For 'Princess,' Disney Returns to Traditional Animation Style," *Wall Street Journal*, November 2, 2009, http://online.wsj.com/article/SB10001424052748704746304574508552919095862.html.

CHAPTER 14: PSYCHO (1998)

1. *Psycho*, DVD, directed by Gus Van Sant (1998; Universal City, CA: Universal Studios, 1999).

2. D-J. "Psycho Path." *Psycho, Collector's Edition* DVD, directed by Gus Van Sant (Universal City, CA: Universal Studios, 1999).

3. Gus Van Sant, Anne Heche, and Vince Vaughn, "Feature Commentary." *Psycho, Collector's Edition* DVD, directed by Gus Van Sant (Universal City, CA: Universal Studios, 1999).

4. D-J, "Psycho Path."

5. Van Sant, "Feature Commentary."

6. D-J, "Psycho Path."

7. Van Sant, "Feature Commentary."

8. D-J, "Pyscho Path."

9. Van Sant, "Feature Commentary."

10. J. Hoberman, review of *Psycho*, Universal, *Village Voice*, December 15, 1998, http://www.villagevoice.com/1998-12-15/film/taking-another-stab/1/.

11. Van Sant, "Feature Commentary." DVD.

12. Ibid.

13. Ibid.

14. Laura Petrecca, "Marketers Hope 666 Will Be Their Lucky Number," *USA Today*. June 2, 2006, http://usatoday30.usatoday.com/money/media/2006-05-31 -omen-marketing-usat_x.htm.

15. Van Sant, "Feature Commentary."

CHAPTER 15: THE MATRIX (1999)

1. *The Matrix*, DVD, directed by the Wachowski Brothers (1999; Burbank, CA: Warner Home Video, 1999.)

2. Aleksander Hemon, "Beyond the Matrix," *The New Yorker*, September 10, 2012, http://www.newyorker.com/reporting/2012/09/10/120910fa_fact_hemon.

3. Ibid.

4. Josh Oreck, "The Matrix Revisited," *The Matrix: The Ultimate Matrix Collection*, directed by the Wachowski Brothers (Burbank, CA: Warner Home Video, 2008).

5. Hemon, "Beyond the Matrix."

6. Josh Oreck. "Making the Matrix."

7. Ibid.

8. Oreck, "The Matrix Revisited."

9. "What Is Bullet Time," *The Matrix: The Ultimate Matrix Collection*, directed by the Wachowski Brothers (Burbank, CA: Warner Home Video, 2008).

10. Ibid.

11. "The Video Cassette Tape," Sony Corporation, accessed June 8, 2013, http:// www.sony.net/SonyInfo/CorporateInfo/History/SonyHistory/2-01.html.

12. "Sony Timeline," Sony Corporation, accessed June 8, 2013, http://www .sony.net/SonyInfo/CorporateInfo/History/sonyhistory-d.html.

13. "Boom and Bust: The First Videocassette Revolution," Total Rewind, accessed June 8, 2013, http://www.totalrewind.org/revolutn.htm.

14. Dave Owen, "The Betamax vs. VHS Format War," MediaCollege.com, May 1, 2005, http://www.mediacollege.com/video/format/compare/betamax-vhs.html.

15. Dennis Lim, "Instant Nostalgia? Let's Go to the Videotape," *New York Times*, January 27, 2008, http://www.nytimes.com/2008/01/27/movies/27lim.html ?pagewanted=all.

16. "Optical Disc," Total Rewind, accessed June 8, 2013, http://www .totalrewind.org/disc/disc_opt.htm.

17. "The Matrix DVD: The First to Sell 3 Million," August 1, 2000, http://web .archive.org/web/20080305104849/http://whatisthematrix.warnerbros.com/rl_cmp/ rl_press_August_01_00.html.

18. "Follow the White Rabbit," *The Matrix*, DVD, directed by the Wachowski Brothers (Burbank, CA: Warner Home Video, 1999).

19. "Wachowski Brothers Transcript," Warner Video, November 6, 1999, http://www.warnervideo.com/matrixevents/wachowski.html.

20. Geoff Boucher, "VHS Era Is Winding Down," *Los Angeles Times*, December 22, 2008, http://articles.latimes.com/2008/dec/22/entertainment/et-vhs -tapes22.

CHAPTER 16: THE BLAIR WITCH PROJECT (1999)

1. *The Blair Witch Project*, Blu-ray, directed by Daniel Myrick and Eduardo Sánchez (1999; Santa Monica, CA: Lions Gate Films, 2010).

2. "Direction," Woods Movie.com, accessed June 8, 2013, http://www .woodsmovie.com/phaseone/direction/directiondocuments_set.html.

3. "The Blair Witch Cult," *Newsweek*, August 15, 1999, http://www .thedailybeast.com/newsweek/1999/08/15/the-blair-witch-cult.html.

4. "Phase One," Woods Movie.com, accessed June 8, 2013, http://www .woodsmovie.com/edjournalphase1.html.

5. Rob Cowie, Gregg Hale, Mike Monello, Daniel Myrick, and Eduardo Sánchez, "Commentary," *The Blair Witch Project,* Blu-ray, directed by Daniel Myrick and Eduardo Sánchez. (Santa Monica, CA: Lionsgate Films, 2010).

6. Rebecca Ascher-Walsh, "The Blair Witch Project: Rhymes with Rich," *Entertainment Weekly*, July 30, 1999, http://www.ew.com/ew/article/0,,272498,00 .html.

7. John Young, "'The Blair Witch Project' 10 Years Later: Catching Up with the Directors of the Horror Sensation," *Entertainment Weekly*, July 9, 2009, http:// popwatch.ew.com/2009/07/09/blair-witch/.

8. "Phase Two," Woods Movie.com, accessed June 8, 2013, http://www .woodsmovie.com/edjournalphase2.html.

9. John Young, " 'the Blair Witch Project' 10 Years Later" *Entertainment Weekly.*

10. "Commentary"

11. "The Beginning," Woods Movie.com, accessed June 8, 2013, http://www .woodsmovie.com/edjournalbeginning.html.

12. "Phase Two," Woods Movie.com.

13. Ibid.

14. Ibid.

15. "Finishing," Woods Movie.com, accessed June 8, 2013, http://www .woodsmovie.com/edjournalfinishing.html.

16. Ascher-Walsh, "The Blair Witch Project: Rhymes with Rich."

17. Ibid.

CHAPTER 17: CROUCHING TIGER, HIDDEN DRAGON (2000)

1. "Wuxia," Webster's Online Dictionary, http://www.websters-online -dictionary.net/definitions/wuxia.

2. Scarlet Cheng, "Art and Action Kick It Up," *Los Angeles Times*, November 12, 2000, http://articles.latimes.com/2000/nov/12/entertainment/ca-50506.

3. *Crouching Tiger, Hidden Dragon*, DVD, directed by Ang Lee (2000; Culver City, CA; Columbia Tristar Home Entertainment, 2001).

4. Ang Lee and James Schamus, "Commentary," *Crouching Tiger, Hidden Dragon*, DVD, directed by Ang Lee (Culver City, CA; Columbia Tristar Home Entertainment, 2001).

5. Lee, "Commentary."

6. Ibid.

7. Steve Rose, " 'The Film Is So Slow—It's Like Grandma Telling Stories,' " *The Guardian*, February 13, 2001, http://www.guardian.co.uk/culture/2001/feb/13/artsfeatures2.

8. Lee, "Commentary."

9. Susan King, "Classic Hollywood: Remembering Bruce Lee and Martial Arts Films," *The Los Angeles Times*, April 15, 2013, http://articles.latimes.com/2013/apr/15/entertainment/la-et-mn-kung-fu-classic-hollywood-20130415.

10. "Zhang Movie Breaks China Record," BBC News, January 13, 2003, http://news.bbc.co.uk/2/hi/entertainment/2653949.stm.

11. BoxOfficeMojo.com.

CHAPTER 18: THE LORD OF THE RINGS (2001–2003)

1. *The Lord of the Rings*, Blu-ray, directed by Peter Jackson (2001–2003; Burbank, CA: Warner Home Video, 2012).

2. Pat Reynolds, "*The Lord of the Rings*: The Tale of a Text," The Tolkien Society, accessed June 8, 2013, http://www.tolkiensociety.org/tolkien/tale.html.

3. Geoffrey Macnab, "John Boorman—A Very English Visionary Is Back," *The Independent*. August 21, 2009, http://www.independent.co.uk/arts-entertainment/films/features/john-boorman—a-very-english-visionary-is-back-1774989.html.

4. Tasha Robinson, "Interview: Ralph Bakshi," *The AV Club*, December 6, 2000, http://www.avclub.com/articles/ralph-bakshi,13690/.

5. Peter Biskind, *Down and Dirty Pictures: Miramax, Sundance, and the Rise of Independent Film* (New York: Simon & Schuster, 2004), 244–45.

6. Robert Levine, "The Ring Leaders," *New York*, accessed June 8, 2013, http://nymag.com/nymetro/movies/features/5508/.

7. Christopher Borrelli, "The Evolving Images of 9/11," *Chicago Tribune*, September 9, 2011, http://articles.chicagotribune.com/2011-09-09/entertainment/ct-ae -0911-images-20110910_1_first-screening-attacks-images.

8. Levine, "The Ring Leaders."

9. "About Massive," Massive, accessed July 8, 2013, http://massivesoftware
.com/about.html.

10. "From Gollum to Avatar," *The Economist*, June 10, 2010, http://www
.economist.com/node/16295602.

11. Phil De Semlyen, "A History of CGI in Movies," *Empire*.com, accessed
June 8, 2013, http://www.empireonline.com/features/history-of-cgi/p1.

12. John Hiscock, "James Cameron Interview for *Avatar*," *The Telegraph*,
December 3, 2009, http://www.telegraph.co.uk/culture/film/6720156/James
-Cameron-interview-for-Avatar.html.

13. Kimber Myers, "Peter Jackson Calls 48fps & 3D a "Gift to His Style of Filmmaking, and Says Fran Walsh Directed the Best Scene in 'The Two Towers,'" *Indiewire*, December 7, 2012, http://blogs.indiewire.com/theplaylist/peter-jackson-calls
-48fps-and-3d-a-gift-talks-new-and-improved-gollum-and-how-fran-walsh-directed
-the-best-scene-in-the-two-towers-20121207?page=1#blogPostHeaderPanel.

CHAPTER 19: FUNNY HA HA (2002)

1. *Funny Ha Ha*, DVD, directed by Andrew Bujalski (2002; Santa Monica, CA;
Genius Entertainment, 2007).

2. Michael Koresky, "Decade: Andrew Bujalski on 'Funny Ha Ha,'" *Indiewire*,
August 16, 2005, http://www.indiewire.com/article/decade_andrew_bujalski_on
_funny_ha_ha.

3. Ibid.

4. Ibid.

5. J. Hoberman, "It's Mumblecore!," *Village Voice*, August 14, 2007, http://
www.villagevoice.com/2007-08-14/film/it-s-mumblecore/.

6. Dennis Lim, "A Generation Finds Its Mumble," August 19, 2007, http://www
.nytimes.com/2007/08/19/movies/19lim.html?pagewanted=all&_r=0.

7. Koresky, "Decade."

8. Ethan Alter, "Sisterly Rivalry: Lynn Shelton Directs Blunt and DeWitt in
Improvised Romantic Triangle," *Film Journal International*, May 29, 2012, http://
www.filmjournal.com/filmjournal/content_display/esearch/e3i06cfcbf80fe0261012
0c28053270282c.

CHAPTER 20: BUBBLE (2005)

1. Mary Kaye Schilling, "Steven Soderbergh on Quitting Hollywood, Getting the
Best out of J-Lo, and His Love of *Girls*," *Vulture*, January 27, 2013, http://www
.vulture.com/2013/01/steven-soderbergh-in-conversation.html.

2. *Bubble*, DVD, directed by Steven Soderbergh (2005; Los Angeles: Magnolia Home Entertainment, 2005).

3. "About Magnolia," Official site of Magnolia Pictures, accessed September 27. 2013, http://www.magpictures.com/about.aspx.

4. Mark Romanek and Steven Soderbergh, "Commentary," *Bubble*, DVD, directed by Steven Soderbergh (Los Angeles: Magnolia Home Entertainment, 2005).

5. Ibid.

6. Ibid.

7. Dustin James Ashley, Debbie Doebereiner, Coleman Hough, and Misty Dawn Wilkins, "Commentary," *Bubble*, DVD, directed by Steven Soderbergh (Los Angeles: Magnolia Home Entertainment, 2005).

8. Romanek, "Commentary."

9. Alex Dobuzinskis and Sue Zeidler, "Disney and UK Theater Chains Reach Deal on 'Alice,'" Reuters, February 18, 2010, http://www.reuters.com/article/2010/02/19/disney-alice-idUSN1810056120100219.

10. Gary Gentile, "'Bubble' Hits Theaters, TV, DVD on Same Day," *USA Today*, January 18, 2006, http://usatoday30.usatoday.com/tech/news/2006-01-18-bubble-theater-threat_x.htm.

11. Devin Leonard, "Scary Movie: Hollywood Goes to War over Simultaneous Release of Film and DVD," CNNMoney.com, January 24, 2006, http://money.cnn.com/magazines/fortune/fortune_archive/2006/02/06/8367927/.

12. Romanek, "Commentary."

13. Ibid.

14. "BUBBLE" Grosses Estimated $5 Million in Opening Weekend with Day-and-Date Strategy," The Free Library.com, accessed June 9, 2013, . . . http://www.thefreelibrary.com/%60%60BUBBLE%27%27+Grosses+Estimated+$5+Million+in+Opening+Weekend+with...-a0141446095.

15. Official site of *The Girlfriend Experience*, accessed June 9, 2013, http://www.girlfriendexperiencefilm.com/.

16. Patrick Goldstein, "Universal's 'Tower Heist' VOD Fiasco: What Went Wrong?" *24 Frames* (blog), *Los Angeles Times*, October 12, 2011, http://latimesblogs.latimes.com/movies/2011/10/universals-tower-heist-vod-fiasco-what-went-wrong.html.

CHAPTER 21: THE HURT LOCKER (2008)

1. *The Hurt Locker*, DVD, directed by Kathryn Bigelow (2008; Universal City, CA: Summit Entertainment, 2010).

2. Kathryn Bigelow and Mark Boal, "Commentary," *The Hurt Locker*, DVD (Universal City, CA: Summit Entertainment, 2010).

3. Bigelow, "Commentary."

4. "Kathryn Bigelow Winning the Oscar for Directing," YouTube video, 5:51, from a ceremony televised on ABC on March 7, 2010, posted by Oscars, March 10, 2010, http://www.youtube.com/watch?v=e-DPBOTlSWk.

CHAPTER 22: AVATAR (2009)

1. *Avatar*, Blu-ray, directed by James Cameron (2009; Beverly Hills, CA; 20th Century Fox Home Entertainment, 2010).

2. Mark Graham, "Steven Soderbergh Endorses *Avatar*," *Vulture*, April 29, 2009, http://www.vulture.com/2009/04/steven_soderbergh_endorses_ava.html.

3. "Quint Has Seen Avatar Footage!!!" *Ain't It Cool News*.com, July 24, 2009, http://www.aintitcool.com/node/41793.

4. Gilbert Cruz, "One Man Spends Four Years Watching Hollywood's Worst Movies," *Time*, November 3, 2010, http://www.time.com/time/arts/article/0,8599,2029135,00.html.

5. Josh Grossberg, "Five New Things We Learned from James Cameron on the Making of *Titanic*," March 30, 2012, http://www.eonline.com/news/305382/five-new-things-we-learned-from-james-cameron-on-the-making-of-titanic.

6. John Patterson, "A History of 3D Cinema," *The Guardian*, August 19, 2009, http://www.guardian.co.uk/film/2009/aug/20/3d-film-history.

7. David Konow, "Making and Editing the First 3D Color Film," Tested.com, June 18, 2013, http://www.tested.com/art/makers/456521-making-and-editing-first-3d-color-film/.

8. Roger Ebert, review of *Avatar*, 20th Century Fox, *Chicago Sun-Times*, December 11, 2009, http://www.rogerebert.com/reviews/avatar-2009.

9. Anne Thompson, "How James Cameron's Innovative New 3D Tech Created *Avatar*," *Popular Mechanics*, January 1, 2010, http://www.popularmechanics.com/technology/digital/visual-effects/4339455.

10. Brooks Barnes, "Growing Conversion of Movies to 3-D Draws Mixed Reactions," *New York Times*, April 2, 2010, http://www.nytimes.com/2010/04/03/movies/03threed.html?_r=0.

11. Tim Masters, "James Cameron: 3D Conversion Best for Classic Films," BBC News, November 3, 2010, http://www.bbc.co.uk/news/entertainment-arts-11683132.

CHAPTER 23: LIFE IN A DAY (2011)

1. *Life in a Day*, Blu-ray, directed by Kevin Macdonald (2011; New York: Virgil Films & Entertainment, 2011).

2. "Life in a Day: About the Production," *National Geographic.com*, http://movies.nationalgeographic.com/movies/life-in-a-day/about-the-production/.

3. Ibid.

4. Joe Walker, "Commentary," *Life in a Day*, Blu-ray, directed by Kevin Macdonald (New York: Virgil Films & Entertainment, 2011).

5. John Young, " 'Life in a Day': Tonight Attend the Sundance Premiere from the Comfort of Your Own Home," January 27, 2011, http://insidemovies.ew.com/2011/01/27/sundance-life-in-a-day/.

6. Kevin Macdonald, "Commentary," *Life in a Day*, Blu-ray, directed by Kevin Macdonald (New York: Virgil Films & Entertainment, 2011).

7. "Me at the Zoo," YouTube video, 0:20, posted by jawed, April 23, 2005, http://www.youtube.com/watch?v=jNQXAC9IVRw.

8. "Wayne Wang Premieres Full-Length Film on YouTube," Marketing Vox, http://www.marketingvox.com/wayne-wang-premieres-full-length-film-on-youtube-041542/.

9. "Statistics," official site of YouTube, accessed June 10, 2013, http://www.youtube.com/yt/press/statistics.html.

10. Macdonald, "Commentary."

CHAPTER 24: MARGARET (2011)

1. *Margaret*, Blu-ray, directed by Kenneth Lonergan (2011; Beverly Hills, CA: 20th Century Fox Home Entertainment, 2012).

2. Joel Lovell, "Kenneth Lonergan's Thwarted Masterpiece," *The New York Times Magazine*, June 19, 2012, http://www.nytimes.com/2012/06/24/magazine/kenneth-lonergans-thwarted-masterpiece.html?pagewanted=all&_r=0.

3. Ibid.

4. Jaime Christley, "Make MARGARET Available to US Critics and Other Pertinent Voting Bodies," Change.org, accessed June 11, 2013, http://www.change.org/petitions/fox-searchlight-make-margaret-available-to-us-critics-and-other-pertinent-voting-bodies.

5. Ibid.

6. Mary Pols, "Director Kenneth Lonergan Emerges to Tell Us He's on Team Margaret," *Time*, December 2, 2011, http://entertainment.time.com/2011/12/02/director-kenneth-lonergan-emerges-to-tell-us-hes-on-team-margaret/.

7. Ibid.

8. Guy Lodge, "Kenneth Lonergan on Why 'Margaret' Shouldn't be Perfect," July 10, 2012, http://www.hitfix.com/in-contention/interview-kenneth-lonergan-on-why-margaret-shouldnt-be-perfect.

9. Christley, "Make MARGARET Available," Change.org.

10. Christy Grosz, "Team 'Margaret' Scores an Awards Season Victory?" *The Vote with Jon Weisman* (blog), *Variety*, December 27, 2011, http://weblogs.variety.com/thevote/2011/12/team-margaret-scores-an-awards-season-victory.html.

11. David Fricke, "The Greatest Rolling Stones Movie You've Never Seen: 'Cocksucker Blues,'" November 20, 2012, http://www.rollingstone.com/music/blogs/alternate-take/the-greatest-rolling-stones-movie-youve-never-seen-cocksucker-blues-20121120.

12. Sheila Muto, "The Fantastic Four Movie You'll Never See," *Wired*, September 1994, http://www.wired.com/wired/archive/2.09/fan.four.html.

13. Russ Fischer, "David O. Russell Quits 'Nailed,'" July 14, 2010, http://www.slashfilm.com/david-o-russell-quits-nailed/s.

CHAPTER 25: RED STATE (2011)

1. *Red State*, DVD, directed by Kevin Smith (2011, Santa Monica, CA; Lionsgate Films, 2011).

2. "The Making of Red State," *Red State*, DVD, directed by Kevin Smith (Santa Monica, CA; Lions Gate Films, 2011).

3. Brenna Cammeron and Soraya Roberts, "Kevin Smith, 'Red State' Director, Slams 'Cop Out' Star Bruce Willis and Hollywood as a Whole," New York *Daily News*, January 24, 2011, http://www.nydailynews.com/entertainment/tv-movies/kevin-smith-red-state-director-slams-star-bruce-willis-hollywood-article-1.149522.

4. Robert Fischer, "The GQ&A: Kevin Smith," *GQ*, August 31, 2011, http://www.gq.com/entertainment/movies-and-tv/201108/kevin-smith-interview-red-state.

5. Jeff Labrecque, "Kevin Smith Is Back: Director Talks His Next Movie, Ben Affleck's Batcave and 'The Most Important Film of 2013,'" *Entertainment Weekly*, September 24, 2013, http://insidemovies.ew.com/2013/09/24/kevin-smith-ben-affleck-batman-the-dirties/.

6. "The Sundance Speech," *Red State*, directed by Kevin Smith, DVD (Santa Monica, CA; Lionsgate Films, 2011).

7. Ibid.

8. Ibid.

9. Ibid.

10. Ethan Alter, "Seeing 'Red': Kevin Smith Brings His Indie Provocation to Radio City Music Hall," *Film Journal International*, March 7, 2011, http://www.filmjournal.com/filmjournal/content_display/news-and-features/features/movies/e3i15cd74f50b02a369390f34ad2e55c308.

11. Kevin Smith, "QT and Me," *The Red Statements*, April 18, 2001, http://theredstatements.com/2011/04/18/qt-and-me/.

12. Karina Longworth, "Kevin Smith's *Red State* at the New Beverly," *L.A. Weekly*, August 18, 2011, http://www.laweekly.com/2011-08-18/film-tv/kevin -smith-s-red-state-at-the-new-beverly/full/.

13. Bryce J. Renninger, "Kevin Smith's 'Red State' to Screen Nationwide in One-Night Simulcast," *Indiewire*, September 2, 2011, http://www.indiewire.com/article/ kevin_smiths_red_state_to_screen_across_nation_in_one_night_only_simulcast.

14. Fischer, "The GQ&A," *GQ*.

15. Kevin Smith, "One Year Later," *The Red Statements*, January 24, 2012, http://theredstatements.com/2012/01/24/one-year-later/.

CONCLUSION

1. Nicholas Kulish and Michael Cieply, "Around the World in One Movie: Film Financing's Global Future," *New York Times*, December 5, 2011, http://www .nytimes.com/2011/12/06/business/media/around-world-in-one-movie-film-financings -global-future.html?pagewanted=all&_r=0.

2. Patrick Goldstein, "Universal's 'Tower Heist' VOD Fiasco: What Went Wrong?" *24 Frames* (blog), *Los Angeles Times*, October 12, 2011, http://latimes blogs.latimes.com/movies/2011/10/universals-tower-heist-vod-fiasco-what-went -wrong.html.

3. Richard Lawler, "Disney Announces Wreck-It Ralph Will Arrive for Download Before DVD, Blu-ray," Engadget.com, January 4, 2013, http://www.engadget .com/2013/01/04/disney-wreck-it-ralph-early-digital-release/.

4. Eliana Dockterman, "Spike Lee Raises $1.4 Million on Kickstarter," *Time*, August 21, 2013, http://newsfeed.time.com/2013/08/21/spike-lee-film-raises-1-4 -million-on-kickstarter/.

5. "Oscar Exclusive: James Franco on Why Andy Serkis Deserves Credit from Actors," Deadline.com, January 8, 2012, http://www.deadline.com/2012/01/ oscar-exclusive-james-franco-on-why-andy-serkis-deserves-credit-from-actors/.

Selected Bibliography

Listed here are all of the 25 films discussed in the book, as well as a selection of additional sources with a focus on specific published books and visual supplements included on DVD editions of the various films. Although the latter section is not a complete list of sources cited within the book, it provides an overview of the types of material that I consulted and suggestions of material that can be read and watched for more information on these particular films and firsts.

1. THE FILMS

Avatar. Blu-ray. Directed by James Cameron. 2009; Beverly Hills, CA; 20th Century Fox Home Entertainment, 2010.

Blade Runner: The Director's Cut. Blu-ray. Directed by Ridley Scott. 1992; Burbank, CA: Warner Home Video, 2012.

Bubble. DVD. Directed by Steven Soderbergh. 2005; Los Angeles: Magnolia Home Entertainment, 2005.

Crouching Tiger, Hidden Dragon. DVD. Directed by Ang Lee. 2000; Culver City, CA; Columbia Tristar Home Entertainment, 2001.

Funny Ha Ha. DVD. Directed by Andrew Bujalski. 2002: Santa Monica, CA; Genius Entertainment, 2007.

The Hurt Locker. DVD. Directed by Kathryn Bigelow. 2008; Universal City, CA: Summit Entertainment, 2010.

Jaws. DVD. Directed by Steven Spielberg. 1975; Universal City, CA: Universal Studios Home Entertainment, 2012.

Life in a Day. Blu-ray. Directed by Kevin Macdonald. 2011; New York: Virgil Films & Entertainment, 2011.

The Lord of the Rings. Blu-ray. Directed by Peter Jackson. 2001–2003; Burbank, CA: Warner Home Video, 2012.

Margaret. Blu-ray. Directed by Kenneth Lonergan. 2011; Beverly Hills, CA: 20th Century Fox Home Entertainment, 2012.

Parting Glances. DVD. Directed by Bill Sherwood. 1986; New York: First Run Features, 2000.

Psycho. DVD. Directed by Gus Van Sant. 1998; Universal City, CA: Universal Studios, 1999.

Pulp Fiction. Blu-ray. Directed by Quentin Tarantino. 1994; Los Angeles: Lionsgate and Miramax, 2011.

Red State. DVD. Directed by Kevin Smith. 2011, Santa Monica, CA; Lions Gate Films, 2011.

sex, lies, and videotape. Blu-ray. Directed by Steven Soderbergh. 1989; Culver City, CA; Sony Pictures Home Entertainment, 2009.

She's Gotta Have It. DVD. Directed by Spike Lee. 1986; Beverly Hills, CA: 20th Century Fox Home Entertainment, 2008.

Showgirls. Blu-ray. Directed by Paul Verhoeven. 1995; Beverly Hills, CA: 20th Century Fox Home Entertainment, 2011.

Star Trek: The Motion Picture. DVD. Directed by Robert Wise. 1979; Hollywood, CA: Paramount Home Entertainment, 2009.

Star Wars. DVD. Directed by George Lucas. 1977; Beverly Hills, CA: 20th Century Fox Home Entertainment, 2006.

Superman: The Movie. DVD. Directed by Richard Donner. 1978; Burbank, CA: Warner Home Video, 2007.

The Blair Witch Project. Blu-ray. Directed by Daniel Myrick and Eduardo Sánchez. 1999; Santa Monica, CA: Lionsgate Films, 2010.

The Matrix. DVD. Directed by the Wachowski Brothers. 1999; Burbank, CA: Warner Home Video, 1999.

The Thin Blue Line. Netflix Instant. Directed by Errol Morris. 1988; Los Gatos, CA: Netflix.

Toy Story. DVD. Directed by John Lasseter. 1995; Burbank, CA: Buena Vista Home Entertainment, 2000.

Tron. DVD. Directed by Steven Lisberger. 1982; Burbank, CA: Buena Vista Home Entertainment, 2002.

2. ADDITIONAL SOURCES

Alter, Ethan. Review of *Avatar*. *Film Journal International*, December 15, 2009, http://www.filmjournal.com/filmjournal/content_display/reviews/major-releases/e3if667a78777fe70e11f6c65ca8ba655c9.

Alter, Ethan. Review of *Life in a Day*. TelevisionWithoutPity.com, July 29, 2011, http://www.televisionwithoutpity.com/mwop/moviefile/foreign-relations/2011/07/life-in-a-day-youtube-goes-glo/.

Alter, Ethan. Review of *Margaret*. TelevisionWithoutPity.com, September 30, 2011, http://www.televisionwithoutpity.com/mwop/moviefile/girls-on-film/2011/09/margaret-the-only-living-girl/.

Alter, Ethan. Review of *Red State*. *Film Journal International*. September 21, 2011, http://www.filmjournal.com/filmjournal/content_display/reviews/specialty -releases/e3ifb2fa3d87f5244467efb12103dcc7d75.

Alter, Ethan. Review of *Red State*. TelevisionWithoutPity.com, September 2, 2011, http://www.televisionwithoutpity.com/mwop/moviefile/i-want-my-vod/2011/09/red-state-9-1/.

Alter, Ethan. "Seeing 'Red': Kevin Smith Brings His Indie Provocation to Radio City Music Hall." *Film Journal International*, March 7, 2011, http://www.film journal.com/filmjournal/content_display/news-and-features/features/movies/e3i15cd74f50b02a369390f34ad2e55c308.

Alter, Ethan. "Sisterly Rivalry: Lynn Shelton Directs Blunt and DeWitt in Improvised Romantic Triangle." May 29, 2012, http://www.filmjournal.com/filmjournal/content_display/esearch/e3i06cfcbf80fe02610120c28053270282c.

"Beyond Tron." Disc 2. *Tron, 20th Anniversary Collector's Edition* DVD. Directed by Steven Lisberger. Burbank, CA: Buena Vista Home Entertainment, 2002.

Biskind, Peter. *Down and Dirty Pictures: Miramax, Sundance, and the Rise of Independent Film.* New York: Simon & Schuster, 2004.

Biskind, Peter. *Easy Riders, Raging Bulls: How the Sex-Drugs-And-Rock 'N' Roll Generation Saved Hollywood.* New York: Simon & Schuster, 1998.

"A Bold New Enterprise." Disc 2. *Star Trek: The Motion Picture—The Director's Edition* DVD. Directed by Robert Wise. Hollywood, CA: Paramount Home Video, 2001.

Bouzereau, Laurent. "The Making of Jaws." Blu-ray. *Jaws*, Blu-ray + DVD edition. Directed by Steven Spielberg. Universal City, CA; Universal Studios Home Entertainment, 2012.

De Lauzirika, Charles. "Dangerous Days: Making Blade Runner." Disc 3. *Blade Runner: 30th Anniversary Collector's Edition* Blu-ray. Directed by Ridley Scott. Burbank, CA: Warner Home Video, 2012.

D-J. "Psycho Path." *Psycho, Collector's Edition* DVD. Directed by Gus Van Sant. Universal City, CA: Universal Studios, 1999.

Hayes, Dade, and Jonathan Bing. *Open Wide: How Hollywood Box Office Became a National Obsession.* New York: Miramax Books, 2004.

Hollander, Erik. "The Shark Is Still Working: The Impact & Legacy of *Jaws*." Blu-ray disc. *Jaws*, Blu-ray + DVD edition. Directed by Steven Spielberg. Universal City, CA; Universal Studios Home Entertainment, 2012.

Kolb, William M. "Reconstructing the Director's Cut." In *Retrofitting Blade Runner*, edited by Judith B. Kerman. Madison: University of Wisconsin Press, 1997, 294–301. Originally published as "Blade Runner: The Director's Cut That Nearly Wasn't," *The Perfect Vision* 6, no. 23. October 1994.

Lee, Spike. *Spike Lee's Gotta Have It: Inside Guerrilla Filmmaking.* New York: Simon & Schuster, 1987.

"The Longest Trek: Writing the Motion Picture." *Star Trek: The Motion Picture*, DVD. Directed by Robert Wise. Hollywood, CA: Paramount Home Entertainment, 2009.

"The Making of *Tron*." Disc 2. *Tron, 20th Anniversary Collector's Edition* DVD. Directed by Steven Lisberger. Burbank, CA: Buena Vista Home Entertainment, 2002.

Oreck, Josh. "The Matrix Revisited." *The Matrix, The Ultimate Matrix Collection* Blu-ray set. Directed by the Wachowski Brothers. Burbank, CA: Warner Home Video, 2008.

"Phase II: The Lost Enterprise." Disc 2. *Star Trek: The Motion Picture—The Director's Edition* DVD. Directed by Robert Wise. Hollywood, CA: Paramount Home Video, 2001.

Pierson, John. *Spike, Mike, Slackers & Dykes: A Guided Tour across a Decade of American Independent Cinema.* New York: Hyperion, 1995.

Sandler, Kevin S. *The Naked Truth: Why Hollywood Doesn't Make X-Rated Movies.* New Brunswick: Rutgers University Press, 2007.

Soderbergh, Steven. *sex, lies, and videotape.* New York: Harper & Row, 1990.

"The Story Behind Toy Story." Disc 1. *Toy Story, Collector's Edition* DVD. Burbank, CA: Buena Vista Home Entertainment, 2000.

"What Is Bullet Times." *The Matrix, the Ultimate Matrix Collection.* Directed by the Wachowski Brothers. Burbank, CA: Warner Home Video, 2008.

"You Will Believe: The Cinematic Saga of Superman." Disc 13. *Superman: Ultimate Collector's Edition.* Burbank, CA: Warner Home Video, 2007.

Index

About the Author

ETHAN ALTER is the chief film critic and editor for the website *Television without Pity*. His movie reviews and feature articles have appeared in such publications as *Film Journal International, TV Guide*, and *GIANT* magazine. He lives, works, and watches movies in New York City.